THE
BUSINESS
HEALERS

THE
BUSINESS
HEALERS

Hal Higdon

RANDOM HOUSE

NEW YORK

For the Baron of Goethe Street

CONTENTS

Contents

THE
BUSINESS
HEALERS

INTRODUCTION

No individual could spend much time examining the business phenomenon known as "management consulting" without becoming aware of ACME, the Association of Consulting Management Engineers. The imprimatur of ACME is the Good Housekeeping Seal of Approval of the consulting world. Belonging to ACME is like belonging to the right fraternity. There are several other associations of consultants, but membership in ACME carries the most prestige—and generates more new business. Thus when I first decided to write a book on management consulting, I journeyed to New York to speak with Philip W. Shay, ACME executive director. Shay received me on this first visit with apparent coldness, as though the idea of a free-lance writer doing a book on consulting bothered him. "I don't see how anybody from the outside can do a book on management consulting," Shay sniffed. "You need to be inside a firm, or at a desk like mine, where you have access to certain figures."

"But isn't that what consultants do," I countered, "come in from the outside and tell people how to run their businesses?"

This seemed to fluster Shay. "That's not the same thing!"

His response, however, reflected well the attitude of many within the management consulting profession who shroud their work under a cloak of mystery—as though they were soothsayers, or practitioners of some sort of black art which gets handed down from father to son. Many members of ACME view reporters as a necessary evil they would rather do without. Thus almost a conspiracy of silence pervades the management consulting profession. Consulting firms desire publicity on a certain level (such as occasional favorable mentions by name in *Business Week*), but they seem to fear anything which might bare the true nature of their occupation to the public. They want publicity, but only on their own terms. "We're about as good at public relations as most doctors are," one vice-president at Booz, Allen & Hamilton, Inc., admitted to me, "and that's not very good."

"We don't want publicity," added the head of a large executive recruiting firm. "We stay out of it, particularly where we have any suspicion that it's going to a mass audience, or where it's going to reflect poorly on the business, and I'm right now in the process of coming close to withdrawing from our professional association because they've

Introduction

got a PR guy* who's gone to *Life* and *Newsweek*, and a bunch of places that don't write to our audience—which is just the few guys that run businesses. We're interested only in maybe five hundred or a thousand company presidents. Those are the ones that we want to know about us, and understand our business—and maybe another group of five hundred or a thousand individuals just below them who could aspire to be president."

While I found few other consultants as outspoken as this gentleman, many share his views. Many, in fact, suffer from what a psychiatrist might describe as "the *Fortune* Syndrome," stemming from the fact that about once every five years *Fortune* publishes a debunking article on management consultants that completely punctures their egos. It takes the consultants about five years to regain their composure then, ZOT! *Fortune* strikes again! In the February 1965 issue, assistant managing editor Walter Guzzardi, Jr., built his attack on the premise that once a consulting firm hooked into a client for a single assignment it never released its grip. "Consultants: The Men Who Came to Dinner" was his article's title, and the accompanying blurb read: "Consulting firms can render a real service to management. But the best service of all is the one they render to themselves."

Reporters who approached management consulting firms in the wake of that broadside were fortunate to learn any-

* He didn't withdraw, but the PR firm no longer handles that association's business.

thing more controversial than the time of day. In trying to arrange an appointment with a member of a Chicago firm specializing in psychological evaluation I was referred to an individual charged with that firm's public relations. I recognized his name. For several years he had served as director of public relations for Booz-Allen and then had left them to establish a public relations firm of his own. Several months before, while he still worked at Booz-Allen, I had written him a letter requesting an interview, and it had gone unanswered. Now I phoned him at his new office. "Well, you know *Fortune* has written a lot of articles highly critical of us," he mumbled evasively when appraised of my purpose for calling. "I'll have to confer with the partners of the firm to see if we're willing to talk to you. I'll call you back."

He hasn't called yet.

According to legend, *Fortune*'s disenchantment with the management consulting profession began many years ago when one of its better-known writers, Perrin Stryker, reportedly appeared unannounced one day at Booz-Allen's New York offices and demanded an interview. He remained sitting outside in the waiting room as panic-stricken partners stumbled from office to office wiping their brows, worrying how to handle him. Finally, after forty-five minutes Stryker, tired of waiting, stormed out, and the management consulting profession has trembled in the backlash of his ire ever since. At least, so went legend.

The story did have an apocryphal ring to it so I contacted Perrin Stryker and asked him for his version. He replied that the story had no basis in fact, but might have been a garbled version of an incident that did occur.

He wrote: "Several months after the publication of my article, 'How Executives Get Jobs' in the August 1953 issue of *Fortune,* I requested and was granted an interview with Booz-Allen on the subject of consultants' problems in preparation for another article, 'The Ambitious Consultants,' later published in May 1954. Accompanied by a *Fortune* researcher, I met with Mr. James Allen himself. After the usual amenities, he pulled out that August 1953 issue and began attacking the reference we had made to Booz-Allen in a separate section dealing with 'The Man-Hunters' Dilemma.' Among other things we had said that 'big man-hunters like Booz, Allen & Hamilton try hard to soft-pedal their success at it. Man-hunting billings may in fact account for 25 per cent or more of their business.' Mr. Allen vehemently denied that his firm got that proportion of its income from recruiting executives, and we replied that our sources—in and out of Booz-Allen—not only said differently, but that the estimate was, if anything, on the low side. Thereafter the discussions of various Booz-Allen policies and views became so sharp that the researcher got up and left, the only such retreat I ever heard of in more than 17 years' experience with such researchers."

In the spring of 1966 I spent several days attending a paper-box convention at the Drake Hotel while on a free-lance assignment for the *Chicago Tribune Magazine.* By sheer coincidence one morning I sat down for breakfast at a table that included a Booz-Allen vice-president who later

THE BUSINESS HEALERS

that day would read a rather dull speech at one of the convention's sessions. He seemed quite friendly and when we passed later in the hall he greeted me by first name, although I couldn't immediately recall his. After his speech I met him again and mentioned my intentions to do a book on management consulting. He paused long enough to mention the name of their staffman in charge of public relations, then fled in another direction.

Later that day I encountered a friend who had served several years as a consultant and mentioned the incident. "These Booz-Allen guys are scared stiff," he commented. "They're like army officers in Vietnam being interviewed. They're afraid of saying something that might get in the papers the wrong way and misrepresent their military posture. First of all, they're users. The minute he learned you were working for a newspaper he was an ambitious guy and wanted to be sure you remembered him, because it might do him some good. But second, he was liable to get quoted, and if he gets misquoted he's dead with the other vice-presidents. It's a rough life, I'll tell you, inside the inner circle."

Because public relations for management consulting firms has been such a one-way street, most of the books on the subject have taken the *Popular Mechanics* approach, that is: How do you use them? Or they've been about as much fun to read as a doctoral dissertation on thermodynamics. Indeed, no balanced analysis of the consulting profession exists. I found a single item on Booz, Allen & Hamilton in the Chicago public library: the published report of a study made by the firm in Wilmington, Delaware, in 1959 entitled "Effective Standards for Institutional Care of the Infirm Aged."

It surprised me that no one at Booz-Allen had bothered either to write a history of that firm or a biography of its founder, Edwin G. Booz, who must rate as one of the most significant business figures of this century. I mentioned this to one of the Booz-Allen vice-presidents. "The suggestion that there be a company history arose at the time of our fiftieth anniversary," he said. "It was vetoed."

Later I mentioned this lack of proper history to Mr. Allen. He shrugged. "You always let your own shoes go unsoled."

In defense of the management consulting firms, however, several sound reasons do exist for their being entirely circumspect about their client relationships. "Like the psychiatrist or the plastic surgeon," _Newsweek_ once wrote, "it behooves the management consultant to be as inconspicuous as possible, and to let clients take credit for whatever good works he may perform."

Most management consulting firms will never reveal the name of a client or even hint at the type of work they might have done for a client whose identity becomes known. "The firm's degree of success," says one Booz-Allen spokesman, "is that when a client comes to Booz-Allen they know we're not going to talk about them to outsiders. One of the factors of our business is that we do keep quiet about client assignments."

A new employee coming to work for McKinsey signs a statement that he will keep his work confidential at all times, and most other consulting firms in one degree or another enforce the same discipline. Booz-Allen staffmen sweep their desks clean of all clutter each night. It's not only because of an obsession for neatness. They fear that spies might enter in the wake of the cleaning lady. Some of the firm's government work is classified Top Secret, and all of its corporation work is considered at least confidential. "We have to watch security here," one Booz-Allen staffman admitted to me. "We rock our people about not taking talk about our work into the elevators and washrooms."

This self-erected wall of silence may seem necessary to avoid offending client presidents who won't admit they wouldn't sharpen a pencil without outside counsel, but it often frustrates the consultants who can't blow their own horn with any degree of success. The director of the management services division of a large accounting firm bragged to me some years ago that his firm had just completed the largest management consulting engagement ever undertaken by man, but he wouldn't say how large, didn't want the type of industry mentioned, and didn't want his firm's name used in connection with it.*

Management consulting firms frequently talk more freely about work done outside the general area of business. John W. Mitchell, a partner of Fry Consultants Incorporated, apparently felt no reluctance to discuss his firm's relationships with Southern Illinois University with me. When one afternoon I called Richard Lopata, who handles public

---

* The facts became known anyway. Peat, Marwick, Mitchell & Co. handled a $3.5 million assignment for the Pennsylvania Railroad.

Introduction

relations for A. T. Kearney & Company, Inc., and asked some questions about their work with hospitals, he sounded genuinely relieved that I had chosen the one area where he could speak with some freedom. Rudy Dallmeyer of Donald R. Booz & Associates talked openly about some work his firm had done for a suicide prevention center.

But even in the seemingly innocent arena of nonprofit organizations and institutions, skeletons remain hidden in closets. In 1964 the U.S. Olympic Committee announced with a flourish that it had retained Arthur D. Little, Inc., to "study ways and means for the long range development and implementation of a more effective United States Olympic program." General James M. Gavin and Dr. Bruce S. Old would supervise the Little research team. Thanks to press releases from the USOC, the news of the study got full coverage in newspapers and magazines. I was interested because of my own involvement in amateur sports as a long-distance runner. Reportedly the study would cost $150,000 and would be completed within a year.

But following the projected completion date, the USOC remained strangely and sullenly silent about the report. When queried about the study, Little predictably deferred to the people who had employed them. When I asked USOC executive director Arthur G. Lentz about the existence of such a report he indicated that no action on it had been taken by their board directors. Another olympiad passed and no sounds yet emanated from Olympic House in New York.

Actually Little did complete a four-volume report which

THE BUSINESS HEALERS

covered the strengths and weaknesses of each of the Olympic and Pan American sports as well as the organization of the Olympic Committee. Apparently Little got into trouble in this last area. The battle between the National Collegiate Athletic Association and the Amateur Athletic Union raged at that time with the USOC in the middle. Like those other two organizations, the USOC is an inflexible and autocratic body. Although some of the suggestions in the four volumes soon were implemented, the public never saw the report. "It's a shame too," said someone who read it. "Its release would have increased its value immeasurably."

Work done by consulting firms for nonprofit organizations and institutions normally doesn't strike such tender nerve cords. Such consulting assignments happen in public view, much more so than in the area of business. But this one hole in the curtain often results in the public's obtaining a distorted picture of the type of work done most often by management consultants. I noticed that in several articles written about consultants, reporters followed the path of least resistance and detailed only the institutional work. Some years ago the business section of *Time* contained a short article on Booz-Allen entitled "The Company Doctors." *Time* cited five seemingly typical assignments beginning with "a current $1,250,000 research job to help the Army biological-warfare experts figure out the best defense against bacteriological attack." The other Booz, Allen & Hamilton jobs were:

Introduction

1. Helping RCA reorganize its divisions, beginning with Victor records, which set the pattern for RCA's postwar growth. The consultants' market studies marked out for RCA the most profitable line to concentrate on.
2. Showing the city of Seattle how to save $3,000,000 a year on its $86 million budget by instituting citywide accounting, starting a driver-training program for city employees that cut accidents 30 per cent, and reading meters quarterly instead of monthly.
3. Pinpointing for the state of Connecticut the reasons why established industries were leaving and new industries were avoiding the state. Some recommendations: adopt a new state water law to allocate water supplies to industry, establish a radioisotope institute at the state university to attract new nuclear industries, simplify corporate taxes.
4. Reorganizing the nonteaching side of Pasadena's $22-million-a-year school budget to save $150,000 a year through such economies as keeping kindergarten-to-college records by IBM machine and stopping a $3,000-a-year loss in stolen gym towels by the simple technique of requiring the exchange of one dirty towel for each clean one.

Having branded Booz-Allen as "Company Doctors," *Time* had managed to list only one actual company case study out of five reported. Booz-Allen's connections with RCA had become known only because of publicity attending the appointment of one of the consulting firm's vice-presidents (John Burns) as RCA president.

Consulting firms occasionally will dodge the issue of their client relationships even when it becomes a matter of public record. In February 1966 it was announced in the House of Commons that the British post office system had engaged the American consulting firm McKinsey & Company, Inc., to review its operations. One staffman showed the clipping from a London paper to Marvin Bower, then McKinsey's managing director, and suggested that perhaps the American public should be apprised of the news. "Oh no," Bower replied. "We never talk about our clients."

Since consultants won't talk about clients, case histories become available only when clients talk about consultants. Unfortunately for the consultants' image, the unhappy client talks more frequently, out of an apparent (although sometimes subconscious) desire for revenge. Therefore, although the great majority of consulting assignments result in the client's being at least satisfied that he obtained his money's worth, you hear chapter and verse quoted mostly on blown assignments. And quite frankly, tales of rape and violence do make the most interesting reading.

When information does appear in the press, often both management consultant and client company appear astounded that the results were leaked. Having read in *Fortune* about McKinsey's handling a $700,000 study for the Metropolitan Life Insurance Company, I approached Metropolitan to obtain further details. "We have always regarded it as a confidential arrangement and have not publicized the results or the fees involved," one of Metropolitan's assistant vice-presidents informed me. "Presumably *Fortune* got their information from McKinsey."

Whether this bears any relationship to the breaching of security or not, the same vice-president now *claims* Metropolitan has not engaged any management consulting firms since. His statement is quite interesting since, of course, Metropolitan *has* engaged a consulting firm since. Discretion forbids me from naming which one.

In Great Britain, companies apparently feel less insecure and have fewer qualms about admitting their relationships with consulting firms. "Rather than being an admission of weakness it's considered a sign of strength," says McKinsey's Everett Smith. "They go around boasting of hiring the McKinseys. Our name hits the *Times* regularly, and quite frankly it scares the devil out of us."

While news of the arrival of even a single consultant will spread through a small company like chicken pox through a kindergarten, many billion-dollar corporations are so large that a consultant may come and go undetected by all except topmost management. Often even not all of an organization's top echelon will be appraised of a consultant's visit. According to D. Reid Weedon, Jr., a senior vice-president at Arthur D. Little: "You go into a company and ask if they use consultants and the company will say no, and the first thing you find out is they have a great big project going with one of your competitors, and you get the answer 'no' because the men you saw weren't involved with the project and didn't even know it was going on."

Perhaps the classic story concerning an invisible consultant was related by Walter Guzzardi, Jr., in *Fortune*. A consultant told of being seated at a dinner next to Frederick Donner, chairman of the board of General Motors. The consultant identified his profession to which Donner promptly replied that G.M. never used consultants. "I told him that as a matter of fact we were doing some work in a G.M. division at that very moment," the consultant recalled.

Donner immediately wanted to know which division.

"I just laughed and wouldn't tell him," said the consultant.

If the chairman of the board can't uncover consultants on the premises, the chance of the average stockholder's learning of their presence seems remote indeed. "You won't find many annual reports that deal with consultants," comments one individual in the investment business. "Companies don't broadcast that they're using them."

In a few instances where news of consultants has been broadcast prematurely it has caused some embarrassment. Arthur D. Little at one time did a study for Great American Industries, Inc., of New York related to corporate acquisitions and options on mining properties. When in the spring of 1966 news of the report leaked to the public, a rush on the company's stock forced the Securities and Exchange Commission to suspend trading.

"I don't think the public as a whole, and particularly the stockholder public, recognizes the decisions entrusted today to names that never appear on proxy statements," adds John H. Smith, Jr., of Communications Analysis, Inc. "The

Introduction

question is, how much influence do these people have on basic decisions? Do they in effect make decisions? How often does this occur and what kind of thinking governs decisions they make, or the influence they exert? You could make a case that consultants ought to be identified. Companies should report whom they have for consultants and what they think those consultants have contributed."

Considering current attitudes within the business community, it seems doubtful that the management consultants will surface before stockholders' eyes, at least in the near future. Nevertheless, consultants do have a determining influence on success and failure in business. This is particularly true today. There was a time when the strong entrepreneur, the Horatio Alger, could fly by the seat of his pants and achieve success. He could, but his son can't. Business has become so complex today, particularly with the advance of computer sciences, that no one man can possibly have all the answers. He is forced to go outside for help to succeed. The most astute businessmen recognize this. And so the management consulting profession has experienced its greatest period of growth within the past decade.

Management consulting, as founded and practiced in the United States, also has gained increased acceptance abroad. Until the mid-fifties, few businessmen outside the United States knew the firm names Booz, Allen & Hamilton, or McKinsey & Company, or understood the nature of their work. Because both these firms, and others, have begun to scatter offices abroad, the international business com-

THE BUSINESS HEALERS

munity has become suddenly aware of management consulting. The thinking has gone something like this: *American businessmen are successful. American businessmen use consultants. Therefore, we must use consultants to achieve success.* In addition, the use of consultants has spread from large corporations to small companies to nonprofit institutions. Management consultants are ubiquitous. During the many years of researching this book, I can't remember encountering a single businessman who was unaware of, or who didn't have a strong opinion about, management consultants. There seemed to be no neutral ground.

Yet many otherwise knowledgeable businessmen still do not completely understand the nature of the consultant's work. Consulting is considered by too many as some sort of magic wind-up toy: You wind up a consultant and he makes you rich. Well, it's not as simple as that. The aim of this book, thus, is to lift the curtain of semisecrecy surrounding the management consulting trade and give the curious businessman a peek inside.

1

The Amorphous Umbrella

The taxicab halted before the headquarters of a medium-sized Midwestern corporation. The cab's passenger, a man wearing a conservative business suit with vest, paid the driver and stepped out into the morning air. As the taxicab sped away he set his tan briefcase down on the sidewalk and reached inside his suitcoat for a leather-covered notebook. Methodically, he jotted down the exact amount he had just paid. Replacing the notebook inside his suitcoat, he regrasped his briefcase and began to walk toward the building. The edge of a white handkerchief showed in his breast pocket. His shoes were black and round-tipped and had been shined that morning. He was a youngish man, about thirty-one years of age, handsome, slender and tall, wearing a hat. His tie displayed in broad stripes the colors of an Ivy League college. He pushed open a glass door.

"Good morning," a receptionist half-smiled at him, remembering his face but not his name. He half-smiled back.

Passing the receptionist without breaking stride, he entered the offices. A few people looked nervously up at him from their desks. Most tried to give the appearance of nonchalant dedication to duty. He entered a cubicle-sized room toward the rear of the offices with no name on the door, no clutter of mementos, and no picture of the wife and children guarding the desk. He had been utilizing the room since arriving in town two days earlier. He placed his briefcase before him on the desk. A secretary poked her head in the door and said: "The president would like to see you as soon as you are ready."

He glanced at his watch and noted with amusement that the president must have arrived at work earlier than usual that morning. He dismissed the secretary with a smile and returned his attention to his briefcase, which with some accuracy might be described as his doctor's bag. He removed from it a file folder of reports that he had spent half the night in his motel room studying, a slide rule, a half dozen pens and pencils, several notebooks, a large pad of lined yellow paper commonly known as foolscap, and a black leather folder that contained another smaller pad which he would inconspicuously bring with him when he went to see the president. These represented the surgical instruments of his trade. He was a Business Healer: more precisely, a management consultant.

●

This scene is being repeated today with infinite variations in corporations, companies, businesses, firms, institutions,

The Amorphous Umbrella

associations, and agencies throughout the United States as well as in many other countries of the world. To today's businessman, a management consultant has become almost as essential as a psychiatrist to a Hollywood star. Executives now increasingly look to consultants for help in running their businesses.

The Association of Consulting Management Engineers estimates a total of 2,700 consulting firms and between 30,000 and 40,000 individual consultants working either alone or within the larger firms. Management consulting firms have grown, in size and profits, at a pace that has outstripped the growth of the economy, particularly in the last dozen years. A 1954 ACME survey indicated that a total of 1,915 American consulting firms did $426 million worth of business in that year. The gross billings by management consulting firms in 1968 (again according to ACME) reached $850 million. This figure includes billings by contract research firms (such as Arthur D. Little, Inc.), but ignores the certified public accountants. Considering the amount of consulting work done by the management services divisions of accounting firms, it becomes clear that management consulting has now become a billion-dollar industry.

In discussing management consulting one has to begin with the Association of Consulting Management Engineers, which serves as spokesman and policeman of the consulting industry. ACME was founded in January 1933 after about four years' discussion by a dozen of the more prominent "consulting engineer" firms (the title "management consultant" not having yet come into prominence). These firms had become concerned over the number of charlatans in their ranks. Considering the general growth in the consulting ranks, this blue-ribbon club has expanded slowly and now includes only forty-five members. Nevertheless, as one ACME member points out, "These are the ones you can see and feel."

Several ACME members get seen and felt more than others. Probably the two best-known management consulting firms are Chicago-based Booz, Allen & Hamilton, Inc., and New York–based McKinsey & Company, Inc. Booz-Allen and McKinsey receive more attention than other ACME members because first, in terms of size and gross billings, they are the Hertz and Avis of management consulting; and second, they operate in the inner sanctum of the largest corporate executive suites, where the action is. These are the Big Image firms, the "generalist" firms, the ones in the mainstream of modern management consulting. Because of the influence of their founders, Edwin G. Booz and James O. McKinsey, these two firms also have played an important part in the historical development of consulting.

Three additional generalist firms normally get mentioned in the same breath with McKinsey and Booz-Allen. Chicago-based A. T. Kearney & Company, Inc., also grew out of the McKinsey branch of the consulting tree and in one sense is more directly descended from James O. McKinsey than the firm that now bears his name. Cresap, McCormick and Paget, with headquarters in New York,

The Amorphous Umbrella

developed from a wartime association of three men, two of whom (Cresap and Paget) had worked for Ed Booz during the thirties. George A. Fry, who founded what now is named Fry Consultants Incorporated, was Ed Booz's first partner back in the twenties. At one time Booz's firm was known as Booz, Fry, Allen & Hamilton. Fry also has headquarters in Chicago. More consultants now operate out of Manhattan near the corporate headquarters of most clients, but the birth and growth of management consulting actually occurred in the Midwest.

Although ACME speaks as the voice of management consulting, many of its members function more as industrial engineers than management consultants. But then ACME does stand for Association of Consulting Management *Engineers*. Not all firms doing consulting work are within ACME. Contract research organizations, such as Arthur D. Little, Inc., or Stanford Research Institute, also have management consulting staffs. Many accounting firms—particularly Peat, Marwick, Mitchell & Co. and Ernst & Ernst —have "management services" divisions which compete head-on with the largest consulting firms and nearly equal them in size. They do not belong to ACME nor does it seem likely at the present time that they will be invited in, since most ACME partners become quite uncomfortable when the subject of accountants in consulting is raised. They also become uncomfortable at the mention of the George S. May International Company, of whose aggressive sales methods they disapprove. One other extremely large consulting firm, Alexander Proudfoot Company, founded by a former May sales manager, also does not have ACME membership.

Early in 1967 five vice-presidents (including the well-known Harry W. Knight) defected from Booz-Allen to form a new consulting organization known as Knight & Gladieux. Within a few weeks of its founding the firm signed a lease in a building under construction to provide space for a staff of one hundred. It is not in ACME, as of this writing, because it is too young. Many other reputable organizations do not have ACME membership because they either do not meet all membership requirements or they have not been asked. A few say they don't want to belong, but they may be rationalizing. About 150 of the consulting firms in the United States are considered "large" by ACME standards. Another 350 are medium-sized. The remainder of the estimated 2,700 consulting firms are smaller specialty organizations. ACME also states that there are several thousand individual practitioners, if anything probably a conservative estimate. This figure would not include the possibly still larger number of individuals who moonlight as consultants, taking occasional assignments in addition to their regular jobs or while they are looking for new jobs. Many college professors also consult.

Determining the numbers of those engaged in consulting is more an academic than a real problem anyway. In fact, it's really a semantic problem. The difficulty arises in defining exactly *what is* a management consultant, or a management consulting firm. Ask a group of businessmen—or

The Amorphous Umbrella

for that matter, a group of consultants—and you'll probably get as many answers as people you ask. The word *consultant* is usually defined as "a person who gives professional or technical advice, as a doctor, lawyer, engineer, editor, etc." Thus a management consultant would seem to be a person offering professional or technical advice to management, a sort of doctor to big business.

For reasons we will discuss in a later chapter, management consultants dislike being thought of as "doctors," although they like the idea of consulting's being considered "a profession." Indeed, most people within the consulting industry define their work in rather grandiose terms. Philip W. Shay, the executive director of the Association of Consulting Management Engineers, attempted a definition in a promotional booklet entitled "How to Get the Best Results from Management Consultants" that ACME distributes to businessmen on request. Shay wrote: "Management consulting is the professional work performed by specially trained and experienced persons in helping managers of various kinds of enterprises solve managerial problems and maximize economic opportunities by systematic analysis of facts and the application of objective judgment based on specialized knowledge, skills, and techniques."

Apparently unsatisfied with that explanation, ACME redefined consulting in one directory of membership: "Management consulting is essentially an organized effort, by specially trained and experienced persons, to help managers solve managerial problems and maximize economic opportunities, through the application of objective judgment based on specialized knowledge and skill and systematic analysis of facts." That particular definition rambled on for several paragraphs beyond that opening salvo, but apparently failed to satisfy most ACME partners, because in a recent directory it has been replaced by a somewhat updated version of Shay's original definition.* The catchphrase that the consultants seem to like, however, is "maximize economic opportunities." It implies that the businessman who hires a consultant eventually will get something for his money, such as increased profits.

Speaking in basic terms, the chief function performed by a consultant is simply to solve problems. Accepting "problem solving" as the skill performed, the chief attribute of the (forty-five) firms either skilled or fortunate enough to belong to ACME is the ability (partly because of size) to offer problem-solving skills for many kinds of problems. In stating their capabilities, consultants usually list areas such as marketing, production, executive recruiting, organization, operations research, executive compensation, and so on into the night. "When you read a brochure for Booz, Allen & Hamilton," the head of a small consulting firm told me, "it reminds you of a lost government looking for a country."

Almost any individual who has worked as a consultant for more than a few months will have developed a further means of defining the scope of his work. "A consulting firm sells the time of intelligent analytical people who will operate in a given situation using the experience of the firm

---

* See Appendix A.

The Amorphous Umbrella

in previous similar situations," explains John W. Mitchell, a Fry Consultants vice-president. "When you talk about business consultants," adds Rudy Dallmeyer, a vice-president for Donald R. Booz & Associates, "you're talking about men who are selling judgment and experience rather than particular expertise." According to F. Lee H. Wendell, an A. T. Kearney & Company vice-president, "Management consulting is the profession that brings special techniques and judgment to help management improve its profit, or in the case of institutions to provide better services at lower costs."

Many businessmen, however, talk about management consultants in less grandiose terms. They look aghast at recent efforts by those within consulting to confer professional status upon themselves and thus bracket themselves with doctors and lawyers. Many businessmen are antagonistic toward consultants. In seeking information for this book I would frequently speak with others about "the management consulting profession," but not everyone would allow this casual reference to pass without challenge. "May I gently chide you," one vice-president for the Chase Manhattan Bank replied in a letter, "for stating that management consulting is a profession. I do not think it is but will be very interested if you can furnish me proof."

One individual with whom I spoke, a person who had spent a year at Booz-Allen before deciding management consulting was not the career he wanted to pursue, said, "I never met a group of people before who had so much brilliance, and so little wisdom."

At one point during my research I interviewed Raymond C. Hagel, who before becoming chairman of Crowell Collier and Macmillan, Inc., had served as a marketing consultant. When I again used the term "management consulting profession," he suggested that "the advice industry" might be a more appropriate description. "Consulting is not a profession," Hagel explained. "It's simply an amorphous umbrella that anybody can get under, and with no price of admission."

Although consultants are accepted more readily today than they were two decades ago, a tendency still exists within the business community to accept consultants for their skills but somewhat look down on them much like the caterers that supply rolls for the executive dining room. This is partly a defensive reaction. Certain executives feel sensitive about having to call in a business doctor for help. They interpret this—or think *others* may interpret this—as an admission of weakness, an abdication of authority. Many a senior executive, who has spent thirty years clawing his way to the top of the pyramid, resents having to pay three hundred dollars a day for the services of someone only several years out of Harvard Business School. Thus I found numerous businessmen who, while admitting that they use consultants, insisted that the consultant performed no function that they or their own staffs couldn't perform as well, or better, if given the time. And many consultants, recognizing their clients' sensitivities, echo this same point of view. "Giving advice to people is no more than updating their skills," suggests Harvey C. Krentzman, a Boston-area

The Amorphous Umbrella

consultant. "Every ten years there's a complete turnover in knowledge. The consultant brings into business what almost any businessman could learn if he had the time to learn it."

I'm not sure I agree completely with that statement. Consultants *are* more than merely talented, male Kelly Girls. Maybe it once was true that consultants only bought the hiring executive time, an extension of his staff, but business and the techniques of management have reached such a sophisticated level recently that for profit-minded companies management consultants are no longer merely a luxury. They are almost a necessity. "I wouldn't want to do business today without access to a consultant," says Rudy Dallmeyer. "It's a competitive weapon. A company president may decide he's smart and doesn't need a consultant, but he wakes up when his competitors start taking off like a skyrocket."

As evidence Dallmeyer cited two food distribution companies located across the street from each other in a Midwestern city. A dozen or so years ago, company number one hired Booz, Allen & Hamilton to carry out a major organization study aimed toward the future and also to analyze certain marketing operations. At intervals of a few years the company either retained Booz-Allen or other consulting firms for additional studies or to update the first ones. The company's sales increased nearly tenfold and profits soared. Its future now seems limited only by how large the Federal Trade Commission will allow it to get. Meanwhile, company number two found itself left far behind. Recently it retained McKinsey & Company in an attempt to catch up.

It would be wrong to assume that Booz-Allen and the other firms that worked with company number one wrought a miracle and it also would be wrong to expect that McKinsey can now intone the proper magic words over company number two and achieve instant success. If the top executives of the first company were astute enough to call in consulting firms at the proper times, they probably were astute enough to be making all the other correct business moves too. Invariably it is the well-managed companies that have more success in their consulting relationships. This is the first law of management consulting.

Part of the success in utilization of consultants comes from choice. There are many types of consultants. If you glance at a classified telephone directory, you may feel that ACME's estimate of 2,700 management consulting firms is even more conservative than is actually the case. A recent edition of the Chicago Yellow Pages, for example, listed 269 firms and/or individuals under the title "Management Consultants." In addition to this listing there were separate listings for "Business Counselors," "Engineers—Consulting," and "Engineers—Industrial." Booz-Allen listed itself under all four headings.

In the broadest definition of the term—as someone who advises management—three categories of management consultants exist:

1. *The Generalists.* Normally this category consists of the larger firms such as McKinsey or Booz-Allen, but some

The Amorphous Umbrella

smaller firms such as Donald R. Booz and Associates or The Boston Consulting Group also would qualify. Firms in this category typically, but not always, belong to ACME. They tend to work in many different areas of advising management. Normally a generalist firm can solve most problems thrown at it, partly because it is selling broad-line analytical skills, and partly because by growing to large size it will have accumulated men covering most specialities. Many individual practitioners and moonlighting professors, however, would be considered generalists.

2. *The Specialists.* Firms in this group concentrate on one particular discipline or sometimes serve one particular industry. Specialist firms normally are smaller than generalist firms. For example, even the largest executive-search firms have only a few dozen professionals on their staff. The giant Alexander Proudfoot Company, however, is essentially a specialist firm. It markets a specific business technique aimed at cutting costs. Since ACME limits its membership to firms providing several disciplines, a true specialist firm, by definition, could not qualify for membership. In many cases the smaller specialist firms work for smaller businesses, although some highly qualified ones work at the highest levels in industry. Many specialist firms list themselves simply as "management consultants," but operate best in certain well-defined areas and recognize that fact. The ethical ones will turn down business outside their area of competence. A few specialist, or semi-specialist, firms recognize they operate best in certain areas, but sometimes the sniff of money lures them outside

their competence. Some specialist firms don't operate well in any area, but hopefully they don't last long.

3. *The Masqueraders.* For this last group the term management (or business) consultant becomes merely a euphemism to cover an activity which, while sometimes giving aid and support to industry, doesn't qualify in the strictest sense as management consulting.

An example of a person who falls into this last category —although certainly with no malicious intent—is New Yorker Ulmont O. Cumming. Several years ago *True* magazine featured a profile story on Cumming, billing him as "the nation's number one business spy." In the article Cumming admitted that when someone at a cocktail party asks about his occupation he replies blandly: "I'm a business consultant." He claims to answer this way merely to avoid discussion. I also know an executive recruiter who similarly identifies himself to strangers. He knows that if he admits he works as a recruiter they usually badger him to find them a job.

A large number of firms, however, exploit the term "management consultant" simply because of its public image. This is frequently true in the personnel field. "I once worked as a member of a firm that referred to itself by the title 'management consultant,'" an employment agency counselor told me. "I never did any actual consulting. I think we only used the title because it was impressive."

"Recently there has been a fuzzing up of the image of what consulting is," says Rudy Dallmeyer. "There are no

The Amorphous Umbrella

licensing or professional requirements. There is no board that certifies practitioners. Anyone can hang up a sign that says 'I'm a consultant.' "

Unemployed executives frequently hide under this label while seeking a job. When pressed by friends as to their present line of work they respond, "I'm working as a consultant." If the friend who asked the question has any tact, he'll change the conversation to a less sensitive area. Many such temporarily unemployed executives actually will consult on a part-time basis while seeking a job, or as a means of obtaining a job. Often they will perform quite competent work if given assignments in areas familiar to them. Executives past the compulsory retirement age sometimes become consultants partly out of boredom, but many times because a demand still exists for their knowledge. Sometimes an executive becomes a "consultant" in the company records, even though his salary continues, as a dodge to avoid compulsory retirement policies. The U.S. Government's Small Business Administration maintains a program called SCORE (Service Corps of Retired Executives), which utilizes retired executives on a voluntary basis to service businesses so small that they ordinarily couldn't afford to pay even the least expensive individual consultant.

Individual consultants come in varying forms. Peter F. Drucker of New York charges fees of $500 a day simply to sit down with top executives and talk business for no other purpose than to stimulate their thought processes. Most universities have faculty members on their staff who, particularly in the areas of business and scientific technologies,

make more from part-time consulting work than they do
from their professorial salaries. Harvey C. Krentzman of
Newton, Massachusetts, operates as an individual practitioner in small and medium-sized firms at fees ranging from
$200 to $300 a day. In a typical five-day week he normally
will have functioned in five different firms. "I can generate
enough activity in a single day to keep the firm hopping for
a week," says Krentzman. "If I stayed there too long I'd be
stepping all over myself. Big consulting firms couldn't
operate that way. If they had to schedule their men on a
day-by-day basis they'd go crazy."

The question of whether to go to a small firm or a large
firm for help is one that constantly bothers businessmen.
Do you seek a specialist or a generalist? And if you choose
the generalist, do you seek the big generalist or the little
generalist? Most major management consulting firms dislike doing small jobs simply because, like any large industry, they have start-up costs. But their dislike for small
jobs only becomes evident as long as they can continue to
get big ones. Booz-Allen claims it rarely bills less than
$10,000 an assignment. Actually it probably accepts more
of these assignments than its partners would like to admit.
Running a management consulting firm is somewhat like
having the golf-cart concession at the country club. Sooner
or later along comes a rainy day.

In his booklet "How to Get the Best Results from Management Consultants," ACME's executive director Philip
W. Shay discusses the question of choosing brand-name
firms as follows: "On the premise that the company's prob-

The Amorphous Umbrella

lems will receive more attention from the principals of a small firm, does this factor outweigh the advantages of the greater facilities and more varied talents that a large firm is likely to possess? Is the problem such that employing a 'name' firm will carry greater weight with bankers, or the company's board, or prospective customers? Could the problem be solved by a qualified individual practitioner? These are questions that top management must decide."

Shay may be leaving the question for "top management" to answer, but he manages to give some very strong arguments in favor of the larger firms.

Not all businessmen can either afford to work with the blue-ribbon ACME firms, or want to work with them. McKinsey and Booz-Allen are delivering what might be classified as a branded product, and like any branded product it costs more than what the average shopper finds at the discount store. While a greater danger of buying inferior merchandise exists at a discount store, a shrewd shopper sometimes can obtain more for his dollar there than at the prestige department store downtown.

He also may save money if he knows exactly what specialized service he wants performed and can go directly to the firm most competent to perform that specialty. For practically anything that a businessman might want to do on a once-in-a-lifetime basis, there exists a specialty firm ready to serve him. Dudley F. King & Company and Georgeson & Company are two specialist firms whose main work consists of handling proxy solicitations for companies fighting stockholders or stockholders fighting companies. Seyfarth, Shaw, Fairweather & Gerlandson, a law firm, specializes in helping companies negotiate with unions. Know Associates will establish door-to-door sales routes for companies. If a corporation seeks to build a new plant or relocate an old one, it can call on The Fantus Company's services. Kei Yamato, president of the International Business Management Company, specializes in helping American companies mate with potential subsidiaries in the Far East. Jerry Verlen, a New York consultant, will walk in the front door of a failing men's retail store, assume its management for several weeks or months, and put it back into the black. In addition, advertising agencies often function as consultants in the area of marketing, while public relations firms often advise companies in the area of communications. All of the above are consultants, but they are not "management consultants" in the strict sense of the word.

There is also practically no limit to the amount of "free" consulting a company can get from whomever it purchases equipment. This is particularly true in the area of electronic data processing. Large corporations often maintain internal consulting staffs. At least one, Distillers Corp.–Seagram, Ltd., maintains an *external* one for the exclusive use of its network of 450 independent wholesalers. In four years, Seagram's consulting arm grew from one part-time staff consultant to a department of five full-time consultants. It breaks even on billings of close to $100,000 a year.

Many specialist firms do consulting for industries or professions that the generalist management consultants normally wouldn't touch. Martin L. Gross, in his book *The Doctors,* estimated there were more than one hundred consulting firms specializing in doctors' business problems. Gross quoted one medical consultant as saying: "Before I can do anything for a doctor I make a survey of his practice. I spend a full day in his office, go over his records, day book, taxes and collections. I sit in his waiting room and make believe I'm a patient. I listen to the girls on the phone making his appointments, and then spend two uninterrupted hours interviewing the doctor. A few days later I deliver a report."

Except for obvious differences in the personnel involved, that's a fairly good description of how McKinsey & Company might handle an assignment for someone like Xerox Corporation. Most typically a management consultant operates in three stages. First, he operates like a vacuum cleaner, sucking in information. Next, he operates like a computer, sorting the information, analyzing it, and comparing it with his past knowledge and experience. Finally, he operates like a tape recorder, playing back the gathered and rearranged information to the client. The typical management consultant might be compared to a business-oriented Ann Landers.

●

The variations in assignments are so many that often the simplest means of explaining the role played by management consulting firms in solving business problems is simply to cite case histories. Take for example the case of a large textile manufacturing company with several dozen mills scattered throughout the South. One mill in a small South Carolina town had been purchased several decades before. The textile company had retained the former owner as plant manager, telling him, "As long as you continue to make a profit you have a job." For sixteen years the mill did show a profit, then the manager died and his son became manager. Within three years the mill began to operate at a loss.

The simplest solution seemed to be: fire the son. But could a different manager do any better? Perhaps a better solution might simply be to abandon the mill. Nobody at the mill was qualified to make the detailed study that the problem demanded and nobody at company headquarters had time. The textile company management decided to go outside for help.

Several weeks later on a Monday morning, a team of three management consultants appeared at the South Carolina mill. They had flown in from New York the previous night. They began to roam through the plant examining its operation and speaking with workers as well as with the foremen and mill executives. The workers talked freely, but with a certain amount of fear, perhaps sensing that should the consultants' decision go against them the mill would close and they would lose their jobs.

Bit by bit, as interview piled on interview, the picture clarified. The consultants discovered that the new manager did not understand textile mill operation as well as his father had. He had purchased too much second-grade

The Amorphous Umbrella

cotton which, when mixed too freely with first-grade cotton, produced low-quality goods, what the industry refers to as "seconds." Poor ventilation caused uncomfortable working conditions, lessening worker efficiency. When one of the consultants climbed atop one of the machines, he nearly choked because of chemical fumes. He mentioned this to the mill executive and was told: "They [meaning the workers] can stand it better than we." The workers sensed this attitude on the part of their superiors, and production suffered.

But all the blame could not be laid on the present management. The previous manager had maintained profits mostly by "running out the mill," that is, failing to spend money to replace obsolete equipment. Even if he had not died, his past sins would have overtaken him. His son's inexperience merely accentuated, rather than caused, the problem.

One of the consultants involved in the textile mill study told me of meeting with a group of night-shift workers in a shack outside the mill. It was December; the night was cold and rainy. "The workers wanted their story told," recalled the consultant. "They spilled out everything they knew. After the meeting one woman who was six feet tall and must have weighed 200 pounds shook her fist in my face. She said, 'After us coming out here in the cold, if something isn't done to improve this place I'm coming after *you* first!' "

The consulting firm, whether because of that woman's threats or not, advised against either relocating or abandoning the plant. The son received a less sensitive job and a more skilled manager assumed command. The parent textile company spent $3 million rehabilitating the plant, which eventually showed a profit again.

Evidence of this particular consulting assignment's success appeared quite dramatically on a profit and loss statement. Not all work done by consultants lends itself to such easy measurement. An executive compensation study, for example, may actually cause corporate profits to shrink somewhat if the conclusion is to raise salaries. It may be difficult a half dozen years later to relate an organization's improved competitive position to less turnover among personnel.

"We're usually planting some pretty long-range seeds," says Rudy Dallmeyer. "It takes many years to see the results of the things we're doing. It's like drawing a map and saying take this road instead of the other one. When you start down the road you usually can't see where it will lead."

Corporations frequently ask management consulting firms to make organization studies. A team of consultants may swarm around a corporation headquarters for months interviewing everything in gray flannel that moves. After their departure, the only visible reminder of the consultants' one-time presence (besides a six-figure canceled check in the accounting department) may be that the boxes, and lines between the boxes, on the corporation organization chart will have been shuffled. If three or four years later profits should rise, no one will be able to say with any justification that the consultants deserve the credit. The chairman of the board, not the management consulting firm, accepts the applause at the stockholders' meetings. At the same time, should the corporation's profits start to sag, that same chairman will know exactly where to point the finger of guilt.

Often the best advice a consultant can give his client is to do nothing. In the early sixties a major oil company on the West Coast considered adding food-vending machines in their service stations. The top executives divided down the middle on what soon became a major controversy within the organization. "It was like trying to watch a badminton game from under a net," one executive caught in the middle said. "We decided to call in an outsider. He could be impartial, and perhaps most important, he wouldn't have to live with the losers after it was all over."

The outsider called in was the management consulting firm Booz, Allen & Hamilton. In keeping with the high status of the corporation (which ranked in the top twenty-five of *Fortune*'s annual list of the 500 largest U.S. industrial corporations), a Booz-Allen vice-president (who ranked high in seniority with the firm) made the initial contacts and interviewed the key executives. Then he left, leaving the assignment in the hands of an "associate," which on Booz-Allen's three-step pyramid is halfway between the bottom and the top. The associate supervised the work of several "consultants" (the title given to the firm's lowest echelon, their so-called bright young men), who interviewed executives of lesser status and began visiting service stations. They also examined what data they could find related to station operation in the corporate headquarters.

With the research completed the vice-president returned to present the final report. He commented that most service stations have little surplus parking space. "Food will merely encourage customers to remain in the stations longer," he said. "The result will be congestion. In addition, local restaurant owners, who buy gasoline too, may be offended." The Booz-Allen vice-president recommended a trial in several selected stations. This would permit the oil corporation executives to determine how successful food vending would be before fully committing themselves. It was a polite way of saying, "Don't touch food vending with a ten-foot pole."

The chief executive decided to accept the report. Whether food vending in service stations could have proved profitable may never be fully proved, but the members of the organization—including those who had favored the now lost cause—seemed satisfied with the thoroughness and objectivity of the report. It also showed that good consulting often is more art than science.

Consultants get hired not only for their objectivity, but also for their anonymity. Executives of a major chemical company which had acquired a new subsidiary decided that they wanted to expand the subsidiary's business in the sale of phosphates, an area of the market previously dominated by a large, well-entrenched competitor. Not wishing their competitors unduly alerted, the chemical company

The Amorphous Umbrella

hired Fry Consultants to serve as a somewhat anonymous fact-finder.

In this instance the information didn't lie within the organization requesting the study, but outside it. The consultants went directly to leading chemical organizations and identified themselves as representatives of another chemical firm. They said they could not reveal the firm's name. "We'd like to discuss various marketing data with you," the Fry consultants said. "If you cooperate we'll give you a quantitative feedback on what we learn." As a result, 95 per cent of the industry agreed to participate.

Fry eventually determined that in order for their client to become competitive, it would have to purchase phosphate mines. The chemical company decided against that course of action and eventually sold the subsidiary.

One significant aspect of the market study was that except for the inquiring company's name and its purpose all information passed above the table. "There's no limit to the amount of information you can wring out of people if you're willing to lie," admits Richard Strubel, who supervised the study for Fry. "But we're not spies. Sometimes a person we're interviewing will open up with information we think our client has no right to know. If so, we won't tell him."

Management consulting firms traditionally refuse to discuss case histories in significant detail. "We would no more reveal the list of our customers than would a call girl," a member of one ACME firm once informed me. The chemical study done by Fry only became somewhat a matter of public record because the chemical company involved felt highly enough of it to allow its use as a case study at the Harvard Business School. Not all work done by consulting firms, however, gets studied at Harvard.

In fact, not all work done by consulting firms gets accepted by the client. Several years ago Booz, Allen & Hamilton studied the operations of a leading manufacturing concern in Louisville that ranked as the leader—at least in terms of reputation—in its industry. The concern's catalog sat on the drawing board of every engineer, and every engineer used that catalog when drafting plans. Frequently they would specify the Louisville concern's part as listed in the catalog, "or an equivalent." But when the contractor on the job examined the specifications, he often would purchase the equivalent part made by another company. The determining factor became price. Booz-Allen suggested revisions in the Louisville concern's pricing schedule and recommended changes in the sales organization. For example, they felt that the concern had too little business in one Northwestern city to warrant a full-time sales representative in that city. They recommended that the territory be covered by someone from the concern's more active San Francisco office visiting the Northwest city once a month.

The Louisville concern failed to adopt the recommendations. "Our report showed them great ideas," said the consultant who worked on the case, "but they had some

The Amorphous Umbrella

extremely conservative people within their organization and wouldn't follow through. Why they wanted our advice in the first place, I don't know."

"We're somewhat like eunuchs," sighs another consultant. "We can tell other people what to do, but we can't do it ourselves."

2

Is There a Doctor in the House?

In explaining the functioning of management consultants, it is difficult to avoid talking in medical terms. Certainly the doctor-patient relationship becomes obvious. Business consultants have been frequently referred to as the "doctors of management" in the popular press. Consultants themselves frequently use medical analogies in their conversation, in articles they write for business publications, and in speeches before management seminars. Medicine has achieved recognition as a profession, and consultants hunger for similar recognition. The picture of the skilled professional ministering to his worshiping patients apparently appeals to many consultants. Yet while they speak glowingly of the therapeutic values of their services to industry, they blanch when reminded that the patient on whom they perform surgery may be suffering something akin to cancer. "We prefer not to be viewed as doctors," says Thomas Roy of Donald R. Booz and Associates. "The idea that con-

Is There a Doctor in the House?

sultants are called in to cure sick businesses is one of the things we have got to overcome. The really sick and dying company cannot afford good consultants. It's too late."

Yet many businesses in trouble, in desperation, will turn to the Business Healers for help. During its last five years the once mighty Packard Motor Corporation reportedly spent hundreds of thousands of dollars on consultants, but they had asked for help too late. By then, the consultants could do little more than say, "You're right. You've had it." But not all of the consultants did just that. At least one large ACME firm studied Packard's problem and sensed that the chief executives wanted to stay in business despite all contrary evidence. In its report the consulting firm told the executives exactly what they wanted to hear.

Even when a sick or dying company obtains accurate advice on how to save itself, it may be unwilling to accept the advice—just as the patient threatened by a possible heart attack refuses to quit smoking or lose weight. I spoke with Carl Devoe, president of Executive House, Inc. As a member of a group of investors, he had purchased control of a once successful auto supplies manufacturing company whose business had been sliding steadily downhill. The new investors discovered that various management consultants had attempted to advise the company. Gathering dust in its files were two or three extensive reports, any one of which if applied might have arrested the company's decline. The reports had gone unimplemented.

"These reports required such massive doses of treatment," Devoe explained to me, "that the people in the judgment area were overwhelmed. As a result they did nothing." The new investors began to apply the recommendations of the consultants one step at a time. Soon the company began to show a profit again. Often the deficiencies in management that cause business failures also cause management consultants either to be not used or misused.

Seymour Tilles, a vice-president with The Boston Consulting Group, once described the problems of a small manufacturer of pyrotechnical devices for the readers of the *Harvard Business Review*. During World War II the manufacturer could barely meet demand, but in the postwar periods profits dropped. The manufacturer had only one client: the Government. He lost money for several years until the Korean War marked an upturn in the armaments business. Peace once more brought a downturn in sales, but this time the pyrotechnical manufacturer turned to a management consultant for help.

The consultant spoke with the manufacturer first to determine his problems. Then he traveled to Washington and spent several days at the Department of Defense talking to government officials about the possibilities of future orders. Next the consultant thoroughly examined the manufacturer's facilities trying to determine whether or not he could manufacture other products. Finally he walked into the client's office and handed him a bound report. "Your only choice is to liquidate," the consultant advised. "That's the only way the money you've made during boom periods won't be lost."

Is There a Doctor in the House?

The client immediately turned purple and buzzed for his secretary. "Put this report in the safe and lock it up," he snorted. "I'm going to sue these bastards!"

Tilles described this confrontation between consultant and client as having happened prior to 1961. Presumably if the pyrotechnical manufacturer survived until the late sixties, when the sum being spent annually for the war in Vietnam had reached $25 billion, he could walk into the Harvard Club and boast to his executive friends how he had ignored some bum advice given him by a management consulting firm.

The image of the consultant's healing mainly sick businesses had its foundation during the depression, a time when many of today's leading consulting firms had begun to take their first toddling steps toward maturity. In fact, management consulting is actually a depression-spawned business. In the thirties, the consultants thrived by serving sick industries that needed help; in the more prosperous sixties the focus of management consulting shifted to more healthy patients.

"It's fairly easy to state what the typical client is," says D. Reid Weedon, Jr., senior vice-president of Arthur D. Little, Inc. "It's always a company that's on the move for some reason or other. I dare say that better than 80 per cent of our business volume is related to change—differentiated from getting out of the hole." According to Robert S. Mason, director of information services for McKinsey & Company, "It's the hot company rather than the sick one who uses our services." McKinsey's William Perkins agrees:

"The bulk of our clients are exceptionally well-managed companies by any yardstick you want to throw against them."

As proof of the pink-cheeked well-being of their clients, the partners of most management consulting firms like to reach into their desks for *Fortune*'s annual compilation of "The 500 Largest U.S. Industrial Corporations." Apparently all have been bitten by the consultant bug.

"If you look at these top 500 companies," says Fry's John W. Mitchell, "we have done work for 130 in the last three or four years. I doubt if many in the top don't use consultants on a regular basis." Booz-Allen deals with 85 out of the top 100 and three-fifths of the top 500. In describing McKinsey's relationship with this elite group several years ago, Arch Patton noted that his firm had served four out of the top five, six out of the top ten, twenty-one out of the top fifty, and 175 out of the top 500. Strongly implied was the fact that the higher the corporation on the industrial-profit pyramid, the more likely you would encounter the well-groomed hands of McKinsey & Company.

Indeed, the impression gained from talking to partners of management consulting firms is that the top 500 corporations use their services so frequently that consultants must be bumping into each other in the halls and in washrooms. If it hasn't happened already, undoubtedly someday a Booz-Allen staff member will knock on an office door, introduce himself to the man seated behind the desk, start asking questions for a survey, and discover only later that

Is There a Doctor in the House?

he is talking to a staffman from Cresap, McCormick and Paget.

In truth, however, the largest corporations use management consulting firms relatively less than do many smaller organizations. They may spend more total dollars on consulting services, but it forms a smaller percentage of their annual gross expenses.

Partly out of curiosity, partly from a desire to check the claims listed previously, I wrote directly to the chairman of the board of the top twenty-five companies on *Fortune's* list. Of the seventeen replies I received, only five corporations freely admitted using consultants on a regular basis. Six additional corporations admitted using them occasionally, but qualified their answers by saying they deal more often with specialists than general management consulting firms. Another half dozen denied employing consultants. A few in this latter group admitted cautiously that their smaller divisions might use them. Those turning thumbs down on consultants included General Motors Corporation, U.S. Steel, Shell Oil Company, and General Telephone & Electronics Corporation. The Procter & Gamble Company indicated that it hadn't used consultants in the last five years, "except, perhaps, in the most trivial fashion."

This survey says less about the actual usage of management consultants by large corporations than it says about their willingness to *admit* they use them. Later I learned that every one of the anti-consultant corporations used either McKinsey or Booz-Allen.

One reason why the billion-dollar corporations actually may not use consultants as extensively as merely multi-million-dollar corporations is that the larger the firm, the better it can utilize the talents of a full-time internal consulting staff. Thus much so-called consulting in firms like General Motors or General Electric gets done by salaried employees. Another factor probably reflected in this survey may be that many board chairmen don't know what may be happening on the outer reaches of their organization.

A third factor may be the still prevalent "sick business" image that pervades consulting. "When a consultant walks into a company," says Rudy Dallmeyer, "many people unfortunately look on it as though an ambulance had pulled up to the neighbor's door." Most chairmen may not want it advertised that consultants are on the premises for fear their stockholders may panic and deflate the value of their stock options. Or they may fear complaints from stockholders who believe the fees paid consultants to be exorbitant. As anyone who has polled businessmen soon discovers, a certain percentage of executives consider the use of consultants a waste of time and money. Thus while the identity of the accounting firm utilized by a corporation appears as a matter of record in the annual report, few, if any, management consultants ever get identified by name. The identity of fees paid them is buried under general headings such as research or administrative expenses.

I discussed this lack of identification with Little's Reid Weedon. He commented: "There's a reluctance on the part

Is There a Doctor in the House?

of many people to admit they use a consultant. It's looked upon as a sign of weakness."

Weedon pondered a few seconds over what he had just said, then smiled: "I must say that from our standpoint we certainly don't look on it that way."

•

The typical management consulting client is, indeed, a healthy business, despite what many executives still believe. "Curiously enough," writes Walter Guzzardi, Jr., in *Fortune,* "only certain kinds of clients are hospitably received. While consultants love clients, they do not love them all equally. The old adage that consultants specialize in sick companies is so far from the truth that today a company really on the skids may have difficulty finding a reputable consulting firm to take its case. Like the doctor who recently refused to treat a man bleeding of a gunshot wound, management consultants dislike death on the premises—it can be messy, and people may draw conclusions that could be bad for business."

Consulting firms recognize that a business's ill health may serve as a symptom of a poor management team, which may be unable, or unwilling, to accept the suggestions that might be proposed. Thus, particularly in times of high demand for their services, consulting firms reject assignments that promise to become problems. One McKinsey partner told me how his firm had been asked to reorganize a company by its chairman of the board. Mc-

Kinsey sensed the problem to be the chairman himself. "Look, you're not going to buy what we have to tell you," they told him, "so let's not even start."

"Some firms hire consultants because of a force outside of management," explains Reid Weedon. "A financial institution with a lot at stake may force the management to go outside for help. These situations almost inevitably turn out badly no matter how good a job the consultant does. You end up with information which the client isn't able to use because he doesn't have the capacity to use it—or because he doesn't *want* to use it. Either way you have an unsatisfied client, and very frequently some people associated with the business will say the consultant did a great job and other people will say he did a lousy job—and the twain will never meet. So that if we saw something like that coming we tend to steer clear of it, because it's really hopeless."

Recently Fry Consultants accepted an assignment with a company in the educational equipment field which had allowed its position in the market to erode through sloppy management. The company president, although not a majority stockholder, controlled a considerable number of shares. Fry analyzed the company's problems and found one of them to be the president. They diplomatically recommended his promotion to chairman of the board, where he no longer would make decisions, and supervised the hiring of a new executive officer. "He agreed to this at first," commented John W. Mitchell of Fry, "but he couldn't quite stomach the idea of someone else's making decisions.

Is There a Doctor in the House?

Within six months he fired the new man and he hasn't talked to us since."

If the result of such an unsatisfactory assignment meant only that the consulting firm would no longer work for that client again, its partners probably would merely shrug and proceed to *Go,* remembering to collect their $200. But like infidelity in marriage, ineffectiveness among consultants may be hard to conceal. It soon gets advertised where it can hurt them the most: in the marketplace. "When you're talking about business reputations it's a small world," says Victor A. Lennon of Lennon/Rose. "We have to do a good job, because one blown assignment can undo one hundred good ones for us."

Because of the ethics of their profession, which considers it infra dig to advertise, most management consulting firms obtain a large share of their new business either directly or indirectly from former satisfied clients. If for one reason or another a client becomes dissatisfied with the surgery performed on his organization, he not only will refrain from referring new business to the consultant whose knife slipped, but he will make certain that all his luncheon dates and golf partners know why. If through botched surgery a patient dies, the consultant's reputation may be irreparably soiled. A patient whose doctor took out his liver instead of his appendix can sue for malpractice. No entirely satisfactory alternative to malpractice suits exists under the framework of half-law, half-handshake, that binds consultant to client, so if the latter is unhappy all he can do is scream.

And as we shall see, sufficient screaming does occur.

●

Although similarities do exist between consultants and doctors, the differences between the M.D. and the unlicensed consultant far outnumber the similarities. When you consider the scope of its practice, Booz, Allen & Hamilton might be compared to the Mayo Clinic, but the real Mayo Clinic probably never would send a team of doctors traveling several thousand miles to visit a patient. On the rare occasions when a client visits the office of a management consulting firm, he encounters large numbers of empty desks. The greatest share of all consulting activity occurs at the client's place of business or in the field. "There's not much you can do at the home office," comments a former Booz-Allen consultant, "except tidy up the final report."

In short, consultants (unlike most medical doctors) *do* make house calls.

Few consulting assignments are exactly alike. Most, however, form a general pattern. A consulting assignment normally begins when the president or chief executive officer of a company discovers that he has some problems that need solving and decides to hire a management consulting firm to solve them. In most cases the president will select a management consulting firm he knows either by reputation or from past experience.*

———

* Most ACME firms indicate that up to 80 per cent of their business is with clients who have used them before.

Is There a Doctor in the House?

According to one Booz-Allen vice-president: "When we begin an assignment, one of our officers first will sit down and chat with the client. Later we may send in one or two other men to determine the scope of his problems and how much work we need to do. Once we've isolated the problem, we return home and write a proposal letter. This would include a cost estimate and what we expect to do. Sometimes we might back out of the assignment if we think the problem doesn't lend itself to being solved."

At Booz-Allen someone at the vice-president level (or higher) makes this initial contact with the client and writes the proposal letter which serves as a contract. At Mc-Kinsey, a "director" handles this transaction. "It's not really a contract," says Rudy Dallmeyer. "It's more of a gentleman's agreement. Our proposal letters simply state what we will do. We don't ask for a written acceptance. If we have one I suppose it amounts legally to a contract. But the essence of our work is again like that of a lawyer or a doctor. If we aren't doing you any good, let's go on to something else. Obviously it can be a precarious existence, especially if the medicine is strong and the treatment protracted. But our profession is healthy." There are exceptions to this no-contract arrangement. Contract research firms such as Arthur D. Little use them and any consulting firm that obtains a government assignment will find that a handshake is not enough.

Like the army, the management consulting profession has a hierarchy of rank. Each consulting firm generally has its own method of designating its consultants by titles, but most firms break responsibilities beneath the managing partners into three levels:

1. The officer of the firm
2. The middle-level consultant
3. The bottom-rung consultant

At McKinsey & Company this three-level hierarchy results in the titles:

1. Director
2. Principal
3. Associate

The chain of command at Booz, Allen & Hamilton is:

1. Vice-president
2. Associate
3. Consultant

Most other firms use similar titles or variations on them. A. T. Kearney & Company uses the same nomenclature as McKinsey, but instead of directors has vice-presidents. Cresap, McCormick and Paget has partners, principal associates, and senior associates. Fry used to follow Booz-Allen's pattern, reflecting a common heritage, but early in 1967 the firm retitled its associates as principals, subdividing them into managing principals and consulting principals.

Levels at one firm cannot always be compared to levels at another. Just as a navy captain outranks an army captain, a McKinsey principal stands higher in rank at his firm than a Booz-Allen associate does at his. A consultant becomes an associate within two or three years at Booz-Allen, whereas

Is There a Doctor in the House?

it takes the bottom-level McKinsey man between six to eight years to earn a title change from associate to principal.

After the officer (whether he be vice-president, director, or partner) has agreed with the client on the scope of the job, he returns to the home office to gather a team of consultants to accomplish the assignment. The average team will consist of three to five people. "We have to make sure we don't get so many men in a company that we disturb the client's business," comments a Booz-Allen vice-president. In the case of the largest corporations, however, the team may consist of several dozen consultants.

This team next journeys to the client company under the supervision of an "engagement director," who may or may not be an officer in the firm. In most cases this engagement director works immediately beneath the officer who "sold" the business and signed the contract. Frequently he is a middle-level consultant who has two to four bottom-level consultants under him. The officer, whose principal activity is development of business, may have more than a dozen engagement directors (on as many different assignments) reporting to him. The bottom-level consultant, on the other hand, has nothing under him except a chair while he is writing his report. If he needs someone to type that report he uses the firm's secretarial pool.

In actual practice this seemingly neat division of authority does not always follow seniority or the organization charts. According to Kearney's Richard Lopata: "Everybody in our firm is a consultant, and works as a consultant, and that goes for the highest partners. As soon as anyone spends all his time administrating we hop all over him. Every man is obliged to consult."

This insistence on the part of most partners that they continue to consult is almost an obsession. It might be compared to the hospital chief of surgery who enjoys making rounds in the wards. Thus C. Lee Walton, Jr., and James L. Allen, the managing directors of McKinsey and Booz-Allen, respectively, will find themselves, despite their high salaries, serving as working consultants beneath other engagement directors. In such a case, the engagement director will be an officer and not a middle-level consultant.

The engagement director ordinarily has two responsibilities: to manage the time of those under him, and to maintain liaison with the client. Since the majority of consulting assignments occur away from the home office, the team of consultants will live in a nearby motel or hotel, the client being billed for their expenses above and beyond their per diem billing rate. Typically they will spend mornings and afternoons on the premises of the client company interviewing executives or other employees and observing operations, but the consultant's day rarely ends at five. He will have reports to read and figures to analyze in the motel. If he spends the evening merely talking with his fellow workers, the subject under discussion will probably be the client's problems.

Friday after work the team of consultants climb aboard the first jet headed home and spend the weekend with their families. The client pays their fare, and it is part of

Is There a Doctor in the House?

the agreement that he do so. Bright and early Monday morning they arrive back on the job. A fair percentage of travelers you meet on Mondays at 6 A.M. at O'Hare Field and Kennedy Airport are management consultants. They are among the most peripatetic commuters in the world.

The impression held by those on the outside as to how management consultants work is that they spend a month or two with their stethoscopes probing the heart of their patient, return to their offices where they enter into consultations on the state of that patient's health, then finally one day appear at the office of the president that hired them and deposit a carefully worded and well-bound report on his desk, much like the goose laying the golden egg.

Most consultants, however, insist that rather than present only a report, they sit down with the client frequently during the assignment to discuss the work in progress. This is known as testing or pre-selling the results. It reduces the chances of the client's throwing the report back at the consultant the day after it is presented. According to Rudy Dallmeyer: "We've long since given up the Pandora's Box approach to consulting in that you open up the box and there the answer is. We like to work with the client so that he could write his own report if he had the time."

Usually the officer of the consulting firm will return to supervise the presentation of the ultimate report to the client president. This report is never merely mailed or handed to the president. It will be read to him, much as the minister reads the Gospel at church on Sunday morning, or at least synopsized in a specially staged presentation with the officer or partner in charge, even though his only connection with the actual work may have been to point the direction for the lower members of the consulting team. This is for a thoroughly good reason. While youngsters can be trusted to uncover facts, they cannot be expected to put their arm around the shoulder of a man thirty years their senior and tell him what to do. This requires a polished professional performance on the part of the partner, much of whose confidence may come from the fact that he has a higher salary than the man hiring him.

One former Booz-Allen consultant described to me how once he had been permitted to give a report to the client president. He admitted that he had botched the job, and the reason he knew was that in the cab heading back to the airport the partner told him so. "He told me I gave a beautiful report," the former consultant explained. "But the client president and I weren't tracking. I gave too much detail and technological information. I wasn't selling him. In fact, I was overwhelming him. The partner was very sensitive to the reactions of the man sitting there. Eventually he did a little recovery, but I had lost him. He told me that's why he was a partner and I was only a consultant." Eventually the firm lost the account.

And eventually the Booz-Allen consultant became a *former* Booz-Allen consultant.

Most firms bill monthly as the work progresses and, in fact, one unarguable statement that can be made about hiring a consultant is that it costs money. It's just like checking into the hospital: you may not be completely cured

Is There a Doctor in the House?

when you depart (you may even be dead), but you will have to pay a sizable bill. In the area of business, however, there is no Blue Cross or Medicare to ease the sting of the final reckoning.

Several years ago Charles L. Quittmeyer, then a professor at the University of Virginia, surveyed a number of mostly medium-sized businesses and determined that the average consulting assignment cost $10,000 with consultants billing their services at $175 a day.* A more recent survey of 202 companies made by The Dartnell Corporation also indicated median per diem rates of $175 with total fees for at least 50 per cent of the companies running from a low of $16,000 to a high of $60,000. Quittmeyer uncovered a high fee of $156,000. One official for a large oil corporation described to me his firm's use of several consulting firms during one recent year for assignments, "none of them very large." They had paid Kearney around $80,000 and Bruce Payne & Associates $25,000. A previous study by The Emerson Consultants had cost $100,000. They had also used Booz-Allen, seemingly indicating their belief that no one consulting firm had all the answers.

Generally speaking, the larger corporations pay larger consulting bills. This is not necessarily because their problems are more difficult, but because there may be more ground for the consultants to cover. The Metropolitan Life Insurance Company once hired McKinsey for a $700,000

---

* Median per diem rates by 1969 had risen to around $200. For a detailed breakdown on what consultants charge for their services, see Appendix C.

market analysis that lasted two and a half years. Shortly after the depression, U.S. Steel paid $1.5 million for what basically was one consulting assignment, although work was subcontracted to several firms including what was then McKinsey, Wellington & Company. Booz-Allen billed the U.S. Government $3 million for work done in the Philippines in the early fifties.

Credit for the largest management consulting assignment reportedly goes to Peat, Marwick, Mitchell & Company, which did $3.5 million worth of business with the Pennsylvania Railroad several years ago. Considering the amount of work Booz-Allen does for the army and McKinsey does for the air force, Peat-Marwick may only be running a distant third. The picture gets fuzzy, however, when you get into the area of continuous relationships with single clients for ten and twenty years.

In terms of dollars per hour, the record may belong to Ben S. Cole, president of Cole & Associates, Inc., a small Boston-based firm. Cole had dinner one evening with the president of a large industrial concern in northern Indiana. They merely chatted about business for several hours. Afterward the president said he felt he should pay for the several hours they had spent together. Cole shrugged the matter off.

Several days later Cole received a check from the president for $2,500. Astounded, he called his client to ask what the check was for. "That's what I figure the advice you gave me that night was worth," replied the president.

Is There a Doctor in the House?

Because of lower overhead costs, the smaller firms usually (but not always) charge less. Lennon/Rose consists of ten consultants whose per diem billing rate is between $175 and $200. The two partners charge $240 a day. Most major management consulting firms charge comparable rates (between $150 and $250) for their bottom-level consultants, but billing rates skyrocket considerably for men with more seniority. Associates (or principals, or engagement directors, or whichever title is placed on the second-level consultants) have a billing rate between $300 and $400. If a partner needs to be called in, his presence may boost charges by $500 a day, or $1,000 a day.

In most cases, the major consulting firms dislike discussing fees in anything but general terms. Booz-Allen consultants keep an hour-by-hour record of their daily activities in a small notebook provided by their firm. If you frisk a Booz-Allen man you'll probably find this notebook in his inside breast pocket. This hourly record is expected to be kept constantly up-to-date. It includes amounts of money paid for meals, taxicab rides, and any other items that eventually will become part of an expense statement. It also shows at what hour the consultant was working for what client. The partners consider this hourly record-keeping so important that if they ask a consultant for his notebook and find it not current within a few hours, it may be grounds for dismissal.

This notebook, however, rarely gets waved in the face of the man paying the bill. Per diem rates are merely for internal use, the client normally will be told. Usually when bidding for a job, a management consulting firm (more like a garage mechanic eyeing your car than a surgeon eyeing your appendix), will quote a general range where its bill will fall. If the actual costs (figured on a per diem basis) run higher than estimated, they swallow the difference—or at least they say they do. If lower, they lessen their bill accordingly. Needless to say, a partner whose estimates prove to have missed the target may find the other partners glaring at him rather sternly. A few consulting firms consider even a preliminary estimate an indignity. "We usually only give an estimate with a new client," I was told by Everett Smith, a senior partner at McKinsey & Company. "An old client won't even ask us."

"I assume they trust you," I commented.

"If not," replied Smith, "they shouldn't work with us."

Not all businessmen agree that consultants are to be completely trusted. Several years ago Crowell Collier and Macmillan, Inc., hired a large consulting firm for one assignment which eventually proved unsatisfactory. When the bill arrived Chairman Raymond C. Hagel, a former consultant himself, noticed what he thought to be disproportionate charges for out-of-pocket expenses. Many consulting firms bill the client for typing and clerical costs of their own staff "above a reasonable amount of time."

"I asked our financial department to ask the consulting firm for a breakdown of these charges," says Hagel. "The firm's reply was that it was the first time in their history that they had ever been asked to do this. They said that if we did not take their word for the charges *we* were not the type of organization that *they* wanted to do business with, and *they* were not the type of organization that *we* should do business with—which mirrored my sentiments exactly."

3

A Bank Account of Talents

A major steel corporation, realizing that its marketing abilities had outstripped its administrative capacity, decided within the last few years to reorganize. The corporation had three divisions, each selling to the same market. Each division had as its head a capable and tough-minded manager, and each of the three managers had developed an extremely loyal staff. Everyone at the top level of the corporation knew that changes needed to be made. The only question was: Who had the guts to make them? "Anyone on the inside who attempted to do the job would have been torn to shreds," commented one observer.

The top executives recognized this as a major obstacle blocking reorganization, so rather than risk an internal fight they looked to the outside for help.

They hired a management consulting firm, in this instance Fry Consultants. Fry completed the study. "The

A Bank Account of Talents

people in each of the three separate divisions might not necessarily have agreed with our recommendations," says Fry's John W. Mitchell, "but there would be no doubt in their minds that we were impartial. They knew we wouldn't take sides."

Too often executives base decisions more on passion and prejudice or political expediency rather than on sound business practices. An executive who has worked and golfed with a companion for a dozen years may not recognize his inability to perform certain jobs—or if he does recognize it he may say nothing, or if he does tell somebody he may not be believed. A company which has been operating with certain methods for many years may be blind to the fact that other methods might prove more profitable. The most successful businessmen are often the ones who realize they don't have all the answers. They are the ones who turn most frequently to outside experts to answer their questions and solve their problems.

The reasons why a businessman might want to hire a management consulting firm are numerous and varied. Nevertheless, certain patterns do prevail.

In a survey of 500 large- and medium-sized companies, business professor Charles L. Quittmeyer discovered that the most popular reason for using consultants was "to get an outside viewpoint." (This certainly was the case with Fry's steel corporation assignment.) The Financial Executives Research Foundation found in a similar study that the desire for an independent opinion, both in analyzing problems and in reviewing management's own conclusions, ranked second.* "Since he is an outsider," the Foundation claimed, "he has the perspective to bypass the company's specialized knowledge or convictions. An independent opinion helps the manager choose among conflicting claims or reconcile differences."

This theory that most managers "can't see the forest because of the trees" frequently is used by consultants themselves when asked to explain the value of their services. "In the beginning when a business operator starts out, he does everything," says former consultant John K. Diederichs. "He even sweeps the floor. As he prospers he begins to divide responsibilities among others and eventually loses intimate contact with what is going on at all levels. When he becomes really big he loses judgment to see his business as a whole."

"Suppose your product is salt, and it's not selling," adds Rudy Dallmeyer of Donald R. Booz and Associates. "You can call in a label designer and he'll provide you with a beautiful package that will make women want to reach for it on the shelf. But if your salesmen are so poorly trained that they can't get your product to the grocer, women will never see it. Or maybe your price is out of line with that of your competitors. What it finally comes back to is the need for a broad guy who can look at design, sales, price, then finally decide that they're all fine, but we've got a bad pouring spout. The women buy the product once and will never do it again."

* Utilization of the consultant's special skills and know-how ranked first.

A Bank Account of Talents

Dallmeyer talks about one assignment he handled for a Midwest consumer company. The company boasted a hotshot sales training director. He used every known device—booklets, seminars, training courses—in teaching his men how to push their products, yet profits had stalled. Finally the company's president hired a management consultant. "If there's one thing you won't have to improve," boasted the president, "it's our sales training. We have one of the top men in the country."

It is one of the duties of the management consultant to listen to the suggestions of the client president, but also to ignore his conclusions. Obviously if the client had all the answers before calling the consultant he never would have called him. Dallmeyer spent several weeks scrutinizing the consumer company with the care of an archeologist uncovering lost relics. Finally he made his recommendations.

"Your training director is doing a good job," he said. "In fact, he's doing *too* good a job. You're spending four weeks a year training your salesmen when two weeks should be enough. Get your salesmen out in the field where they can do some good." The consultant also rearranged the sales territories, balanced the work load, and advised pushing certain neglected products. Sales soon increased.

Ranking second on the Quittmeyer survey were two interrelated factors: the lack of skills or experience of regular employees, and the lack of time of regular employees. A businessman may not need either the talent or the time of an analyst with a master's degree in business administration on a year-round basis, but at specific intervals this need may present itself. "The client who engages us," explains Harland Riker of Arthur D. Little, "is like a man who opens up a bank account and the bank is full of talents instead of dollars. When he opens this account he has drawing power on this fantastic range of talents in the amounts he wants them. And when he doesn't want them he can turn them off, and the meter isn't running."

"We deal with problem situations," says Walter Foersch, president of his own consulting firm in Rochester, New York. "A problem might be a problem simply because you don't have the hands and minds to apply to it, so you hire the consultant for an extra pair of hands and minds. This solves the problem of limited manpower, and I think this is a very good and legitimate reason for hiring consultants."

Management consulting firms frequently add more specialists to their staffs as they grow in size. The major firms now see the need for additional expertise where previously they thought only judgment skills were needed. As a result many management consulting firms have begun to reach out for specialists to be brought into their firms at a relatively high level. Previously most men became officers, or partners, by starting as staff consultants and working their way up. Within the last few years, however, McKinsey brought David Hertz, a former professor of industrial engineering at Columbia, into the firm as a principal. Hertz joined the firm as a specialist in operations research and the management sciences, and later assumed responsibility for computer systems as well. Almost a quarter of the assignments in McKinsey now involve the development of

A Bank Account of Talents

models and various uses of electronic data processing techniques. Six or seven years ago, this percentage would have been near zero.

As consultants continue in tenure with a firm (rising from bottom- to middle- to officer-level), they find themselves building a background of specific knowledge which becomes extremely marketable. A consultant who achieves status as an "expert" in his field, whether it be economic predictions or executive compensation, becomes a sizable asset in selling prospective clients.

Paradoxically, consulting firms often find themselves unable to make maximum use of their expertise. A firm that had just made a thorough analysis for one company of the automotive parts industry, for example, seemingly could peddle its knowledge throughout that industry. However, the Code of Professional Ethics followed by ACME members (as well as common sense) prohibits a consulting firm from bouncing from one company to another within a single industry.*

Certain exceptions do exist. A firm that made a market study for one company might reorganize one of its competitors—but only with permission from the first. In talking to the partners of the top management consulting firms you sense a certain sadness at their literally having to flush much of their hard-earned knowledge down the drain. Yet because of necessary confidences, they realize that a lawyer

---

* "We will serve two or more competing clients at the same time on problems in a sensitive area only with their knowledge," so states Article IX of the Code.

can't work for a murderer and the district attorney at the same time. This inability on the part of any single firm of consultants to cannibalize entire industries has been one factor limiting the growth of individual management consulting firms within the United States. Much of the recent single-firm expansion has occurred by establishing offices abroad and tapping new clients in different industries. Firms such as Booz-Allen or McKinsey cannot grow too large without losing both effectiveness and maneuvering room. Some observers feel that they may already have expanded beyond what might be considered optimum size.

In addition to the need for an outside viewpoint, temporary help, or particular skills, many other reasons cause businessmen to seek consultants. Often a businessman with a specific question will run to a consulting firm to have it answered. "Suppose I have $2 million cash," says John K. Diederichs. "Should I develop my own product line or buy a new company? Sometimes a consultant will come in and say, there is no answer! But that's an answer."

"One reason why you have consultants in is you don't know any answers," adds Richard B. Port, president of the Hanes Corporation's knitwear division in Winston-Salem, North Carolina, "or you have all the answers but don't understand the questions."

Still another reason why businessmen hire consultants is to help accelerate growth. According to Walter Foersch: "We have for a client a bank that wants to grow to over a million dollars. Now they're going to reach that goal with

A Bank Account of Talents

or without my presence. The only reason I'm here, is to help them reach it faster."

"Management consultants are very good when business either is going up very fast or down very fast," says Donald R. Booz. "When business is stable there is less demand for consulting help. The kinds of problems on which we can help best often are postponed. When the pressure is on, people reach for consultants and listen to them."

Ben S. Cole, president of the Boston-based Cole & Associates, claims that the work done by management consultants falls into three categories. "The first category is analysis and fact finding," he claims. "Any intelligent and educated person, if given carte blanche, can find out what the true problems in a given company are. If he hears the same complaints repeated often enough there's probably some basis in fact. The primary skill you need in consulting is the ability to listen and a reputation as a person who can be trusted."

Cole continues: "Second is the determination of solutions. This requires more experience. The consultant must determine what should be done, what will work? The answer to this is easy: there is no correct answer. Any one of twenty solutions may prove successful if the executives follow them through. Some decision has to be made. It doesn't matter, for example, if while you're planning a transportation system you decide to have a monorail or a tunnel. The important thing is to decide *which one*, then have a program and policies for implementing that decision. That's the final category: the area of persuasion, the implementing of policies. You can find all the problems, determine all the solutions, but if you can't convince the executives in charge to follow your advice you've wasted your time and their money. We consider persuasion, not the written report, to be the end product. We believe it part of our function to persuade people what they should do."

Cole, however, believes that a more basic and general reason for businessmen to hire consultants is to learn the truth. "It's a commodity that's almost impossible for people to get," he says, "particularly people in power. Their faults are multiplied by success. Everyone beneath them may be afraid to tell them the truth for fear of getting fired."

Telling the truth can prove hazardous. Cole tells the story of one president that retained Cole & Associates to do an organization study. Cole noticed that all of that company's top executives had reached their sixties. No younger men had been trained to replace them. Cole walked into the president's office carrying a set of actuarial tables detailing the mortality rates of men in their sixties. He compared the company to a college with all the members of its football team ready to graduate in the spring. Cole suggested that the company make a concentrated effort to hire and promote younger executives. "The president of that company has not talked to me since that day," says Cole. "We hurt his feelings. He followed our advice, but he didn't like it, and I don't blame him for not liking it." Cole paused. "Still, you've got to tell the truth."

A Bank Account of Talents

Part of the success of a good management consultant is an ability to sugar-coat the truth so the client can swallow it. "I once had a professor at Harvard who gave our class some good advice," says William Hocking, president of Fry Consultants. "He said you always have to call a spade a spade, but you don't have to call it a goddam shovel!"

There is a story that has become part of the consulting legend about the president of a Wisconsin company that wanted to choose a successor and hired Booz-Allen to do the job. The president was nearing retirement age and there were five vice-presidents beneath him. Booz-Allen was to evaluate all five and name the one most qualified to run the company.

Shortly after completion of the report, but before it could be acted upon, the president died. The board of directors (not realizing the report existed) met and voted on a new president. On his first day at his new position, the president opened the top drawer of his desk and found the Booz-Allen report inside. He noticed that the man selected was not him.

According to the story he picked up the intercom and buzzed for his secretary: "Miss Smith, have someone go out in the factory and see if there are any Booz-Allen men around. If so, tell them they're fired!"

●

Perhaps the most valuable asset that a consultant brings into any assignment is his own intensity. Management consulting firms carefully seek as employees individuals who possess this particular attribute. They want men who not only have the ability to focus laser-like on one particular problem, but who can hold that focus for long periods of time. "One reason for the effectiveness of consultants is that they often spend sixteen hours on the job," says former Booz-Allen consultant H. M. Tuttle. "A consultant away from home on an assignment sleeps for eight hours, but the rest of the time, even when he's eating dinner, he continues to think about the company's problems, so he's giving sixteen hours of effort while being paid for eight."

Many consultants I interviewed insisted that, rather than spend their evenings in a movie or at a bar when away from home, they often will continue working on their assignment into the night, either at the office of the company employing them or in their motel. Presumably because of this bred-in intensity and because of their desire to move upward in the business world, consultants fall prey to the vices of the world less often than either traveling salesmen or visiting conventioneers. Assuming this to be true, a company president seeking a consulting firm might wisely skip past the one with the branch office in his city. A consultant commuting home to wife, children, and a lawn that needs cutting may be personally happier and psychologically better adjusted, but he may not find time for those sixteen-hour work days. A president who pays travel expenses for a visiting consultant may find his bill slightly higher, but may profit in terms of value per dollar. When I mentioned this unproved theory to several individuals familiar with the consulting profession they denied

A Bank Account of Talents

its truth. "Consultants work sixteen-hour days even when they're at home," said one. If so, perhaps it is the consultants' wives who are not psychologically well adjusted.

"I worked for Booz-Allen for three-and-a-half years," one high-level consultant, now head of a large recruiting firm, commented to me. "I've also been in industry, and at reasonably high levels of industry. And there's no place where you get more effort per dollar spent than among reliable consulting firms. Part of it is because these guys are young, and the application is fantastic."

Another former consultant told me, "I think every organization we did any work for was better off because of our going in there." In describing the value of their work, consultants normally talk in abstract terms. They have to, because positive results are difficult to document. The head of one small consulting firm, however, showed me an illustrated presentation in a leather-bound notebook that he used while talking to prospective clients. One of his selling points was that the companies that hired him had received a return of $4.80 in tangible payroll benefits for every dollar spent. At the same time, he would not flatly promise any new client to achieve such results. He was merely citing statistics.

With certain notable exceptions, most consultants avoid guaranteeing savings or profits. "We will present our qualifications to prospective clients solely in terms of our ability, experience, and reputation," says Article III of ACME's Code of Professional Ethics. "We will not guarantee any specific amount of cost reduction or increase in profits from our efforts, nor will we accept an engagement where the fee is related to any cost reduction that may result."

"A legitimate consulting firm does not promise results," the vice-president of one ACME firm informed me. "We do say that here is what we are going to do, these are the actions we will take, but we don't guarantee that when we're through the company will double its sales. One of the trademarks of the less reputable organization is to promise the sky."

Most management consultants thus promise nothing but their time. Nevertheless, when you hear them speak, it seems obvious that their time may be the most valuable commodity in the world anyway. In fact, you get the impression that many consultants think of themselves as very fine fellows. A management consultant will not come right out and tell you that his work is the result of divine inspiration—but don't press him.

Without question, over the years the major consulting firms have devoted considerable time and effort to building an image of impartiality and detached efficiency. The Big Image consulting partners have succeeded in endowing their firm names with certain mystic qualities. Brand awareness exists on the part of executives hiring consultants, just as it does among housewives buying detergents. Far from being a symptom of a diseased business, the proper use of the proper consultants within the last few years has taken on respectability. It's like the ambitious executive who needs to belong to the right club. A certain prestige transfers to the company able to hire the right

A Bank Account of Talents

consulting firm. "Cresap's working with us now," a president can mention casually while relaxing in the sauna room of the Chicago Club, and his business friends will be impressed. No longer will they rush to sell their stock in his company; they may phone their broker to buy more. The ability to hire McKinsey has become a sign of affluence.

The partners of the Big Image consulting firms exploit their hard-won reputations as much as possible. The better a firm's reputation, the easier it becomes to sheathe its newest (and therefore lowest paid) employees with an air of credibility. When the chairman of the board who has hired McKinsey & Company meets the bright-eyed associates assigned to work with him he may blanch at their youthfulness, particularly if he compares their experience with what he will pay for their services. But he has purchased not merely the temporary availability of a pair of one-time Baker scholars, he has purchased the McKinsey name and reputation.

McKinsey probably achieves greater success in having its fresh-out-of-college consultants accepted by corporate executives than any other firm. This is for two reasons. Because it is the Rolls Royce of the consulting profession, McKinsey probably attracts as employees the most impressive individuals both from a standpoint of talent and ability to exhibit that talent. Second, because of McKinsey's past reputation for high-quality work, executives assume that the young consultant facing them would not be working for the firm if he did not have something to offer. The advantage of having a brand product also operates with the other Big Image firms: CMP, Booz-Allen, Kearney, and Fry. Of the four, CMP probably comes closest to matching McKinsey in impressiveness of its staff members. For lesser known firms, ACME membership is a form of brand identification. The Association consists of only forty-five members, and rejects an average of sixty applications for new membership a year rather than dilute its image. ACME firms thus operate with a built-in edge over smaller and less well-established consulting firms. In many instances these firms may be equally competent, but may have a harder time convincing management.

Prestige and brand image, however, do count for something other than attracting business. A firm's name and reputation—real or imagined—may become particularly valuable near the end of an assignment when it comes time to stuff an unpopular decision down management's throat. In this area McKinsey & Company operates with particular effectiveness. "The president will hire McKinsey and write the firm a blank check to do what he wants," one ex-McKinsey consultant told me. "Nobody below dares offer any overt resistance. People who don't like McKinsey's ideas can keep things from happening, but it's not wise to make a frontal attack. It's much easier to let their programs in and then nibble at their shoes. Few lower executives will openly fight McKinsey. They're represented as the experts."

"Occasionally, management will be tempted to call in a consulting firm for the sake of its prestige," admits Philip W. Shay, ACME's executive director, "for instance, to back

A Bank Account of Talents

up an unpopular decision or to serve as a scapegoat in taking disciplinary action against some individual. All reputable consulting firms resist such assignments whenever they foresee them, feeling that such maneuvering prostitutes their services."

Nevertheless, businessmen frequently utilize consultants —sometimes out of necessity and sometimes out of cowardice—as sounding boards for their own ideas. Charles L. Quittmeyer in his survey on why companies used consultants quoted the head of a public utility as saying: "Frankly we have more experience than the consultant. However, the people concerned will buy a new idea more readily from an outside expert. It's well worth the money to get your story across." At a business convention I shared a table with an executive from Detroit's J. L. Hudson department store, a user of McKinsey's services. He admitted to me that it was often worth the price paid consultants simply to convince those above that what you're doing is right. Whether those above would think it worth the price might be another question.

"There's another side to this," cautions Little's Reid Weedon. "People often don't give full weight to ideas that originate in their own organization. It's against human nature. It means a lot more to get advice from the outside, and it carries more conviction. They feel, well, we've paid somebody specifically for this. Maybe we ought to carefully consider their ideas and do something about it instead of just letting it drift away."

The public relations value of having a consultant walking behind you also has been recognized by various branches of the armed forces, which have been frequent users of management consulting firms since Secretary Frank Knox hired Booz-Allen to reorganize the Department of the Navy early during World War II. I spoke with a colonel in the U.S. Air Force, one of McKinsey's leading customers. "Consultants lend a lot more credibility to what you're doing," he said. "A fellow who works for us at a billing rate that amounts to $166,000 a year is making ten times my salary. This lends him a certain amount of stature. You can use a consultant as a communications aid."

But use of consultants as communications aids (i.e., to impress the officer above you in the chain of command) is not the only reason various branches of the Government use consultants. In 1961 the Comptroller General of the United States surveyed management consulting within government and quoted one official: "I think it wise . . . to build in some independent review and appraisal of our efforts as we go along. This is useful not only in checking our own thinking, but may also prove most advantageous in any future defense of decisions reached. . . ."

Thus hiring a management consultant becomes a form of buck-passing. An officer need not risk his career by taking sole responsibility for a decision. Should things turn wrong, he can look over his shoulder and lo, there stands the friendly management consultant, his pockets stuffed with taxpayers' money, available to take the blame. Before we all rise in indignation and start writing our Congressmen, however, it might be well to remember that this form of

A Bank Account of Talents

buck-passing quite often also serves as Standard Operating Procedure in private industry.

The question might be raised: If a consultant is being used, does he realize it? And if he realizes it, does he care, or does he accept it as part of the price he pays for his home in the suburbs? Some years ago I had lunch in New York with a vice-president from one of the largest and best-known executive recruiting firms. Sitting over coffee we began to discuss the relationship between consultant and client. He talked about one particular executive who upon assuming the presidency of a company needed to hire five high-level assistants. He contacted the executive recruiting firm. My luncheon companion visited the president and spent a half hour discussing the specifications of the five men to be employed. "It was the strangest thing," mused the recruiter. "While he was talking I realized he didn't mean what he was saying. He knew he had to reorganize, but he wanted his own team. We sent him two top men, but he rejected both of them with hardly a look." Finally after two months, the new president informed his board of directors that the executive recruiting firm had failed. The president next suggested five men, who apparently already had begun to clean out their desks two months ago. The recruiter told me that he responded to the president's game, "by sending him a whopping big bill." For what it is worth that vice-president is no longer with the recruiting firm.

Writing in the *Harvard Business Review,* Seymour Tilles quoted a consultant who had been engaged by a small manufacturing firm with a personnel problem. "They wanted to fire one of their employees," said the consultant, "but felt they couldn't because of that employee's social standing in the community in which they were located. We wrote them a letter suggesting it and got them off the hook!" The consultant apparently had some mixed emotions about accepting money for such services. "I'm not happy about that sort of thing," he told Tilles. "It's prostituting the profession."

One alternate choice for the consultant might have been to write the letter but not accept the fee; that would have made him only a whore.

"Businessmen often try to hire consultants because there's some real tough work to do," I was told by Walter Foersch. "If there's a backlash they want to blame it on the consultant rather than someone in their organization. I think that shows lack of courage, intestinal fortitude, and manhood on their part.

"Another reason for hiring a consultant that smacks of that but really isn't, is where internally there's a personality clash which keeps the organization from getting work done. So they run an outsider through who has no ax to grind and who is after no one's job, and who can bring a completely independent and unbiased point of view. It isn't that he's any smarter, or wiser, or more gifted, or qualified than someone internally. It's just that he comes in, gets the job done, and gets out and no one has time to get awfully mad at him."

Foersch paused a moment and a frown came across his

A Bank Account of Talents

face. "I think an example of what I consider completely un-acceptable reasons for hiring consultants is to chop heads. I presume there are consultants that work along these lines. They come in and get rid of everyone that isn't doing a job and replace them with more qualified people. If this is what the company wants, I think they can do it just as well themselves."

4

—

Muddy Footprints on the Rug

Rare is the business executive who fails to harbor some
sort of opinion on management consultants. While researching this book I spoke with an individual who served
as a vice-president on the national board of the Boy Scouts
of America. Some of the highest-ranking executives in
America served with him. During one board meeting someone suggested that they hire a management consulting
firm to survey the national scout movement. "I never heard
a greater uproar," the board member told me. "It was obvious to me that at least half—if not three-quarters of those
present—wanted no part of management consultants."

Several studies have attempted to determine the attitudes of businessmen toward management consultants:

• The editors of the monthly business magazine *News
Front* queried a group of small business executives as to
whether or not employment of part-time professional management consultants had been a profitable experience.

Muddy Footprints on the Rug

Sixty-four per cent of the respondents answered "yes," with no apparent doubts. But 24 per cent had definite reservations and 12 per cent found the experience of no value whatsoever.

• The American Management Association surveyed 115 companies and learned that among executives, 27 per cent think that "a substantial number of management consultants are fakes," while 67 per cent believe "a small minority" are fakes. The remaining 6 per cent divided between those believing all consultants to be fakes and those believing none fakes.

• The Dartnell Corporation, after asking a number of companies about their success in working with management consultants, discovered that 29 per cent of those reporting expressed some dissatisfaction. "Of the disenchanted," reports Dartnell, "27 per cent are completely so, and most of these would not hire a consultant again under any circumstances."

Dartnell's survey had been aimed mainly at smaller businesses, ones whose chief executives would almost never be invited to lunch by a Booz-Allen partner. Of the companies participating in its survey, only 6 per cent had more than 25,000 employees. However, when I surveyed the top twenty-five corporations, as ranked by *Fortune*, I discovered attitudes that reflected the same percentages as these previous studies. If you approach three business executives, apparently at almost any level, you will find two inclined favorably toward management consultants and one who either doesn't use them, or won't use them, or refuses to talk about them.

Indeed, one can't snoop around the business community very long without uncovering numerous incidents where consultants have left muddy footprints upon the rug of some concern. Early in 1966 I visited Rochester, New York, to make a luncheon address before the Chamber of Commerce. I breakfasted with two local businessmen. One, an executive with a printing concern, told me how a consulting firm had spent six months redesigning all their order forms and shifting desks and jobs. Within nine months after the consultants had left, all the desks had gravitated back to their previous positions. So had the people involved in the job shifts. "We still use the forms because we printed so many of them," said the executive somewhat bitterly.

My other breakfast partner once worked as a radio announcer in Worcester, Massachusetts, and had as one of his advertisers a merchant who had successfully operated a bridal shop for twenty-five years. A consultant examined the merchant's business and shook his head. "There can't be enough brides in Worcester," said the consultant. "You should diversify." The merchant diversified by adding a line of men's wear. Within six months his business failed.

The history of management consulting contains several classic goofs. Although the incident occurred in the Dark Ages of business—that is, long before most of the current consulting firms were even gleams in their founders' eyes—the consulting profession still suffers the blame for the group of industrial engineers asked by General Motors

Muddy Footprints on the Rug

shortly after World War I to report on all its properties. One recommendation by the engineers was to liquidate Chevrolet, because it "could not hope to compete in its field." Chevrolet still rubs salt in the wounds of this unnamed firm by continuing to retell the incident in a brochure you can get at your neighborhood auto dealer—which probably causes many consultants to rush out and buy Fords.

Booz, Allen & Hamilton still winces in embarrassment at mention of the Vornado fan. An inventor from a Midwest farm state had designed a circular fan that would sit in the middle of the room and throw air in all directions. He paid Booz-Allen $20,000 for a market study that said in short, forget it. The inventor stuffed the Booz-Allen report in his wastebasket and went ahead to produce what became the most successful fan in history. "Yet it was an honest piece of market research," alibis one former Booz-Allen consultant. "You can't be perfect 100 per cent of the time, and we were just wrong."

While Dwight D. Eisenhower served as president of Columbia University, he retained a firm of consultants to study the school and make recommendations concerning its improvement. The consultants' report, Eisenhower later commented, "subsequently became the most expensive and least read document the University's library ever acquired."

Another tale, which has been repeated in articles on the management consulting profession by both the *Wall Street Journal* and *Fortune,* describes the problems of a furniture manufacturer who engaged a consultant to advise him how to increase the sales volume of his "small but profitable business." The manufacturer's top line consisted of couches and chairs. The company utilized left-over wood to make ironing boards. The couches and chairs produced a 10 per cent profit, while the ironing boards barely broke even. The consultant compared the relative profits of these two areas of the business and deduced that if the manufacturer dumped the ironing boards and concentrated on expanding production of the couches and chairs, profits soon would soar to new heights. The consultant suggested that the manufacturer establish a chain of retail stores to sell the additional furniture being produced.

Production soon increased as predicted, but so did costs. According to those who have retold the story, costs increased because the manufacturer no longer utilized the waste wood in making ironing boards. Sales increased too, but the furniture executives discovered they did not have the experience to manage properly their new retail outlets. They needed a hard-headed collection department to help solve the problem of extending too much customer credit. Before the furniture manufacturer could successfully establish one, bankruptcy resulted.

The moral of this story? Seemingly, keep making ironing boards. Yet it would be wrong to presume that the consultant deserves all the blame for this business failure. Perhaps the manufacturer did not obtain *poor* consulting advice as much as he simply may not have obtained *enough* consulting advice. "The main problem with consulting in these days," says Kenneth R. Andrews of the Harvard

Muddy Footprints on the Rug

Business School, "is not crookedness, but rather superficiality."

A repeated charge lodged against management consulting firms is just that: in their vacuum cleaner approach to accumulating information they merely suck in surface dust without comprehending the dirt lodged within the rug's fabric. Charles L. Quittmeyer quoted one dissident company president (who had spent $50,000 on consultants) as saying: "They came in knowing little about our problem, talked to the help, repeated their opinions, and closed knowing no more than when they came. A complete waste of money."

While visiting Winston-Salem, North Carolina, I spoke with a Reynolds Tobacco Company vice-president. Had Reynolds used management consultants, I asked? Indeed they had. Reynolds, worried about the relationship between cigarettes and lung cancer, asked Booz-Allen for help in planning diversification. "They went around asking questions and looked at our business," the vice-president informed me. "They said we should diversify into consumer products. We eventually did buy Hawaiian Punch. Well, hell, it didn't take a great deal of intelligence to discover that."

Of course, if the answer had been that obvious, why had Reynolds bothered to ask Booz-Allen to hold its hand in the first place? Presumably the cigarette firm must have obtained some value from the consulting arrangement, although the particular vice-president with whom I talked might not have been at a high enough level to realize it.

"Client corporations often complain that they weren't told anything different than what they already knew," says Edwin C. Johnson, a former Booz-Allen consultant, now an executive recruiter. "This is where client corporations are way off base. Suppose the management consulting firm tells the president nothing more than what he had already suspected. Well, at least he's got his money's worth. He knows he was right in his feelings, assuming that the consulting firm is honest and neutral. The only place where this runs into a fallacious area is where you have consultants who polish their report to say what they think the president wants to hear."

Naturally it becomes easy, after a consultant's report has been submitted, for someone within the client organization to raise his hand, look hurt, and say: "I thought of that first." Quite often some of the ill will directed against consulting firms, particularly by members of middle management, is that their ideas have been borrowed and replayed to the company president, who then thinks the consultant thought of the idea. "They never give any credit to the people who originated the ideas," a General Dynamics executive complained to me. But consultants insist that part of their interviewing technique is to assure the person being interviewed that he will *not* get the credit—and thus the blame for controversial suggestions. This theoretically permits people to speak with more freedom than otherwise might be true.

Actually it is the task of the consulting firm many times not merely to originate ideas, but uncover ones that have been lying around unnoticed. The executive who claims that his ideas have been pirated may have been unable previously to get the president to listen.

Reid Weedon of Arthur D. Little told me the story of a single-product company whose executives recognized that they should broaden their product line. At every annual meeting at least one stockholder in the audience would rise and make the statement: "We ought to diversify." The chairman of the board would nod and reply that plans to do just that were under consideration, and the subject would be dropped—until the next annual meeting. Then by chance one year, a member of the Little market research staff encountered the statement about planned diversification while reviewing the annual reports of companies within the industry. He discovered that for seven consecutive years one stockholder or another had suggested diversification and those same seven years the company officers had announced their willingness to diversify—but nothing had happened. One of the Little officers approached the company with the seven annual reports under his arm and in his most diplomatic way said, in effect, put up or shut up. As a result the company diversified with Little's help.

"I quite frequently tell a client, don't expect us to come back with something you don't already know," Reid Weedon explains. "We sometimes try to help companies identify new products that they might add to their product line. I'll warn a client against expecting us to develop a list about which they can say, we never thought of that before.

Let's say they're in the consumer products business. They can easily get a list of the full line of products carried in every supermarket, read it, then say: we thought of every item that's now in a supermarket. While our firm may come up with an idea for a better and entirely different household cleanser, it's still a household cleanser. I think it's important in the consulting business to make it clear to the client in the beginning what he's apt to get out of a job."

Perhaps a more serious charge that might be thrown against consultants is that, far from stealing ideas from people within the client company, they steal ideas from previous client assignments. Because a course of action worked for Company A, the consultants may assume it will work for Company B. Several consulting firms such as WOFAC Company advertise themselves as applying proven methods to industrial problems, but at least in theory most generalist management consulting firms sell their analytical skills rather than their experience. John Cooper now works on the staff of the *Wall Street Journal,* but at one time he labored in public relations for Booz, Allen & Hamilton. "I had a chance to read quite a few of the consultants' reports in the library," he informed me. "There seemed to be a tendency to borrow the conclusions of one report and adapt it to another. I don't know how you would prevent this or whether it was a bad thing."

"Some work we did for Philco was written up in *Fortune* a few years ago," explains Reid Weedon. "The president of Philco was quoted in that article as saying he looked at

Muddy Footprints on the Rug

various management consultants, and the reason he hired Arthur D. Little was that we had never done a general management organization study for a company anywhere near the size of Philco before. Therefore he could be sure that we weren't going to reach into the files and pull out an organization chart we had done for somebody else, doctor it up a bit, put Philco names on it, and submit it." The number of consulting firms with doctorable large corporation organization charts in their files, needless to say, has now been reduced by one.

Another occasionally aired gripe is that management consulting firms always lead with their suavest partners—who then disappear. The partner discusses the assignment with the client and presides over the signing of the proposal letter. He may even conduct one or two of the initial interviews. Then he climbs on the first jet bound for the next client and in his place appear several eager-eyed youngsters only two years out of the Harvard Business School. Or the partner may be followed into the job by experienced second-level associates who then will be followed by the youngsters. "Consulting firms send out real sharp men at first," groused one industrial engineer whose company frequently hired A. T. Kearney & Company. "They get you hooked, then send out a bunch of trainees to finish the job."

Yet apparently so skillful are the consulting firm partners at selling businessmen on the skills versus experience theory, that in most instances their bright young men encounter surprisingly little resistance. "The thing that always amazed me," a former Booz-Allen man confesses, "was that at a place like Johnson Wax, I could walk into the office of the vice-president of sales, give him some answers, and be regarded as an oracle who would solve all his business problems."

However, a former International Telephone & Telegraph executive with whom I spoke, a man in his sixties, was not enamored with young consultants. McKinsey & Company had been retained by IT&T to help it relocate in a new corporate headquarters building, and most of those the executive met from the firm impressed him as being "very keen, but also very young." As part of the assignment to reallocate space, the McKinsey consultants scrutinized the law library to determine which books got used least frequently. "They found dozens that hadn't been consulted in five years," complained the executive. "They wanted to throw them all out. That's like throwing out volume fourteen of the encyclopedia or all the X's in the dictionary!"

Part of the resentment felt by older executives may be the comparatively high billing rate charged by consulting firms for men still in their twenties. Professor Charles L. Quittmeyer found: "On a per consultant per day basis (client companies) are paying consultants what many of their higher executives are averaging in salary themselves. Although consultants often do top management types of jobs, it may be difficult for some managers to consider them as more than special hired hands and so wonder at the rates they are able to get."

A department store executive with whom I spoke lodged

Muddy Footprints on the Rug

a complaint against consulting firms: "They're expensive and you spend a lot of money educating them about your business. By the time they're educated you know the answer yourself."

At least one other executive, however, considered this to be as much an advantage as a disadvantage. Carl Devoe, president of the Chicago hotel, Executive House, Inc., had hired Lennon, Rose and Company to improve his food and beverage operations. According to Devoe: "Before the study was completed 80 per cent of the solutions had been put into effect by the people on the job. The consultants analyzed the schedules and while seeking information energized the people on the job to look at the things they should have been looking at. When they were through there was no question that they had made huge savings in cost. They turned a deficit operation into a profitable one."

I also spoke with the manager of a large candy company, who at one time twenty years before had labored under the Booz-Allen aegis. He now had risen to a position where he was hiring management consultants. "We've used consultants for marketing research and have come away with mixed feelings," he told me. (His firm had hired Fry and Booz-Allen on two separate studies.) "I thought they were too loose and too fast with their talk without being able to back it up with facts." He claimed better results when, while installing a data-processing system, he had hired the accounting firm Ernst & Ernst.

It would be wrong to conclude from this one man's experience that Ernst & Ernst, or for that matter any other consulting firm, could have outperformed either Fry or Booz-Allen on the marketing studies. "Management consultants are simply just one more tool for the managerial class to use," says Carl Devoe. "A tool does only as good a job as the person who uses it. Two persons handling the same tool are not going to get the same results."

Take for example the case of one Midwest-based company that maintained annual sales of $8–9 million and thus realized $450,000 a year in profits after taxes. All prognostications indicated that this company could maintain this same relative prosperity and mild growth for the next several decades, but there was one problem: the owner and president, a man we'll call Junior.

When his father, the founder of the company, died in 1940, Junior inherited a $100,000 annual salary and a $15,000 expense account. His wife received $18,000 as officer in the company and his two sons, after graduating from college, earned $15,000 each. Junior, however, was a heavy drinker and one of the great spenders of all time. He sponsored expensive golf tournaments for the employees and purchased for $125,000 a company airplane which rarely got used. Soon he began to drain money from the company to pay his personal income tax. "He'd appear at the directors' meeting," remembers his former vice-president. "He'd show us his tax bill and say, 'Unless you give me enough money to pay it I'll go to jail.' What could we do?" Having used added dividends to increase his income to pay taxes, Junior would find himself faced with still higher taxes the following year. The spiral continued to

Muddy Footprints on the Rug

where he siphoned a half million dollars a year from the company. At this point, Junior decided to hire a management consulting firm to help boost profits.

The company's attorney suggested the name of one of the most reputable ACME firms. The company executives awaited the arrival of the consultants with eagerness. But the eventual success of the consulting assignment was threatened at the start by the simple necessity that the final report would be made to one man: the president, Junior.

"When they came in, it was to put on a show," says the production manager, "and I think it was deliberate. They were given the second swankiest office in the building. How many they sent in I don't know, but it seemed like there were six or eight men and they were all over the building at once."

"They interviewed each one of us," another former company employee remembers. " 'Tell me about your job,' they'd start. Then they would get nice and sly: 'Mr. H., this is a nice organization, but there must be something wrong. What goes on here?' Before you knew it, you were spilling your guts."

"They drew up beautiful charts," recalls one former department head. "Their reports were beautifully typed and bound within fine covers. It was only the quality of the recommendations that was bad. They made the assumption that we could reach 5 million sales, about five times our present market. It just wouldn't work with our particular product."

Several specific recommendations involved reshuffling personnel. The consultants decided that the executive vice-president carried too much responsibility, so they decided to split his duties in half. They recommended hiring an administrative vice-president at $40,000 a year. Noticing that the sales manager was in his sixties they decided to replace him. Since the management consulting firm also specialized in executive search, in effect, they had fattened their pot by hiring themselves to recruit two new men.

However, the search proved troublesome. The money offered looked good, but many otherwise qualified candidates rejected what was obviously a "trouble job" because of the president's alcoholic and financial habits. Thus the consulting firm spent a disproportionate amount of time in filling these jobs. Because of the excess effort required, the fee charged to recruit one administrative vice-president and one sales manager came to $25,000.

One important recommendation made by the consulting firm was the installation of an electronic data-processing system to handle accounts. The cyclical nature of the Midwest company's business seemed to favor EDP. Most of the billing department's work occurred during the fall, at which time the help could barely keep pace with orders. At other times of the year, not enough work existed to keep everyone busy. Installation of EDP seemingly would smooth the work load. But rather than install the new equipment during the off season, in the spring and summer, the consultants installed it during the busy fall. This re-

Muddy Footprints on the Rug

sulted in no actual dollar losses, but strained relations with those in the billing department. Installation of EDP also at least temporarily strained profits. Its cost was $80,000 the first year of operation. The executive vice-president fought successfully against several other consultant recommendations. "They would have tacked another $200,000 to the cost of our doing business," he claimed. By this time the golden glow around the consultants had begun to dim.

The final bill submitted by the consulting firm (including their fee for executive search) reached $125,000. The chairman of the board of the average corporation on *Fortune's* 500 list might have quivered a bit if handed a bill that size. For the small Midwest company the bill represented more than a quarter of the organization's annual profits. Even at that, the money would have been well spent had prospects for the future been improved. But the main problem still remained: the president. Junior. "What disturbed me most about the consultants," remarks the executive vice-president, "was that they didn't have enough integrity to call a spade a spade and tell the president he should step out. They must have been abundantly aware that he was the main trouble, but they never made any such assertion."

If cowardice were the only sin that could be laid against the management consulting firm, most businessmen might at least nod and understand. But far from even maintaining its previous position of stability, the company began to slide downhill. The increase in costs as a result of the consulting firm's recommendations had failed to produce immediate increases in profit. The first year after the consultants exited, the firm's net profits dropped by a half. Thus less money remained for Junior to reward himself with dividends. His income tax problems continued to mount. Eventually he was compelled to sell out to a larger corporation based in New York. He retired to Palm Beach, Florida. As one of their first moves, the new owners eliminated the EDP billing system.

Of the two executives recruited by the consulting firm the administrative vice-president lasted only two years before moving to another job. The sales manager proved even less a blessing. Almost immediately he added four new salesmen to his staff, thereby further increasing the costs of that department. However, even with this increase in personnel, he failed to outperform his predecessor. Sales went neither up nor down. Several years later his superiors discovered him taking kickbacks from suppliers. They fired him. He went to work for one of the suppliers and later, as a result of another adventure on his part, the supplier was sued and went bankrupt. This individual is still bouncing around the executive job market today.

The first reaction one might have to a case history such as this would be to lay the blame squarely on the shoulders of the management consulting firm. Admittedly it may have been a botched assignment. But the problems were such that no consultant could have accepted such a job and walked away with honor. To begin with, it was simply a poorly managed company. Without question, the best consulting jobs get performed at the best managed com-

Muddy Footprints on the Rug

panies. There is no substitute for chief executives who understand the functions of management consultants and employ them accordingly.

It is because of cases such as this, however, that many individuals bitterly denounce consultants. "My attitude toward consulting is it's a futile gesture," one executive told me. "A consultant is called in to solve major problems, like a physician called in to heal the sick. I think cures through consulting are minimal and often prolong the catastrophe. In general, I feel that consulting only exists because of poor management. I think the original idea was fine. The pioneers in the field were excellent, but the standards are degenerating. The firms are hiring low-caliber men and the whole thing has become degraded into a rather parasitic function!"

Yet the question might be raised: is the average businessman who talks about management consultants in a position where he can adequately understand them and their profession? The picture most executives have of consultants is colored at most by one or two first-hand, and often second-hand, experiences. Frequently they must rely only on what they've learned while sweating in the steam bath at their downtown athletic club. Because management consulting is so like the elephant touched by the seven blind men (each of whom pictured the beast differently), probably only a minority of businessmen clearly comprehend consulting in all its totality. Only a few truly can picture the beast.

A businessman's conception of management consulting

will further be colored by his own particular position on the executive ladder. In talking to management men at all levels, I discovered that the lower on the ladder the executive, normally the lower his opinion of consultants. Generally speaking, people at the middle-management level dislike management consultants the most.

And occasionally if those within middle management are antagonistic to the work of a consultant they may threaten the success of his assignment. Some years ago a large consulting firm attempted to reorganize B. F. Goodrich & Company and improve its marketing operation. According to a former employee, one change was to double the sales force. One sales force worked with dealers and the other served the company's own chain of stores. New and young executives were recruited at the corporate level. But the older executives within middle management dug in their heels and resisted the changes. Within two or three years, many of the younger corporate executives, finding themselves unable to make any progress, moved on to other jobs. Eventually the marketing operation resumed its previous monolithic structure.

The arrival of a consultant may pose, to the middle-management executive (and to a certain extent also to his boss), a threat to job security. A reorganization study can result in an executive's being swept into a new job (which he may or may not like), or in some cases simply being swept out the door. A man having been fired because of the work of a consulting firm may not carry a warm picture of them in his heart the remainder of his business career.

Muddy Footprints on the Rug

On the other hand, the top executive employing the consulting firm sometimes may overrate and overpraise their work. Essentially they operate by his will, and if they fail it becomes his failure too, whether he wants to admit it or not.

Management consultants claim that when they enter an organization seeking information, generally the people at both extremes of the executive ladder talk most freely. The ones on the bottom apparently have nothing to lose with their frankness. The ones (or one) on the top have nothing to lose either since ultimately they will accept or reject the proposals. But men at the middle-management level (consultants claim) sometimes act overprotective about what they know. They hesitate to give information that may in the end be used against them. And quite frankly, who can blame them? In the end, however, the skilled management consultant, using all the black arts of the reporter's trade, will penetrate most defensive shields and the middle-management executive may find himself more vulnerable because of his original unwillingness to cooperate fully.

But this reluctance on the part of middle-rung executives to talk is true within consulting firms too. In visiting all the major management consulting firms I found that almost always the top officers talked more openly and frankly than those below them on their staffs. The bottom- and middle-rung consultants knew that the officers knew that they were being interviewed and feared saying something that when repeated in print would smudge their firm's image before the outside world and lessen their chances of being officers some day. Thus they quite often spoke as though aware their office had been bugged.

Another factor that prevents middle-management men from obtaining a proper perspective of consulting is that frequently after the consultant exits, they may not be in a judgment position to assess the value of work done. They may note that the consultant failed to slice their cost of doing business, so may consider his presence a waste of time. Middle management does not suffer this blind spot alone, however. Often top management will judge a consultant's work from immediate results without realizing that benefits may not accrue for years.

One executive, who at one time had served in a middle-management position with a paper company in the Midwest once recited for my benefit the sad, sad story of how a team of Booz-Allen consultants had appeared on the front doorstep one morning and had proceeded to cut a terrible swath through the company, chopping heads right and left, and hiring new executives of their own choosing, who after only a few years on the job fled like thieves in the night. It sounded like a good, bloody tale of a consulting firm gone power mad.

When I pressed the executive for details as to how many people had been fired, however, he began to alter his story. "Well, they weren't fired so much as shifted into other jobs," he admitted. The newly hired executives thus arrived not as replacements but as necessary reinforcements for a firm that had grown in billings from $20 million in 1940 to $80 million in 1947 when the reorganization occurred. All the work done by Booz-Allen could not have been as bad as my friend believed, since ten years later the paper company had further increased its business to $180 million.

But another consulting assignment undertaken by Booz-Allen early in the sixties resulted in more significant middle-management disapproval. The assignment involved a nonprofit association in the legal field with headquarters in New York. The chairman of the association had proven himself a poor administrator. When internal dissension threatened to split the association, rather than resolve the problem himself he called a meeting of the executive committee which consisted of outside businessmen. One of the businessmen happened to be the partner of a relatively small Philadelphia management consulting firm. Whether buttering his own bread or not, he suggested: "What we need is a management consultant."

"Well, if we're going to hire a consulting firm, we might as well get the best," announced the chairman. Apparently his definition of the best didn't include the consultant from Philadelphia. Three firms were asked to make presentations: Cresap, McCormick and Paget; McKinsey & Company; and Booz, Allen & Hamilton. After some discussion the association chose Booz-Allen.

When I discussed what happened with one of the association's middle-management executives, he condemned the work the consultants had done. "They sent in a bunch of youngsters," said the executive. "They had the courtesy to assign one of their vice-presidents to the chairman. The rest of us were visited by these young fellows. They came in with a preconceived notion of what to do. Then they talked to the people on the staff and picked up all the internal gripes."

One of the earliest recommendations made by the consultants was that the chairman should resign. He apparently accepted this with grace. Booz-Allen's executive recruiters next undertook a search for a new chairman, a search that failed. The association eventually hired the chairman's cousin.

The consulting assignment had begun on a note of hope, but now rumors began to fly through the association's corridors that a secret report existed calling for mass dismissals. "We were afraid at one time that our business was being taken over by Booz-Allen," one executive told me. These rumors, needless to say, proved false.

When the executive board finally did receive copies of the report, rather than act on it immediately they distributed it to the middle-echelon executives for comment. These executives next proceeded to claw it apart. "The report was full of errors," I was told. "One division of the firm was a big money-maker. Another lost money. But we're a public service firm. What the consultants apparently failed to realize was that the entire purpose of our association was in that low-profit division.

"In my opinion," continued the speaker, "there was not one good idea in the report. It was an unhappy time for the association. We've done well since, but mostly because the ideas the consultants gave us were disregarded."

Muddy Footprints on the Rug

The association paid a fee of $30,000, reportedly low considering the amount of time the team of consultants had spent. "But on the other hand," said another executive, "I'm afraid we got only a $30,000 report." A former Booz-Allen partner and a friend of the association, who had helped in the selection process, also felt that the assignment had been badly handled. He expressed distress that another partner, who he thought more qualified, hadn't been given the assignment.

Yet although there seemed to be almost unanimous gnashing of teeth among the middle-echelon association executives, several of the higher-ups saw at least a few rays of sunshine penetrating the gloom. "I thought their report contained a lot of inaccuracies," a vice-president informed me. "There were amazing misstatements of facts. They said some things that were just not true. But if nothing else it seemed to get people on their toes. We got a fresher direction. The end result now that we're five years away was that it did serve to get some of us angry, and maybe that was good. It served to remove the cobwebs and shake us out of our lethargy, and make us realize that none of us were indispensable."

One problem of being a management consultant is that you can't openly advertise your successes, but dissatisfied clients may complain loud and clear about your failures. It is the same with the medical profession. A doctor can perform a thousand successful operations, but everyone remembers the one where his scalpel slipped.

5

"You Can't Forget a Name Like Booz"

The mammoth among management consulting firms today, without question, is Booz, Allen & Hamilton, Inc., whose home offices are in Chicago. At the beginning of 1969, the firm founded by Edwin G. Booz could count a staff of 2,000 people, 1,200 of them considered "professionals." Booz-Allen's total billings, although a carefully guarded secret, probably easily exceed $50 million. As recently as the early thirties, however, Ed Booz's firm had fewer than a dozen employees. The staff frequently would meet at his home in suburban Evanston and sit around a circular dining room table discussing business into the night. As the firm expanded it became too large to meet in Booz's home, so to maintain continuity with the past, Ed moved the table into his downtown offices. Following his death, the dining room table eventually got moved into the library of the firm's present headquarters, where it remains to this day. "When a young consultant sits down with a book in that library,"

"You Can't Forget a Name Like Booz"

I was told, "he is bellying up to an awful lot of tradition." Although Ed Booz frequently receives credit for being the father of modern management consulting some people have attempted to trace the profession's birth back to the third century B.C.

Han Fei Tzu, founder of the so-called legalist school of ancient Chinese philosophy and advisor to the emperor, has been called the first consultant. On the other hand, the public accounting firms insist that accountants in the mid-fifteenth century deserve the credit. But to attempt to identify *management* consultants much beyond the present century is to stretch a point. Only after mass production became fairly common toward the end of the nineteenth century did a number of industrial engineers begin to pioneer the use of scientific management principles. They used stopwatches to gauge the efficiency of work, and the label "efficiency experts" still gets hung erroneously on consulting firms and consultants today. Some of these early efficiency engineers included Frederick W. Taylor, Henry L. Gantt, and Carl G. Barth. Taylor, who had been fired by Bethlehem Steel for promoting his time-study methods too vigorously, died in 1915. Five years previously, Louis D. Brandeis had served as an attorney in the Eastern rate case before the Interstate Commerce Commission. "These railroads could save one million dollars a day simply by applying new scientific principles of management," claimed Brandeis (later, justice of the United States Supreme Court). Brandeis had obtained the figures from consultant Harrington Emerson.

Attending Northwestern University at about this time was Edwin George Booz, son of a timekeeper from Reading, Pennsylvania. The Booz family name had become well-established in America even before that time, but not for anything connected with traditional business practices. According to Ed's son, Donald R. Booz, early members of the family had worked as glass blowers and most Booz males still have enormous chests and lung capacity. Several have become champion swimmers. Near the time of the Civil War, Ed Booz's great grandfather manufactured bottles for a whiskey distillery in Kentucky, and he put his last name on the bottles. Soon "booz" became a sort of generic nickname for all liquor.

Booz-Allen chairman James L. Allen, however, relates the legend with a slightly different twist. He claims that a distiller named E. G. Booz (whether related to the consultant Booz or not, he isn't sure) was a leading bootlegger during the Whiskey Rebellion in the late eighteenth century. He produced a brew called "E. G. Booz Whiskey" or "Booz Log Cabin Whiskey" and eventually all the liquor produced by the bootleggers got to be known as booz.* The name Booz has provided a mild source of embarrassment to several members of the present firm who have often wished that the name on their door sounded less earthy. "We've even thought of streamlining our firm name to its initials, like IBM did," one executive at Booz, Allen &

* On the other hand, most dictionaries link "booz" or "booze" with the Saxon word "bouse" or "bousen," so the connection of the Booz family with the generic term for liquor may be more coincidental than actual.

"You Can't Forget a Name Like Booz"

Hamilton informed me, "but I'm afraid that 'BAH' is not much of an improvement." Jim Allen, however, doesn't share these feelings. "I've always thought the name to be an asset," he says. "You can forget a name like Allen, but you can't forget one like Booz!"

While at Northwestern Ed Booz encountered Walter Dill Scott, then chairman of the psychology department. Scott had produced a pioneer marketing study in 1906 for the magazine *Woman's World*, and he profoundly influenced Booz's thinking. The psychologist recognized the value of the Taylors and Gantts, but believed it less important to time a job than to obtain the *right person* for that job. This focus on the individual is the principal difference that even today separates the generalist management consulting firms from those that specialize in industrial engineering.

At Scott's suggestion Booz applied for a job at *Woman's World* after graduating in 1912. He worked there two years, accumulating a master's degree in psychology from Northwestern at the same time. In 1914 (which Booz-Allen lists as its founding date) Ed Booz joined with an individual named Anderson Pace in a firm called Business Research Service. One early study involved Pace and Booz's traveling through the state of Illinois examining operations for the Illinois Central Railroad to justify a rate increase. The firm name changed in 1916 to Business Research and Development Company, but the following year Ed Booz joined the army as a private.

Walter Dill Scott also was in the service charged with

establishing a system by which the army might classify personnel. Scott received the Distinguished Service Medal for his success with this program, which consisted mostly of fitting round pegs into round holes, and Booz worked under him. Scott left the service in 1919 and with five of his army associates (Booz wasn't included) organized a business consulting firm known as the Scott Company. It survived only a short period since the following year Scott accepted an invitation to become Northwestern's president.

Booz meanwhile established a one-man consulting firm under the name Edwin G. Booz Business Engineering Service. According to one story, while acting as a buyer for his fraternity, Booz had established credit with the State Bank of Evanston. He approached that bank for a $5,000 loan.* "What is it you want to sell?" the bankers reportedly asked Booz. When he explained his theories that business problems were mainly people problems, they hired him to study their bank. Booz earned a fee of $150, but more important he impressed the bankers sufficiently so they granted him a loan. One of the members of the bank's board of directors was a man named Sewell Avery, who later would play an important part in the rise of the young Northwestern graduate's firm.

In 1924 the one-man consulting firm was known as Edwin G. Booz Surveys. That same year George A. Fry graduated from Northwestern University and, at Walter Dill

---

* Booz-Allen historians believe Booz received the loan and founded his firm in 1914, thus their birth date. However, Booz's partner of later years, George Fry, insists Booz didn't found his firm until after leaving the army.

Scott's urging, became Booz's first assistant. Booz then had an office in downtown Chicago, which he shared with a man in the textile business who sold bath towels. Towels were stacked throughout the office and a single secretary typed and answered the telephone for both businesses.

In 1925 Sewell Avery, remembering Booz from his earlier survey of the State Bank of Evanston, engaged him to help reorganize U.S. Gypsum. Booz and Fry took three months and visited each of the approximately fifty U.S. Gypsum plants scattered across the United States. When they presented their recommendations, Avery asked Booz to join the organization to implement the report. Booz declined, preferring to remain his own boss.

During the late twenties U.S. Gypsum continued as a principal client of the firm. Booz also worked for the *Chicago Daily News,* whose publisher at that time was Walter A. Strong. When Strong wanted to know whether or not his newspaper should erect an office building Booz said yes, then moved into the building as one of its first tenants.

Management consultants had not achieved the acceptance in the 1920s that they have today. In fact, no one yet called them "management consultants," a term that has achieved popularity only during the last few decades. First, they were known as "business counselors" or "management engineers." More often businessmen referred to them as "efficiency experts," a term of derision as much as of definition. A good share of the work done by early "consultants" indeed revolved around making businesses more efficient: taking a task involving five minutes' labor and determining how to do it in one minute. Many management consulting firms (including Booz-Allen) continue to do time and motion studies today as an important part of their total practice, but two factors caused the inheritors of the principles of Taylor and Gantt to fall into disgrace. First, several unethical consultants had begun to prey on businessmen as much as aid them. They overpromoted themselves, promising savings they could not produce. Second, some businessmen began to misapply time and motion studies and use them as a club over the heads of union laborers. To protect their reputation and establish a set of ethics for their profession, a dozen consulting firms began a series of meetings in 1929 that resulted four years later in the establishment of the Association of Consulting Management Engineers, better known as ACME. Also in 1929, James Lane Allen joined Ed Booz's firm as a junior staff assistant. Jim Allen, a former accountant and economics teacher who had been born on a farm near the small town of Somerset in southeastern Kentucky, eventually would do more to shape the current firm of Booz, Allen & Hamilton than its founder.

Only four persons worked for the small consulting firm at this time. In addition to one secretary there were only Booz, Fry, and Allen. But the staff slowly began to expand. In 1934 Booz hired a young man named Richard Moscrop Paget (pronounced Page-it), who had enrolled at Northwestern University at age sixteen, graduated at nineteen, worked at the school for a year, and joined Booz before reaching his twenty-first birthday. For his first assignment, Booz sent Paget to the Martin Oilcloth Company in Peek-

"You Can't Forget a Name Like Booz"

skill, New York. Martin was on the verge of bankruptcy and numerous suppliers and stockholders had claims on the assets of the company. Paget had to go to court to obtain approval for the transactions he suggested. Then only twenty, he was quaking over the thought that someone might ask his age. No one did. The following year he re-organized the *Washington Post*.

Also in 1934 Booz hired Mark Winfield Cresap, Jr., a Chicagoan whose father was the president of Hart Schaffner & Marx. Cresap was two years older than Paget and had attended Williams College before graduating from the Harvard Business School. That same year the firm was re-named Edwin G. Booz and Fry Surveys. In 1935 Carl Lewis Hamilton joined the firm. Hamilton was forty-seven years old at the time and had risen to vice-president and general manager of General Timber Service, which serviced the Weyerhaeuser Company in the area of auditing, merchandising, and advertising. In addition to its four senior partners (Booz, Fry, Allen, and Hamilton) the firm had seven staffmen at this time.

In January 1935 George Fry moved to New York City to establish the firm's first branch in a small office at 285 Madison Avenue. Cresap and Paget accompanied him. In 1934 Jim Allen had left Booz to become secretary-treasurer of Ditto, Inc.; when he returned in 1936 the firm name became Booz, Fry, Allen & Hamilton, the order on the letterhead apparently determined by seniority. Allen also moved east to New York, but remained only a year in Manhattan. He returned to help Booz on a major and difficult assignment at the Chicago Title & Trust Co. In 1939 Cresap left Booz-Allen to become merchandise manager of the John B. Stetson Company in Philadelphia.

In contrast to the frequently colorless persons who have followed in his footsteps, Ed Booz was a hard-nosed individualist who didn't hesitate to state bluntly what he thought. One thing that particularly annoyed Ed Booz (according to his son Don) was the smell of cigarette smoke. If someone would reach for a pack of cigarettes in his presence and ask, "Do you mind if I smoke?" Booz's answer would be an unqualified, *"Yes, I do mind!"* Booz also shunned liquor and in fact had a compulsive fear of it because of his father's heavy drinking habits. Whether because of a tradition started by Ed Booz, or because of a wish that *nothing* should take the edge off their ability to think, few Booz-Allen consultants today will order a cocktail for lunch, unless it is forced on them by a client.

One story involving Ed Booz's bluntness concerns his relationship with Sewell Avery, who had assumed control of Montgomery Ward & Company. The mail-order company had difficulty remaining solvent during the depression, so Avery hired Booz in 1932 and moved him into an office at Ward's to attempt to improve profits. At one point Avery reportedly called Booz into his office and asked what was the mail-order company's main trouble. Booz answered in his most straightforward manner: "You!"

That reportedly ended Booz's consulting association with Montgomery Ward & Company. Jim Allen brands the story as apocryphal, but says that Booz wouldn't have hesitated to say that to Avery. George Fry also denies the story and claims that Booz actually was "scared to death of Sewell Avery." Nevertheless, the story has become a part of the consulting folklore and the fact that Booz apparently did lose the client may be a contributing reason why today's managing partners cultivate "blandness" as a style.

Another of Booz's clients from the early days would have a considerable influence on the development of the management consulting profession. Booz had maintained a relatively close relationship with the *Chicago Daily News*. Walter Strong had died and had been replaced as publisher by Frank Knox. In 1940, with war imminent, President Franklin D. Roosevelt appointed Knox (who was a Republican) as Secretary of the Navy. When Knox asked Booz to reorganize the Navy Department, Booz accepted and moved to Washington.

Booz's total involvement with the Navy Department, however, precipitated a split with George Fry. Fry and Booz had been drifting apart for several years. Fry accused Booz of ignoring their industrial clients, who also needed help in gearing up to war production. Booz accused Fry of ignoring the Government's needs. As James L. Allen diplomatically describes the split: "Essentially George and Ed Booz were not exactly copasetic."

For some years Allen had served as a buffer between Booz and Fry, but in 1941 he left their firm to become vice-president and director of Hall Brothers, Inc., of Kansas City. According to Fry: "That's when I made the decision to separate the business. Hamilton was ill and Booz was acting badly. I tried to persuade Allen to stay, but he declined."

Fry formed his own consulting firm in 1942 under the name of Fry, Lawson & Company, which became George Fry & Associates in 1946. Fry located his new firm's offices in the same Chicago building where Booz-Allen was, and is, located: the Field Building at 135 South LaSalle. A. T. Kearney & Co., until 1967, also had its offices there. According to Fry, he and Booz divided their former firm, with Fry taking a certain number of clients, consultants, secretaries, files, records, and even desks. Booz, and later Allen, tried to underplay the importance of Fry's leaving. "The firm was not divided down the middle," Allen says. "George wanted it to look as though it was a split. Actually it was more of a chip."

Allen returned from Hall Brothers in 1943 and the name of the firm became what it remains today: Booz, Allen & Hamilton.

Whether split or chip, it was accompanied by angry words on both sides. "As long as we're in ACME you'll never get in," Booz reportedly told Fry.

"As long as you're in ACME, we *don't want* to get in!" Fry retorted.

And as long as Fry remained a consultant his firm did scorn ACME membership. In 1955, however, he retired from consulting at age fifty-five, selling his interest in the firm to his partners. George Saum, who recently retired himself, became managing partner of George Fry & Associates, which then quietly applied for and was accepted into

"You Can't Forget a Name Like Booz"

ACME membership. After retirement from consulting, George Fry rented an office on the same floor as Booz, Allen & Hamilton, "so he could be near his old buddies," according to one source. The angry words had been between Fry and Ed Booz, and he still maintained cordial relations with others in the firm.

Fry is now chairman of the board of Hurletron, Inc., and currently divides his time between a home in Vero Beach, Florida, and one in Chicago. A third generation of management under the direction of William Hocking has now assumed leadership in the Chicago-based firm which was renamed Fry Consultants Incorporated in 1966. Although it maintains high standards, Fry Consultants Incorporated has failed to match Booz, Allen & Hamilton either in growth or prestige. At the end of 1967 Fry Consultants was sold to ARA Services, Inc., a large food and vending concern.

"The war proved to be a tremendous impetus for the management consulting business," says George Fry. "Everyone went off to war and tremendous problems developed for those operating businesses. When businessmen looked around for help they found they could get it from firms such as ours." Businessmen, once introduced to management consultants out of necessity because of wartime production needs, continued to use their services. In addition, many businessmen had seen how effectively consultants had been used by the armed services. Lastly, as the consulting firms expanded, they hired young men who eventually returned to industry already indoctrinated to the use of consultants. Management consulting as a profession could not help but expand, and it probably has not neared maximum growth even yet.

Another key consulting firm evolved during World War II, founded by two men who had worked as staffmen for Ed Booz during the thirties. Booz had named Richard Paget as the partner in charge of the reorganization of the navy and after Pearl Harbor Secretary Knox awarded him captain's stripes to enable him to obtain information more easily. Paget, who had become a Booz-Allen partner at age twenty-seven (a record no one else has matched), found himself at age twenty-eight the youngest four-striper in navy history. Assigned to Paget as an assistant was a man some nine years older, William F. McCormick, who had worked for U.S. Steel and Remington Rand before the war. Mark Cresap left Stetson to become a colonel in the army and work in its management services project. Cresap, Mc-Cormick, and Paget developed a close friendship because of their service jobs, and one night toward the end of the war attended a dinner at the home of James V. Forrestal, who had become Secretary of the Navy following Knox's death in 1944. "It's a shame that you three can't stay together after you get out of service," Forrestal reportedly remarked. Whether prompted by those words or not, Cresap, McCormick, and Paget did establish their own consulting firm in 1946.

Edwin G. Booz's firm, following World War II, changed considerably. Carl Hamilton died in the spring of 1946. Fry had left. Booz devoted less and less time to active management of the firm, spending his winters in Palm Springs,

"You Can't Forget a Name Like Booz"

California, and his summers in Michigan. In 1951 he died. James L. Allen, the sole surviving partner of the four whose names had identified the firm in the mid-thirties, now began to remold Booz, Allen & Hamilton in his image. Many of the older consultants that the firm had utilized during the war were politely retired and in their place came the phalanxes of bright young men, individuals valued more for their analytical abilities than for their experience. Of course men like Ed Booz and Jim Allen had been "bright young men" in their time, but youthful though they were, they also ran the business. Booz-Allen continued to expand with senior partners on top and younger men in vast numbers beneath. Ed Booz's son, Donald R. Booz, joined his father's firm in the mid-fifties after having taught at the Harvard Business School and worked for Jewel Tea Company. After several years, however, he left, feeling that the firm had changed drastically from his father's original concept. He founded Donald R. Booz & Associates in 1961 and within five years had built a staff of two dozen men, a considerable percentage of them Booz-Allen alumni.

Although more people now work in its Manhattan Office, Booz, Allen & Hamilton continues to maintain corporate headquarters in Chicago, the city of its founding. The seventeenth floor of the Field Building at 135 South LaSalle consists entirely of Booz, Allen & Hamilton offices, and the firm also has begun to spill over onto the sixteenth and eighteenth floors.*

---

* A. T. Kearney and Fry Consultants, who also had headquarter offices in the Field Building within a few floors of Booz-Allen, found recently they

A visitor to the headquarters of Booz, Allen & Hamilton can't help but be impressed with the appointments. The doors are brown leather with brass buttons. In the waiting room the rugs are green. Provincial-looking prints of places like Versailles hang on olive-green walls. You sit on green leather chairs. Everything seems to be the same color as money.

Green doesn't prevail entirely through the offices, however. The rugs in the areas where the lower- and middle-rung members of the Booz-Allen hierarchy labor are a dull and well-worn tan. As the firm members sometimes express it, "When you step on a green carpet you're in officer country."

James L. Allen, a man in his mid-sixties, has been chairman of his firm's executive committee since 1945. The day-to-day operation of Booz, Allen & Hamilton, however, rests in the hands of the president, Charles P. Bowen.

Bowen, who lives in Greenwich, Connecticut, divides his time evenly between the Chicago and New York offices. Four executive vice-presidents are under him: two of them in New York, one in Chicago, and one in San Francisco. Next on the chain of command are about 150 plain, old, ordinary vice-presidents. Although many of them have considerably more responsibility than others (in that they

---

had to move into newer office buildings near the Chicago River to solve their expansion problems. Consultants apparently enjoy clustering together. Booz-Allen, Cresap, McCormick & Paget, as well as McKinsey all have offices in the same building at 245 Park Avenue in New York. Each firm uses a different bank of elevators, however.

"You Can't Forget a Name Like Booz"

may supervise branch offices), all labor under the same title, but not with the same salaries. Beneath the vice-presidents are the associates and consultants and eventually the secretaries and cleaning ladies.

Although he still remains professionally active, Jim Allen now divides his time between his home in Winnetka, a North Shore suburb of Chicago, and another home in Delray Beach, Florida, which is more or less considered another branch office of the firm, although you won't find it listed on the letterhead. Despite the time spent by Allen in Florida, there is no question on the Booz-Allen staff as to who ranks as top man. "He is God," says one staffman. "The name of this firm really should be: Booz, God & Hamilton." Allen is also sometimes referred to as the man on Mount Olympus.

"He's cautious, conservative, and meticulous," adds another Booz-Allen staffman, "but his thinking is far in advance of anyone else in the firm, with the possible exception of Bowen. He's quite concerned with what the image of Booz, Allen & Hamilton will be ten years from now."

Unlike many corporation presidents (but quite like most management consultant partners) Jim Allen flees from publicity. Some consider him to be the worst public speaker to have ever mounted a podium, but then he mounts them infrequently. "The nature of this business is confidential," says Allen. "An individual can't work in it and expect to reach for the limelight." *Business Week* once carried a photograph of Allen on its cover, but considering the amount of influence he wields in American business, his appearances in the public press could be considered almost negligible. In 1959 *Time* published a picture of Allen sitting at a desk, wearing a dark suit, a dotted tie, a white handkerchief in his breast pocket, thin-rimmed glasses, his hair slicked back over a thin forehead, notebooks, pads and pencils before him, and with a surprised expression on his face. The photograph seemed blurred, leading one to suspect that perhaps *Time* hired a window-washer to take it.

Jim Allen could hardly be considered a Howard Hughes. Nevertheless, numerous hurdles were placed in my path when I attempted to see Allen. When I requested an interview, a Booz-Allen staffman asked how soon was my deadline. "About two months," I replied.

Several weeks later he called back with the answer to my request. "Mr. Allen is going to be jammed up for the next two months." Suggestions that I be allowed to speak with Mr. Bowen met with similar rebuffs.

It seemed inconsistent with good reporting to write a book on management consulting and fail to interview, among the Booz-Allen hierarchy, at least Jim Allen, one of the two individuals (the other being McKinsey's Marvin Bower) most responsible for the profession's growth over the past two decades. I expressed this thought in a letter directed to Allen at his Winnetka home and enclosed an early draft of this chapter dealing with the history of his firm. Several weeks later I received a letter from the Booz-Allen chairman cordially agreeing to an interview and saying he had been unaware I had been reaching for him.

Much of Chicago had been immobilized by three feet

"You Can't Forget a Name Like Booz"

of snow the day of our scheduled interview, and not many
people had made it to work, but Allen was sitting behind
his desk awaiting me. It was the typical consultant director's desk: that is, more table than desk. It was devoid of
all foreign matter except the letter I had sent him. Three
recessed spotlights in the ceiling immediately above provided illumination in lieu of a lamp. When Allen needed
to make a note he reached behind him for a fresh pad of
paper and a pencil that seemed to have been sharpened
only once.

Allen was deeply tanned, having just returned from
Florida. He is a slender man with almost smallish features
and an oval-shaped head that somehow reminded me of
Jiminy Cricket in the Walt Disney cartoon of Pinocchio.
Later when Allen rose to say goodbye I was surprised to see
how tall he was. While no stranger to the consultant's uni-
form of dark suit with vest, Allen will on occasion appear
at the office in a garb that might be described as "conservatively tweedy." "He's the only guy in this firm who
dares wear loafers," says one staff member.

Allen leaned over his desk deep in thought, straightening
and unstraightening the bends of the paper clip that had
been attached to my letter. Finally he threw the clip into
the wastepaper basket. "The thing that gave management
consulting its greatest impetus," began Allen, "was the approach that Ed Booz took, that is: thinking in terms of
people and the organization of them as being the key factors in successful management. This has been borne out by
many individuals who founded great corporations."

He paused with his eyes closed as though framing his words around his thoughts. He tugged at one ear. Finally he continued: "And this is an area where the head of a business needs good counsel. He has no one to talk to about his men and what they are doing and whether or not they have the spread of talent to enable them to reach the goals they are shooting for.

"This whole field of bringing up a man to succeed the head of business is of great importance. Industry has made great progress, but this is a field where we as management consultants can be helpful and save a great deal of expense. I think that the contribution we have made from the beginning was to put the emphasis on men rather than on techniques. We've grown from that to put emphasis on a wide spread of activities. Management problems have not simplified in the last couple of decades. If anything they have grown more complex."

Allen indicated that after he had become chairman in 1945 he had made a conscious effort to organize his firm's activities as a business rather than as a collection of individual consultants. "We've had to round out our own organization in talent and knowledge to satisfy the client," he says. "We approach it all from a top-management point of view."

Ed Booz's firm has come a long way from the time when he used to share offices with a man who sold bath towels. Indeed, Booz-Allen now has begun to resemble a colossal consulting octopus. It has several corporate entities. Booz, Allen & Hamilton, Inc., exists as the parent organization as

"You Can't Forget a Name Like Booz"

well as the basic consulting group with offices in eight American cities.* Booz, Allen & Hamilton International, Inc., serves clients, both American and foreign, overseas from offices in London and Düsseldorf. Booz, Allen & Hamilton of Canada, Ltd., operates out of Toronto to service Canadian clients. The firm also has separate offices in Mexico City and Rio de Janeiro. Then there is Booz, Allen Applied Research, Inc., referred to as BAAR-Inc. (pronounced Bar-ink), with operations offices in three cities and project offices in seven others including Bangkok and Saigon. BAAR-Inc. specializes in research and development for industry and government and competes particularly with contract research firms such as Arthur D. Little, IITRI (Illinois Institute of Technology Research Institute), Stanford Research Institute, etc., in the area of basic and applied research. Its office in Bethesda, Maryland, just outside Washington, functions almost exclusively for Government projects and particularly for Defense Department projects. Security clearance is required to get inside the door. Perhaps one of the most significant contributions to come out of BAAR-Inc. was the development of PERT (stands for: Program Evaluation and Review Technique), a computer-based project management system originally designed to keep Polaris missile planning on schedule during its development. The same managerial techniques used to develop the missile have since that time been adapted to industry. In the meantime, one divi-

* New York, Washington, Cleveland, Detroit, Chicago, Dallas, Los Angeles, and San Francisco.

sion formerly known as Booz Allen Methods Services, Inc., which specialized in the area of industrial engineering, has ceased to exist as a separate entity.

While Booz-Allen has grown to its present size largely because of expansion from within, the firm also has folded one or two other companies under its wing, among them the Glenn L. White Company of Falls Church, Virginia, which specialized in construction management, and Foster D. Snell, Inc., a group of chemists, engineers, and biologists who specialize in research concerned with the life sciences. Glenn L. White lost its identity; Foster D. Snell has retained its. Among Snell's most unusual pieces of test equipment is a cigarette-smoking machine used to analyze smoke components such as tar and nicotine.

Two other identities have also been added to the firm: Design and Development, Inc., of Cleveland specializes in product development for Booz-Allen clients; BASIS, Inc., which more or less derives its name from "Booz-Allen Systems," specializes in computer systems work for public health, medical, and educational facilities. Rumors periodically filter through the business community that Booz, Allen & Hamilton, Inc., will go public, that is, sell shares outside the firm rather than have all the stock in the names of the active partners. In 1969 a spokesman for the firm assured me for perhaps the third or fourth time that there was no truth to such rumors.*

Booz, Allen & Hamilton, Inc., has grown so rapidly in the last two decades that it has lost part of its identity as servant to Big Business to become Big Business itself. One of

"You Can't Forget a Name Like Booz"

the few links to the firm's humble beginnings, of course, is the Booz family's former dining room table around which Ed Booz, George Fry, Jim Allen, and Carl Hamilton used to gather and plan strategy. I had been told about the table by Ed's son, Donald R. Booz. Don said it was still in the Booz-Allen library, but when I inquired, nobody on the present staff seemed to remember much about it. So I decided to take a look accompanied by Sam King, a member of the consulting firm's public relations staff. The single consultant sitting studying a report looked puzzled when I entered the library and got down on my hands and knees to examine the circular table more closely. It was the same table all right, recognizable from its four-footed, worn, wooden base, but above had been attached a modern formica top. Ed Booz never would have recognized it.

---

* On the exact date of publication of this book, Booz, Allen & Hamilton placed ads in the *New York Times* and *Wall Street Journal* announcing the issuance of 500,000 shares of common stock priced at $24 per share. "It was almost," as one consultant later told me, "as if they wanted your book to become instantly out of date."

6

―

"McKinsey Was a Tall, Imposing Man"

In the fall of 1966 I attended a press conference sponsored by McKinsey & Company at the Princeton Club in New York City. The event served as somewhat of a departure from normal practice since most large consulting firms attempt to keep the press at arm's length. Five McKinsey men appeared as panelists discussing the application of computer sciences to business management and unconsciously provided an instant Nielsen poll of the makeup of the second largest management consulting firm within ACME. Four wore gray suits. Three wore vests. One smoked a pipe. Two had attended Harvard; one other had a daughter enrolled in Harvard Medical School. One of the five was British, reflecting the fact that because of recent expansion overseas one-quarter of McKinsey's staff at that time was foreign-born. However, he was one of those who had attended Harvard.

During cocktails before lunch I talked with one of the

"McKinsey Was a Tall, Imposing Man"

panelists and he admitted that McKinsey had become somewhat concerned about its all-Harvard image. Several years before the firm had surveyed the educational background of its professionals and found roughly 100 out of 250 to have attended Harvard. I asked him what the proportion might be today.

The McKinsey panelist thought for a few seconds and then smiled. "About two out of five," he said.

Several reasons exist for the predominance of crimson men at McKinsey. Particularly because of its case study approach to learning, Harvard has produced graduates not only ideally suited to enter consulting but quite sympathetic to consulting as a career. McKinsey's headquarters are in the East, and former managing director Marvin Bower attended Harvard and still serves on the university's executive board. Bower's successor, C. Lee Walton, Jr., attended the University of Texas, but he and other high-level McKinsey consultants are hardly strangers to the Harvard campus. Members of the firm frequently volunteer their services. "I remember one marketing class," a recent Harvard graduate told me. "A McKinsey man took over the class for two days. The regular instructor simply disappeared. And McKinsey men were always appearing for seminars. This built up a lot of PR and good will. The students got a look at these pros and would want to work for the firm. And McKinsey only sent in the real pros; they didn't send up any spring chickens. In return, McKinsey could obtain a lot of information from the faculty to identify the top students."

At the end of the 1968 school year McKinsey made offers to twenty-seven Harvard Business School graduates. Fourteen accepted, a phenomenal acceptance ratio. Six of these were foreign-born, further underlining the firm's international interests.*

While most other management consulting firms have preferred to hire only men with four or five years' business experience in addition to whatever degrees they possess, McKinsey always has stood first in line at the graduate business school doors. Partly this reflects the heritage of James O. McKinsey, who founded his consulting firm while working as an economics professor at the University of Chicago. McKinsey was born in Gamma, Missouri, on June 4, 1889. While a student at State Teachers College in Warrensburg, Missouri, he suffered temporary blindness and for several months could only continue his studies by having his classmates read to him. Eventually his eyesight improved, although many years later his doctor warned him that if he did not forsake the many cigars he smoked each day he might again suffer blindness. No one who knew McKinsey remembers him obeying the doctor, since like Ed Booz, he was a particularly strong-minded individual who disliked taking others' advice. "I have to be diplomatic with our clients," one associate recalls him once saying,

---

* Consulting proved to be the second most popular profession for 1969 graduates of the Harvard Business School. Fifty students, or 2 per cent, chose consulting as a career. Only manufacturing, with 33 per cent of the students, outranked consulting. Consulting also ranked highest in median starting salary levels at $15,000.

"McKinsey Was a Tall, Imposing Man"

"But I don't have to be diplomatic with you bastards!" If a report displeased McKinsey he often would hurl it in the wastepaper basket and dictate a new one himself.

"McKinsey was a tall, imposing man, even though he frequently stood and walked in a stooped manner," remembers James M. Phelan, now the president of A. T. Kearney & Company. "He was somewhat formal and reserved and only his close associates and top business friends dared to call him 'Mac,' and never by his first name. He had a very analytical and perceptive mind and tremendous powers of concentration and organization. He used to claim that the trouble with most people was that they were mentally lazy and unwilling to do plain, good, hard thinking about a subject. That wasn't one of *his* weaknesses, however."

McKinsey accumulated an impressive string of advanced degrees at the University of Arkansas and later at the University of Chicago, where he became a member of the faculty in 1917. He served in the army during World War I, rising from private to lieutenant, and after his discharge obtained certification as a public accountant in 1919. "At heart he was a teacher," says Phelan.

Between 1920 and 1929, McKinsey wrote numerous articles and four books, the best known being his *Budgetary Control,* published in 1922, the first definitive book on budgeting. This volume later would stimulate considerably his consulting practice, particularly with large corporations. McKinsey joined the accounting firm Frazer & Torbet in 1924 and soon persuaded George Frazer to give him

$1,500 to open a New York office. Frazer agreed and Mc-
Kinsey took a leave of absence from his teaching job.
McKinsey met his first client on the train going to New
York, stayed in that city a year, and returned with $5,000
and the decision that he didn't want to remain an ac-
countant.

In 1926 McKinsey founded his consulting firm, James
O. McKinsey & Company, but he continued teaching at
night, until 1931 when the demand for his services as a
consultant became too great. The depression actually provided a strong stimulus to the growth of James O. Mc-
Kinsey & Company, as well as to other consulting and
accounting firms. Much of McKinsey's practice at this time
came from banks and other financial institutions whose
defaulted loans arose in many cases from inept management. In 1932 the firm opened a New York office, taking
over the office space from the branch of a defunct Chicago
investment firm. By that time McKinsey had hired Tom
Kearney.

A. T. Kearney, a director of commercial research for
Swift & Company, joined McKinsey's growing consulting
organization in 1930. "Tom was a very gentle fellow, who
would lean over backward to give the other person the
benefit of the doubt," recalls F. Lee H. Wendell, vice-presi-
dent-director of A. T. Kearney & Company. "He was almost
the exact opposite in personality from McKinsey. His great
strength was in dealing with people, and so he comple-
mented McKinsey, whose main weakness was this same
area."

"McKinsey Was a Tall, Imposing Man"

One other individual who would profoundly affect the history of consulting joined James O. McKinsey & Company during the early thirties. Marvin Bower had been born in Cincinnati on August 1, 1903. He graduated from Brown University in 1925, obtained a degree from Harvard Law School in 1928 and Harvard Business School in 1930. As a corporation lawyer with Jones, Day, Cockley & Reavis in Cleveland he served for several years as secretary for bond holders' committees, gaining first-hand knowledge on why companies had defaulted on their bonds. It provided good experience on how businessmen should *not* run their businesses.

"During the course of that activity," remembers Bower, "I concluded that there was the need for a truly professional firm that could study a business and advise top executives on management problems, much as lawyers advise them on their legal problems. I didn't realize that such firms already existed." While handling a law case in Chicago, Bower encountered J. O. McKinsey, who offered him a job. Marvin Bower, who would later shape the personality of McKinsey & Company more than its founder, went to work in the firm's New York office in November 1933.

In 1934 Marshall Field & Company, the Chicago department store, retained McKinsey's firm to thoroughly examine its business, which in addition to retailing at that time also included manufacturing and wholesaling. McKinsey supervised the study with Bower second in command. Together with a small team of consultants they determined that Field's should abandon its wholesaling and manufacturing businesses to concentrate on maintaining retail leadership. Marshall Field's board of directors not only accepted the recommendations, but in late 1935 they asked McKinsey to become chairman and chief executive officer. The opportunity to become a "doer" instead of merely a "teller" apparently was too tempting for McKinsey to resist. He accepted. "He walked in there like Punjab in Little Orphan Annie: chopping heads in all directions," one business associate informed me. Nevertheless, McKinsey's regime at Field's resulted in the sale of a number of unprofitable factories, the sale of one store with a poor sales record, and generally laid the foundations for the successful department store of today.

But in 1937, at age forty-eight, McKinsey contracted pneumonia. Taken to the hospital one Saturday night, he died on Monday morning. Tom Kearney accompanied his body back to Missouri.

After McKinsey had assumed the chairmanship of Marshall Field & Company several other firms had contacted him suggesting mergers. He accepted the offer made by Scovell Wellington & Company, an accounting firm with offices in Boston and New York. J. O. McKinsey, who of course was a certified public accountant, had included some accounting as part of his practice since his own firm's establishment in 1926, so the merger resulted in a half-accounting, half-consulting organization, with the consulting part named McKinsey, Wellington & Company. Bower helped manage the office in New York; Tom Kear-

"McKinsey Was a Tall, Imposing Man"

ney remained in Chicago. At this time United States Steel
had hired the consulting firm of Ford, Bacon & Davis as
prime contractors on what A. T. Kearney & Company
describes in one internal history as "probably the largest
contract ever let for professional management services."
The consulting fee paid by U.S. Steel reportedly reached
$1.5 million, although it may have been higher. Subcon-
tractors for the job included Robert Heller & Associates in
the marketing area and McKinsey, Wellington & Company,
which mainly concerned itself with procedural matters including a revision of order handling.

When McKinsey died in 1937, however, a split developed among the partners in the merger. The U.S. Steel
assignment ended the following year and billings dropped
so drastically that (according to the Kearney history) "for
the first and only month in its history the firm went into
the red."

Tom Kearney decided that the firm should reconsolidate
in a single Chicago office, but Marvin Bower disagreed. He
felt a retreat to Chicago would be a mistake, so with Guy
Crockett and F. R. Fletcher, the two other New York
partners, he reorganized McKinsey & Company in New
York. Crockett became managing partner. The Chicago firm
became McKinsey, Kearney & Company with Tom Kearney
as managing partner. Scovell Wellington & Company remained in Boston, retaining the accounting practice which
previously had been conducted by James O. McKinsey.

The two McKinsey firms remained affiliated by contract
and in 1944 even established a joint San Francisco office

under the name McKinsey & Company. Shortly afterward McKinsey & Company opened offices of its own in Los Angeles and Washington, and in 1946 approached Tom Kearney with a proposal of reconsolidation. Kearney declined. McKinsey & Company subsequently purchased the name, reportedly for "a sizable sum," and McKinsey & Company of Chicago became A. T. Kearney & Company. That firm thus has as much, if not more, claim to the title of heir to McKinsey as the firm bearing his name. But the point is only of historical importance. The imprint on the firm McKinsey & Company is that of Bower not McKinsey, just as the imprint of Kearney has begun to fade somewhat beneath that of the current president of A. T. Kearney & Company, James M. Phelan. An interesting sidepoint is the fact that Kearney lists its founding date as 1926, or the year J. O. McKinsey first established his consulting practice, whereas McKinsey dates its founding as 1910, relating it to the birthdate of the accounting firm Scovell Wellington.[*]

The two firms continued to develop in different directions. McKinsey & Company opened a Chicago office shortly after its divorce from Kearney but for many years found it difficult to compete in the Midwest, at least in volume, with more firmly established Kearney or Booz-Allen. Only recently have McKinsey's Chicago offices begun to grow. For many years the other firm maintained an

[*] This "one-upmanship" thus permits McKinsey & Company to be "older" than Booz, Allen & Hamilton, whose 1914 founding date is also somewhat fictitious.

"McKinsey Was a Tall, Imposing Man"

office only in Chicago under the capable but conservative direction of Tom Kearney. In 1960 A. T. Kearney & Company finally recanted its one-office policy, and expanded to Washington. By that time Tom Kearney was ill with hepatitis and was no longer taking an active part in the management of the firm. He died in January 1961. The firm eventually added offices in San Francisco, Los Angeles, New York, Washington, Cleveland, Düsseldorf, Milan, Paris, and London.

McKinsey & Company had preceded Kearney abroad, opening a London office in 1957 largely because of a major study for the Royal Dutch Shell Group, which Bower personally directed. Within a few years the London office was serving other British concerns including the Imperial Chemical Industries, Rolls Royce, and Dunlop Rubber. McKinsey next added offices in Paris, Amsterdam, Düsseldorf, Zurich, and Melbourne. As of 1969 McKinsey & Company had established itself as *the* name in international management consulting. By then one-third of its staff was foreign-born, and reportedly one-half of its billings came from outside the United States.

Perhaps a more subtle difference separates J. O. McKinsey's two offsprings in addition to *how soon* and *where* they established branch offices. With Marvin Bower pointing the direction, McKinsey & Company has developed its practice at the executive-suite level of mostly the elite companies. On the other hand, A. T. Kearney & Company has built its reputation as more of a nuts-and-bolts firm whose consultants didn't fear shedding their vests and striding out into the factory or traveling with their client salesmen. Perhaps this is partly a result of geography since corporate headquarters tend to be located in the vicinity of Park Avenue in New York, while manufacturing factories are more often scattered around the Midwest.

The tone at McKinsey & Company, however, very definitely has been set by Marvin Bower, who retired as managing director in October 1967. Bower's early training as an attorney influenced his approach to consulting. "To fully understand Marvin Bower you almost need to be a lawyer," one McKinsey consultant commented to me. "Even the reports we write for our clients follow a lawyer's brief. First, there's the presentation of our case. Then the argument. Finally the recommendation of what to do."

During one visit to McKinsey headquarters in late 1966 I spent some time talking with Marvin Bower. He sat behind a green-leather-topped table, round except for the side he sat behind. He explained that he had copied his desk from a luncheon table. He liked it round because more people could fit around it. He discussed the philosophy of McKinsey & Company.

"I wanted to manage this firm to be attractive to high-caliber people," he explained. "We wanted an atmosphere where quality counted—an atmosphere of nonpolitical activity and where performance was the main criterion for advancement. To be successful we had to get high-caliber people and we had to offer them a career. We set out to raise standards and we are still in the process of raising them. We started to upgrade the caliber of our clients and the caliber of our people on a truly professional basis without any solicitation or advertising. This took a long time to do. Now we're in a position where we can select our clients."

"You can't do a good job for a bum client," I was told later by Everett Smith, one notch below Marvin Bower and one of three men with him in McKinsey's "executive group." Richard F. Neuschel and Gilbert Clee were the other two. "Our best success is with the best clients," says Smith. "Consulting is a two-sided thing. The last several years we have had to turn down a lot of work. We've been flat out for three or four years now. We always did turn down work, but now we're turning down work we'd like to do. The controlling factor is not to spread ourselves so thin that quality is going to suffer."

Without question McKinsey & Company has attained recognition in the business world as being tops in terms of prestige. Whether because of their Ivy League heritage or not, McKinsey consultants appear to be taller, straighter, and better dressed than most others within the consulting ranks and have an air about them which, depending upon your point of view, can be interpreted as either confidence or snobbishness. This causes them occasionally to rub others at rival firms the wrong way. For example, I had lunch with one individual who, when he became interested in a consulting career, had interviewed for jobs at Fry, McKinsey, Booz-Allen, and Kearney. "I got the impression that the people at McKinsey were very able people," he said, "but they didn't have to keep telling me over and over again."

All consultants at the major firms seem to favor suits with vests, but the number of vests per square inch at McKinsey headquarters seems higher than at most. Sartorial discipline normally does not get enforced from the top, either by memo or by direction. It is a rule, however, that no McKinsey man will be seen anywhere without a hat. Also, that hat will not have a feather in the band. "Legend has it," Robert D. Spriggs, a former McKinsey consultant explained to me, "that one day Marvin Bower expressed a word of disapproval about someone with a pretty feather in his hat. Whether this actually happened or not, you'll never find a McKinsey man with a feather. Sooner or later someone on the staff will inform him of the legend."

While Marvin Bower may or may not have frowned on feathers, he has taken a more open-minded view than most about criticism leveled at consultants. Following one particularly critical *Fortune* article in 1965, he wrote a soothing memo to his staff: "Reading the article may make us wince as our cherished beliefs are attacked or belittled, but I suggest that instead of becoming needlessly exorcised by it we treat it as a challenge for us to try even higher professional standards."

Bower also commented: "The management consulting profession is now in the same 'favored' category as public accounting firms, law firms, and many prestigious corporations that have earlier been the focal point of *Fortune's* tongue-in-cheek type of article writing."

"McKinsey Was a Tall, Imposing Man"

"Marvin Bower has drilled into his staff that consulting is a profession," says Bruce McLagan, a former McKinsey consultant, now head of his own firm, C. B. McLagan & Company. "He's written thousands of words and the word 'profession' is used continually. You query a McKinsey man after he's been there three months and he's fully aware of his membership in a profession."

McLagan continues: "They pay their people somewhat more and work them somewhat harder. I'm sure every consulting firm is set up this way, but McKinsey tends to enforce their discipline more."

Indeed, while the business landscape at times seems cluttered with the wreckage of companies who, if not pillaged by, at least suffered from poor consultant advice, it is difficult to lay many wreckages on McKinsey's doorstep. There are several good reasons why this is so. Although the firm doesn't like to admit it openly, McKinsey has been known to lower its fee when it feels that the quality of its consulting work is below standard. A client may pay $40,000 for what on a per diem basis may have amounted to $80,000 worth of work. He may, or may not, realize his bill has been discounted. Since on only rare occasions does a consulting assignment turn out 100 per cent bad, the wounded client probably can shrug and say with few hard feelings: "Well, at least I got my money's worth." More often, if the McKinsey partners sense an assignment going awry, they will smother the client firm with more highly qualified consultants in an attempt to retire, if not with a profit, at least without dishonor.

But one other subtle reason helps to promote not only the quality of McKinsey's reputation, but also the quality of its performance. The firm has a self-admitted reputation for working with the uppermost of those on *Fortune's* 500 list. The president of Union Carbide Corporation, for example, will not complain to the Better Business Bureau if he gets stung. More important, the more successful a company and the more competent its officers, the more likely that its utilization of consultants will be successful. Good management tends to complement good management consulting, and vice versa.

McKinsey also has been less prone to display what *Fortune* has described critically as "the men who came to dinner" syndrome, that is, the tendency by consultants, once they get a foot in a client's door, to stay on and on and on. McKinsey abandoned retainers many years ago. "We don't want any hold on our clients except their desire to use our services," says Marvin Bower. "If that desire fades then we want to steal out silently into the night to serve someone else."

7

"The Most Brazenly Resourceful
Self-Publicist of Our Time"

There is no doubt about the identity of the black sheep of management consulting. It is the late George S. May. Among all consulting firms, none has caused as much controversy as the one he founded: The George S. May International Company of Park Ridge, Illinois. Yet, until just before his death in 1962, May's company outearned all other competitors. May also led the invasion of Europe by consulting firms, establishing an office in Düsseldorf in 1955. Most ACME firm partners shudder when reminded of the flamboyant May, who promoted golf tournaments as an adjunct to running his business and succeeded more than any other individual within consulting in attracting publicity—both good and bad.

It is difficult to find anyone in the business community who has not heard of May or who does not have an opinion of his firm. Many businessmen complain about high-pressure tactics used by May salesmen. Others grouse about the competence of the men employed by the firm. A

Milwaukee restaurant owner complained about what he felt to be excessive charges. Yet a businessman I met on an airplane flight into Cleveland said May's team had visited his company, and "everyone was quite satisfied with their work." One ACME consultant told me that out of curiosity he traced the work of one May engineer through a Minnesota town and found three satisfied customers.

The only incontestable fact about the May Company is that it does both good and bad work. The same might be said about *any* management consulting firm—McKinsey, Booz-Allen, and all other members of ACME. It then becomes a question of percentages: how much good work and how much bad work? Dale S. May, president of the firm from his father's death in 1962 until he resigned in June 1968 to start his own management consulting firm, contends that dissatisfied customers comprise only a small percentage of their total business. When I cited examples of several successful May assignments to one ACME consultant, however, he snorted, "Even a broken clock is right twice a day."

May achieved sufficient prominence during his heyday to receive the full *Fortune* treatment: a critical article by Perrin Stryker. *Fortune* titled its article "The Relentless George S. May Co." The accompanying blurb read: "The 'world's largest business engineering organization' is run by George S. May, one of the most flamboyant promoters alive. His hard-selling company is scorned by the orthodox management consultants—and does more business than any of them."

"The Most Brazenly Resourceful Self-Publicist"

Fortune listed the May Company's 1953 earnings as $7,157,248 in fees from 3,760 clients. Within the next dozen years, May could list offices in nine different European countries in addition to the United States and Canada. The firm reportedly employed 1,200–1,500 people, and surveyed 6,000 businesses a year. Gross billings at one point reached $20 million. One May brochure states that in its more than forty years of operation, the firm has surveyed 150,000 business concerns, thus earning $200 million in fees.

These successes came despite the *Fortune* article, which hardly favored May. Perrin Stryker wrote: "Some May clients have been grateful for the company's help, and have returned for more. Others have called the business 'an out-and-out racket' and some have sued for damages—but very few of them have ever collected." Stryker stated that "orthodox consultants regard the (May) company as a vast embarrassment to their trade." He referred to May himself as the *bête noire* of consulting, and hinted that one reason ACME was organized in 1929 (four years after May established his company) was "to avoid precisely the kind of hard-selling publicity that the George S. May Co. has thrived on. ACME has not officially condemned the company's business methods, but reports on the company by Dun & Bradstreet and several Better Business Bureaus have cited clients' lawsuits against the company and other unfavorable information." Stryker described May's techniques of uncovering customers through mail-order solicitation and blind calls by salesmen paid on a commission basis. He also aired charges that May engineers were undertrained and that "the company encourages its men to overstate the size of the savings possible by its methods and to overstate the time really needed to accomplish such savings."

The article was so unfavorable in tone that *Fortune*'s editors huddled before publication to discuss the dangers of incurring a lawsuit. "Time, Inc.'s legal counsel finally urged publication," Stryker later informed me, "on the grounds that even if a suit did cost the magazine a bundle of money, *Fortune* ought to stand up for what it had found to be true. No suit or threat of one materialized, however."

What did occur shed some light on the shrewd business mind of George S. May. Shortly after the article appeared in June 1954, Stryker learned from some former May consultants that the firm had bought copies of the article and had underlined any favorable or uncritical facts so its salesmen could present the *Fortune* text as a promotion piece. May realized that few prospects would bother to read the whole text before signing to accept a survey.

Then in February 1955, more than eight months after the article appeared, Stryker received a personal letter from George S. May. It was a brief note in which May chattingly brought Stryker up to date concerning the effect on business of *Fortune*'s publication of "The Relentless George S. May Co." Businessmen, upon reading the article, had not boycotted the May firm. Far from it; they had

"The Most Brazenly Resourceful Self-Publicist"

practically trampled down the door to get May's expertise. May enclosed a copy of an advertising brochure called "The Red Book of Business Engineering" and suggested that Stryker not miss page 17. On that page, May indicated, the writer would discover that the May Co.'s sales had increased 110 per cent in three years and that the firm had earned $1,000,000 more in 1954 than it had in 1953. May also cited the opinion of his managers that the *Fortune* article had contributed greatly to this increase.

In telling me of the incident Stryker commented, "I framed that letter as a masterful retort by one of the most brazenly resourceful self-publicists of our time."

I first visited May's "world headquarters" one morning late in 1966 and was greeted by the executive secretary, J. J. Coffey, Jr. A slim, silver-haired man in a dark, conservative business suit, Coffey exhibited as much polish as any ACME firm partner that I had met during my previous travels. We sat down in his office and he began to reminisce about the late George S. May, whom he referred to as the Old Man. Coffey spoke almost reverently about how the Old Man had begun on his own, with a minimum of education, and had built his consulting business to mammoth size. As sole proprietor of a business that grossed close to $200 million in his lifetime, May probably reaped riches unequaled by anyone else in management consulting.

He also reaped more publicity. Pictures of May (usually clad in a floral-patterned Hawaiian shirt) appeared frequently on Chicago sports pages because of the "World's

Championship of Golf" staged at his country club. "George S. May's Tam O'Shanter country club" read the signs outside its entrance. May never missed an opportunity to promote his name, and thus his business. At least in Chicago, May was a major celebrity.

Coffey recalled the good times at the club. Executives with the May Company obtained free green fees at Tam O'Shanter. There were parties and fashion shows for the wives. "The Old Man couldn't break a hundred to save his soul," said Coffey, "but he loved the sport." The Old Man also couldn't get in ACME to save his soul. Coffey admits: "We are not members. We never attempted to join. We realized that advertising as extensively as we did, we wouldn't have been considered acceptable."

Coffey continued: "I visit Phil Shay and lunch with him. He has indicated that the ACME firms have expressed slighting remarks on occasion. I think that probably it's not so much because of our standing as consultants, but because they thought Mr. May a glamorous personality. He was extremely colorful. Newspapers built him up. Any man who started from nothing had to have a hell of a lot on the ball."

"Do you think their disapproval is because of professional jealousy?" I asked.

"I think it's more a misunderstanding."

●

Certainly George Storr May led not only a glamorous but also a stormy career. He was born to a farm family in

"The Most Brazenly Resourceful Self-Publicist"

Windsor, Illinois, on June 5, 1890, and at the age of fifteen entered Eastern Illinois Normal School (now Eastern Illinois University) in nearby Charleston. He was an average student, but left school in 1909 at age nineteen, without having graduated, to sell Bibles for the Cross Reference Bible Company, following Billy Sunday's caravan. Six years later May was arrested and charged with forgery. May pleaded guilty and was sentenced to the Illinois State Penitentiary in Joliet, where he reportedly served eleven months before being released on parole.

May's prison record seems still to embarrass his family. When *Time* did a one-paragraph obituary on him in its "Milestones" column, the prison sentence got mentioned, thus irritating his son. "He paid his debt to society," says Dale. "It was just a family quarrel involving an uncle that didn't like him."

"He got into management consulting almost by accident," explains Coffey. "He bumped into a former classmate from Eastern Illinois and this chap was associated with the Barber-Coleman Company in Rockford. He asked Mr. May what he was doing, and he said selling. So the Old Man went over there at Barber-Coleman in the capacity of foreman of one of the departments. He displayed such an aptitude for systematizing things he came to become recognized as something of an expert in problems of efficiency. Shortly thereafter he began to do some outside assignments on his own—mostly in the area of cost reduction."

While working on a consulting assignment at Hart Schaffner & Marx, May became acquainted with the L. V.

Estes Company, a firm of consulting management engineers. He worked at Estes and later for the Robert-Pettijohn-Wood Corporation. May was thirty-five years old and earning a respectable $625 a month in 1925 when he quit to enter consulting on his own. He composed a sales letter, which he mailed to fifty prospects. Two replied; one of them the Chicago Flexible Shaft Company (now Sunbeam Corporation), his first client. Initially he worked from the basement of his home on Chicago's north side, then built a three-flat next door which became headquarters for his rapidly growing organization. Within two years of the May Company's birth he opened an office in New York. Shortly afterward he moved into Toronto and then San Francisco.

In these early days May worked for a number of companies on *Fortune's* 500 list, including International Salt, Hoover, Gillette, Indian Motorcycle, Eagle Pencil, and McKesson & Robbins. Coffey tells the story of how in the late thirties the May Company ran an ad in the *Wall Street Journal* boasting about the expansion of its business. This prompted Ed Booz to comment to a friend that the ad wasn't factual. At that time Coffey was working in May's New York office. The friend knew Coffey and suggested that Booz visit him on his next trip to New York, which Booz did. Coffey reached into a drawer for the May Company's year-end statement and showed it to his visitor. Booz reportedly examined it in detail and commented: "Frankly if I didn't see it, I wouldn't believe it. My compliments to Mr. May."

Although the May Company continued to prosper it was

not by maintaining an association with the larger organizations the company had served during its early years. According to Coffey: "At the end of the war, Mr. May made an astute judgment and said that with the tremendous growth of small businesses, these businesses are going to have real problems and constitute a tremendous market for a firm of consultants that specializes in their problems. We slanted our approach to small and medium-sized firms. Today I would say that 98 per cent of our business is with firms having fifty to five hundred employees."

The George S. May International Company differs considerably from the typical ACME firm. May consultants operate under titles: senior executives, supervisors, and staff executives. Whereas several ACME firms recruit on campus, May hires mostly men thirty-five years and older. "We've employed Harvard Business School graduates," comments Lawrence Block, a May Company director. "Compared to a man with only a college degree but ten years' business experience, they don't do very well. We've found that we do better by hiring men with practical experience who can analyze a company without considering the economics on the London exchange."

But a more basic difference between May and the more conventional management consulting firms is the former's methods in obtaining clients. "Most consultants assume a primly professional attitude toward clients," wrote Perrin Stryker in *Fortune*. "In the George S. May Company, the client is hotly pursued. Indeed, few companies in any industry have dared to sell their services so hard, so blatantly, and so indiscriminately as does the George S. May Company."

Three departments exist at May: sales, survey, and management services. Although it might be truthfully argued that a Booz-Allen partner sells and surveys clients as well as consults with them, ordinarily the first two departments do not exist as separate entities in the typical ACME firm. At May, however, duties in these three areas do not overlap. The salesman has no function other than to sell prospective clients on the idea of allowing a May survey engineer in the door to make a preliminary survey. The salesman gets paid on commission depending upon the number of prospects he obtains.

Businessmen previously paid May a hundred dollars for what amounted to a two- or three-day analysis of their business problems. Recently the May Company raised the price of this preliminary analysis to $250. Even at that price a thorough business analysis would be a bargain, but this represents only the bait on the hook. The prospective client will receive from the May survey engineer no sleekly polished written report, but rather an oral report during which he learns just enough about his problems to be convinced that to solve them he better hire a May consultant whose services are price-tagged at $38 an hour (up from $25 an hour a few years ago). The May survey engineer, like the salesman, has a vested interest in seeing that the businessman proceeds to the third step, since his salary also depends on commission based on how many assignments result from his surveys. According to Coffey, four out of

"*The Most Brazenly Resourceful Self-Publicist*"

every ten surveys result in assignments. When they do the news of who sold the survey, and where, will be announced like the ball scores over the loudspeaker at the May World Headquarters in Park Ridge. "They play the game like the dance studios," one former Better Business Bureau official told me. "You come in for one lesson and they sign you up for the samba and fox trot."

Actually, despite ACME's ethical posture, there is nothing technically illegal about selling consulting services in this manner. The question of illegality would arise only should the salesman or survey engineer promise profits, or reductions in costs, or benefits, which fail to materialize. Even then the existence of any real or imagined promises may be difficult to prove in court, as several disgruntled May customers who have tried unsuccessfully to sue the firm have discovered. The businessman who finds himself paying for consulting work which he considers of little value may find, at least from a legal point of view, that he has only himself to blame. This is as true with clients of McKinsey and Booz-Allen as it is with clients of May.

"While the term 'high pressure' is constantly used with this company," says John Waldron, a May director, "the ability of the client to cancel the assignment at any time offsets it. Actually a high-pressure sales approach can be very salutary for small businessmen who otherwise might not have the incentive to approach a consulting firm. The fact that they can walk away from us at any time makes it a very satisfactory arrangement for small businessmen."

In one report on the May Company, the National Better

Business Bureau commented on a letter Dale S. May had sent to several BBB's: "Mr. May . . . pointed out that the contract offered the client covering May Management Service 'is probably as fair a document as could be drawn' since it stated that the firm did not guarantee results; was cancelable upon payment of fees owing up to the hour of cancellation; and that a written report of progress is given the client weekly which he is asked to approve or disapprove."

Indeed, after having been visited by the salesman and having agreed to the $250 survey, the businessman can change his mind before the survey engineer arrives and exercise an option to withdraw. After hearing the results of the survey he can pay his $250 and still retire, with embarrassment perhaps but with no further obligation. When the men from the management services department arrive, they remain on the premises only as long as the client so wills. At the end of each week on Friday the May engineer will submit a written report, stating what they have accomplished as well as what they plan to accomplish the following week. The businessman must sign this report, and if he fails to do so by Tuesday of the following week, all work ceases until he has signed. Moreover, at any moment during the consulting assignment the businessman can shout for it to stop. "When a client agrees to a 150-hour job," says John Waldron, "he can cancel it in the first hour, even if his own reason is he doesn't like the color of our man's hair." If the businessman expresses his displeasure at the end of an assignment, an adjustment engineer will visit

"The Most Brazenly Resourceful Self-Publicist"

him to attempt to soothe his hurt feelings. Some of these "reforms" are relatively recent. Nevertheless, regardless of this contractual agreement to terminate the relationship at any minute, it may take more knowledge and self-assurance than perhaps the average, typically small business client possesses to recognize an assignment going awry and call off the troops.

Management consulting, because it tends to upset established patterns and procedures, is controversial at any level of business. On several occasions May clients have complained to their local Better Business Bureau. May concentrates mostly on small- and medium-sized companies, thus any cries of dissatisfaction resulting from the firm's work would naturally come to BBB ears. A larger corporation might not be more sophisticated in its use of a consultant, but for fear of embarrassment (and for fear of parading its mistakes before stockholders' eyes) would not holler if and when stung. In addition, for a consulting firm that boasted six thousand clients a year, even a 1 per cent margin of error would result in sixty nettled clients.

At the height of his success, George S. May frequently found himself beset by enemies. In 1953 May complained to the National Better Business Bureau about reports on client dissatisfaction that were being circulated by local bureaus. In reply, the National BBB offered to make an impartial survey of clients if they would be allowed to pick the names at random. On the advice of its lawyers, May declined to allow the National BBB access to its records. In passing it should be mentioned that even the bluest of the blue-ribbon ACME firms guard their client lists as though they were the Dead Sea Scrolls.

Two years later, faced with continued inquiries about the consulting firm, the National BBB decided to conduct a survey without May's cooperation. It asked its local bureaus to write all companies that had made recent inquiries about the May Company and ask "whether they had engaged the services of this company, and if so, whether they were satisfied, or dissatisfied." The results were unfavorable to May.

When apprised of the survey, May understandably complained of the methods used in conducting it. The National BBB offered to select three hundred names at random from the May files. Again May declined. In replying to this last National BBB request, one of the May officers remarked that the firm had done business for thirty-one years and had served about 45,000 clients, mostly in North America. The officer indicated that far from having ninety-nine dissatisfied clients (the number uncovered by the National Bureau), they probably had 3,000 clients who for one reason or other had complained about services rendered. This worked out to about 7 per cent of the entire May client list, which did not (though they claimed differently) seem unduly high or any higher than the dissatisfaction experienced by other consulting firms.

The May officers suggested that their other customers had no reason to report their satisfaction to the bureau.

In a few instances May actually did provide local bureaus with names of clients. The Chicago BBB contacted

"The Most Brazenly Resourceful Self-Publicist"

twenty-six "satisfied customers" and fifteen wrote commending the firm's work. A few among the dissenters qualified their remarks. One customer felt that some good was accomplished although he expressed displeasures with the eventual results. Another customer felt that the firm's greatest fault was its tendency to hang around too long. He felt May's men should have accomplished what they did in much less time. (These same criticisms, of course, are made quite frequently of ACME firms.) Surveys of May customers made by the New Orleans BBB in 1955 and the BBB of western New York in 1959 uncovered a percentage of dissatisfied customers somewhat higher than that found in Chicago. Nevertheless, the National BBB stopped short of direct condemnation of the May Company, recommending to inquiring businessmen that they check with other May clients in the area.

The history of George S. May has not been written entirely in business ledgers. In 1931 May joined the Tam O'Shanter country club in Niles, a suburb northwest of Chicago. The club at that time was owned and operated by a group of doctors who had difficulty maintaining its financial health. May began by subsidizing the club's operations and later bought a majority of its stock. Under his efficient hand the club began to prosper. He added swimming pools and a watering system for the golf fairways. In 1940 when the Chicago District Golf Association sought a location for its open tournament, May volunteered Tam O'Shanter. The following year he expanded the tournament to national proportions. May's "World Championship of

Golf" soon became the top money tournament on the golf circuit and at its height in the mid-fifties dispensed cash prizes each year totaling $210,000, approximately four times more than the second richest golf tournament. May also became a heavy contributor to the Chic Evans scholarship fund to provide caddies with college educations. To encourage Tam O'Shanter members to donate money, he matched their contributions. He also made a significant financial donation to the High Ridge YMCA.

May's name and face appeared frequently in the sports pages during this time, yet even in golf circles he stirred controversy. In order to stimulate fan interest he made all entrants in his tournaments wear large numbers on their seats. Those who refused received smaller prizes if they won. His was the first major tournament that allowed Negroes to compete. Charlie Sifford got his start at Tam O'Shanter. Joe Louis also played. I recall journeying to Tam O'Shanter several times during the late forties to join the thousands following their golfing heroes: Byron Nelson, Ben Hogan, Sam Snead, Lloyd Mangrum. Since my interest in the newspaper at this time ended at the sports pages, I considered George S. May only a flamboyant golf promoter. But May connected his golf promotions solidly and shrewdly to his business. The winner of his tournament received a contract for fifty exhibition matches at $1,000 apiece. "It was a sales promotion device in that chambers of commerce collaborated in the staging of exhibitions," says Coffey. The magic of the George S. May name appealed to many small businessmen whose knowledge of the

"The Most Brazenly Resourceful Self-Publicist"

news also failed to transcend the sports pages. May's business prospered partly as a result of his golf promotions.

Golf also led May overseas. In 1953 May and his wife visited Europe to attend the Ryder Cup matches and was introduced by golfer Fred Corcoran to textile manufacturer William Schneewin, who asked May when he planned to do business in Europe. May admitted that he had begun to give it some thought. "If you ever do come to Europe," Schneewin reportedly said, "I'll be your first client."

"The next year," Coffey explains, "Mr. and Mrs. May returned to Europe and became so impressed with the industry and determination of the German people that he made up his mind to open an office in Germany. Düsseldorf is the headquarters of our European operations today."

In expanding overseas the May Company became one of the first American consulting firms to exploit the European market. The United States, particularly since World War II, had achieved a reputation as being the fountainhead of business knowledge. European firms seemed more willing than anyone had anticipated to buy American expertise. May, arriving early on the scene, profited because of this. At about this same time several ACME firms began to open offices in Europe, ostensibly to serve their American clients abroad. Soon these firms discovered themselves doing more business with European clients abroad than American ones. Much of the current expansion within the management consulting ranks has been due to demand for American business knowledge abroad. Many ACME consultants, however, express distress that May's having preceded them has reflected on their image and hint he expanded to Europe only because he had run out of clients to serve at home. "I guess the only place left for May to go is to the moon," one consultant told me.

May meanwhile had begun to attract headlines beyond either the sports or even business pages. The night of July 4, 1950, the police surprised a reported 2,500 people in the clubhouse at Tam O'Shanter and confiscated twenty-seven slot machines. Gambling existed in varying degrees at many Chicago-area clubs and at Tam O'Shanter it had flourished profitably for years. Records seized at the time of the raid indicated that gambling profits for the previous eighteen months amounted to $181,177. Forty per cent reportedly was retained by the club; the remaining 60 per cent was grabbed by the crime syndicate. May and several other Tam O'Shanter employees testified before Judge Julius H. Miner, who branded May (then a member of the city of Chicago's planning board) as a discredit to the community and said that Tam O'Shanter should be put out of business as a public nuisance. When May appeared reluctant to discuss gambling at the club, Miner fined him $1,000 for contempt of court.

The following year the Senate Crime Committee (better known as the Kefauver Committee) sought to have May testify at hearings then being conducted in various parts of the country. Although May salesmen and survey engineers made themselves readily available to prospective clients, it took the Kefauver Committee four months to locate and serve a subpoena on the boss. Finally on May 28,

"The Most Brazenly Resourceful Self-Publicist"

1951, May traveled to Washington to testify. That same day Murray (the Camel) Humphrey and Rocco Fischetti appeared before the Committee. The papers noted dutifully the next morning that May, Humphrey, and Fischetti all had taken the Fifth Amendment. One of the questions that May declined to answer was whether or not he was a member of the country club. For his refusal to provide information May was cited for contempt of Congress and fined $1,000. A year and a half later May succeeded in overruling this verdict in a federal district court. He failed, however, to overthrow Judge Miner's contempt of court citation against him, even though he appealed his case as high as the Supreme Court.

One Chicago alderman attempted to have May banished from the Chicago Plan Commission. Even though he rarely attended meetings, May at first refused, which merely extended the controversy and generated additional unfavorable newspaper publicity. Several months later, after the dispute had simmered down, May resigned his commission membership quietly. In 1953 the Internal Revenue Bureau charged May with avoiding $1,206,601 in taxes because his firm wasn't a "bona fide partnership." The Government claim against May was finally settled for $17,816.

In 1958 May was at war again: this time with the Professional Golf Association. The dispute concerned whether they or he should be allowed to retain the entry fees paid by golfers playing in his tournament. May felt that, considering the size of prizes offered at Tam O'Shanter, he should be allowed to pocket the entry fees. The PGA felt otherwise. Whether this represented the actual reason or not, May discontinued his tournament and his name and face retreated from the news.

He reappeared again as though for one last hurrah. Over the years Tam O'Shanter had earned a reputation not only for its golf tournaments but also as a hang-out for Mafia members. Whether May welcomed the mobsters to his club or whether, as frequently is the case, the mobsters welcomed themselves would be difficult to prove, but on Labor Day in 1961 the most notorious members of the Chicago crime syndicate descended on Tam O'Shanter for the wedding reception of the son of John (Jack the Lackey) Cerone. Invited guests that evening included Tony Accardo, Sam Battaglia, Phil Alderisio, Marshall Caifano, and Joe (Gags) Gagliana. Uninvited guests, who stationed themselves at the door of the club, included a battery of newspapermen, television cameramen, and policemen recording the license numbers of those in attendance. One of the license numbers recorded during the eight-hour party was that of George S. May, whose chauffeur had stationed himself up the road to warn arriving gangsters of the police observation point.

The gangland wedding served as a swan song in the press for George Storr May. Six months later on March 2, 1962, he died of a heart attack at his club shortly before noon. He was seventy-one years old.

Since George S. May's death his consulting organization has become somewhat of an enigma. His son and two daughters inherited the family business, with Dale S. May

"The Most Brazenly Resourceful Self-Publicist"

as president. In 1963 the organization was incorporated in Delaware, becoming the George S. May International Company. Tam O'Shanter was sold to a group of investors who planned to use the land for an industrial park. That transaction became clouded with a controversy over whether or not the property could be legally rezoned for industrial use. A lawsuit ensued, involving the developing company and the village of Niles on one side, and residents of that village on the other. The industrial park, however, eventually became a reality.

In the summer of 1966 the George S. May International Company moved from the two or three floors it had once occupied in a downtown Chicago office building to a modern but relatively small two-story building in suburban Park Ridge. May closed its New York office and returned all executives stationed there to Park Ridge. This Midwest office, in addition to being "world headquarters," serves the United States from the Atlantic to the Rockies. One other office in San Francisco covers the remainder of the country. In Europe, May has reduced the size of its offices in Düsseldorf.

When I spoke to Dale S. May about the visible reduction in office and personnel, he admitted that the May Company grossed slightly less than eleven million dollars in 1966 compared with a high of twenty million at about the time of his father's death. But he indicated that this represented a necessary consolidation of an overextended organization. Dale says that they actually make more profit off the eleven million gross than they had made grossing twenty million.

He also insists that the firm now has started to concentrate on quality control and the hiring of better men. Certainly in the area of complaints made to Better Business Bureaus, May seems dormant. Several BBB presidents with whom I talked indicated that they now receive few complaints about the firm.

Thus the enigma: Has May reformed or is the firm simply doing considerably less business than Dale S. May would like to admit? One person within ACME expressed the belief that May's gross billings may have sunk as low as two or three million dollars annually, but then ACME never has spoken charitably of May. When I spoke with J. J. Coffey in 1969 and asked if he wanted to update the 1966 figure of eleven million dollars, he declined to do so.

In the meantime, J. J. Coffey still reminisces about the good old days when Tam O'Shanter became the center of the golf and business world, its colorful owner parading up and down fairways in floral-colored shirts, president of the biggest and certainly most controversial management consulting firm of all time. "Here's a man who came off a farm," says Coffey. "He had a limited education, but a tremendous imagination. I think that history will have to say that the Old Man was a person of tremendous accomplishment."

8

"A Rare and Treasured Human Being"

"Consulting has become a queer sort of status symbol," explains John H. Smith, Jr., president of Communications Analysis, Inc. "You can be fired and out of a job, but if you have enough money to go into consulting your friends accept it. They'll ask you, what do you do? 'I'm a consultant to management,' you can answer. People are impressed. It's better than being just another vice-president at the bank. It indicates an acceptability for consultants that didn't exist twenty years ago."

"Many consultants think their job has a very impressive social impact," claims executive recruiter Edwin C. Johnson. "Say you're with Booz-Allen. Everyone thinks you're making millions of dollars. It's socially acceptable and a lot of guys get kicks out of being at a cocktail party and when someone asks them what they do, they can reply in a deep, authoritative voice, 'Well, I'm with Booz-Allen.'"

"Being a consultant lends you an air of mystery," says

Dick Hespus, an associate with McKinsey & Company. "People you meet casually will want to know your occupation, so you answer, 'I'm a management consultant.' Then they want to know what you do, so you answer, 'I'm in operations research.' Then they kind of look at you funny."

Rufus Allen, an individual practitioner from Raleigh, North Carolina, claims that people that he meets casually at social or business gatherings often want to classify all consultants as either oracles or shysters. "I'd be hard put to choose which label or stereotype is most distasteful," he says. "The typical comment of the former group is, 'Oh yes, you tell everybody what they are doing wrong.' The latter group is likely to ask: 'How did you get into such a good racket?'

"Of the two appraisals, I suppose the latter is somewhat more likely to be true, since there is considerable evidence that shysters are much more easily found than oracles."

Allen says that often he has to be careful before accepting an assignment from a new client of the oracle school to be certain his expectations are not unrealistic in terms of what can be accomplished and how quickly. According to Allen: "There seem to be businessmen around who are quite anxious to find someone on whom they can hang a halo and to whom they attribute all the qualities of a magic wand." These persons, he finds, will not be happy clients unless they can be given a realistic appraisal of the problems and whether or not a consultant can affect their solution.

"The group who sees us as shysters, of course, are no

problem," adds Allen. "They never become clients in the first place!"

Whether they think of management consultants as shysters or oracles, most people do find them fascinating individuals. One Booz-Allen vice-president, who apparently had tired of the constant explanations to strangers, told me how he erected defenses to avoid conversations with his seat partners on jet airplanes. Before departing from the airline terminal he would walk up to the magazine counter and buy a newspaper, any newspaper. At his seat he would unfold the paper and read it from first to last page, every word, even the marriage announcements. He had found that a seat partner wanting to talk would ignore a paperback book or a magazine in his hands, whereas an unfolded newspaper presented a formidable wall against conversation. He even would continue to read it during meals.

Nevertheless, most management consultants probably relish the role of being looked upon in awe by many of their fellow citizens. A very definite "consultant mystique" does exist. The hurdles placed before a candidate wishing to enter one of the major consulting firms are of such height and of sufficient number so that a person clearing and passing all them may indeed feel himself the equal of an Olympic decathlon champion.

Many people I met who never had been consultants, but knew a bit about the type work they did, expressed a nostalgic interest in the profession. "I've always thought that if I didn't have a family I would have enjoyed being a consultant," said James A. Gray, president of Old Salem,

Inc. "I would enjoy seeing what made a business tick. I liked the case study methods when I attended the Harvard Business School."

Tom Mahoney, who wrote an early article on consultants for *Fortune,* told me: "If I were a young man bright enough to pass all the hurdles, if I didn't have a clear and definite idea of what business to choose, it would be an ideal spot to work. There are a lot of big people who at one time worked as consultants."

But a businessman wishing to be a management consultant might be compared to a draftee with desires to be a paratrooper. It's one thing to say you would like to wear the boots and bloused trousers and strut down the street with wings on your chest; it's another thing to jump out of an airplane. "Consulting isn't necessarily glamorous," says Richard E. Peterson, a principal at A. T. Kearney & Company. "Most of it is tough work where you bang your skull up against complex management problems."

Most consultants, however, don't enter the field looking for easy work. Almost without exception, the typical, successful management consultant is a high-energy individual whose main attribute is not necessarily sheer brainpower but drive and a fiery ambition to make thorough use of whatever natural-born attributes he possesses. On a football field they would call it desire, the indefinable something that makes it possible for a 180-pound defensive back to slam into a 230-pound fullback.

"I know people who become intoxicated with their work," says Harold W. Peterson, Jr., a consultant with

"A Rare and Treasured Human Being"

Albert Ramond and Associates. "They get a glow on from work. It makes them feel good and relaxed. A lot of consultants are simply compulsive workers. There are some lazy bums, but they don't last too long."

Dr. Charles McDermid, president of Management Psychologists, Inc., does the psychological evaluations of job candidates for the Chicago offices of CMP. From talking in depth to more than a hundred individuals who later became consultants, he feels he has a good picture of the factors involved in their makeup. "A consultant has everything that a successful businessman has got, but more of it," he says. "It's a question of degree. They have to be superior individuals. They should be, by virtue of their job, a lot taller. They should be good-looking and aggressive. They're going to tell other executives how to run their businesses so they have to be better men."

"The individual who possesses the attributes for a competent consultant," claims Howard L. Green, a Detroit-area consultant, "is a rare and treasured human being, indeed. He attains these skills only after long business experience combined with an excellent education. Added to these qualities must be a warm, ingratiating personality and a keen mind! Obviously these qualities are not likely to be combined completely in a single human being, and we must come to expect something less than perfection."

"The key factors making for success in the field (of consulting)," wrote D. Donald Daniel of McKinsey & Company in the *Harvard Business Review*, "are qualities of character, intelligence, judgment, the ability to express oneself persuasively, self-confidence, self-discipline, and an attractive personality."

"To the fellow that's able to cut the mustard," says McKinsey's Everett Smith, "he gets involved in higher levels of things much earlier in the game than if he went into industry. Basically our men enjoy the opportunity to challenge themselves and be independent. The consultant knows that his success depends entirely on what is contained between his two ears."

The distance between those two ears may increase the longer a person remains—or is allowed to remain—in consulting. The individual who accepts the average executive position will find that with relatively little exertion he can claim a spot that—barring a merger or similar calamity—will provide him security (including profit-sharing and a pension) for life. It is usually only the ambitious ones who exert themselves and get fired—or make president. No such security exists within a consulting firm. After only a bare two years to prove themselves, embryo consultants are shed from their desks like water droplets from the back of a dog. Those few who through perseverance or personality survive the cut and move on to the partnership level may indeed think themselves well above the cut of mortal man. "To hear some consultants tell of it," wrote Walter Guzzardi, Jr., in *Fortune*, "their appearance on the scene ranks with the Second Coming."

Even if he does possess an uncommon amount of humility, the young consultant may find it difficult to keep his perspective when he discovers how readily men twenty and

"A Rare and Treasured Human Being"

thirty years his senior are not only willing, but eager, to accept his advice. "I wouldn't go back into consulting if it were the last thing on earth I could do," says John Zeisler, an investment banker who worked two years for Booz-Allen. "At the same time it's one of the most rewarding things to have a president of a large corporation sit down with you and say, 'John, what do we do?'"

"I think at certain levels of immaturity," says executive recruiter Spencer Stuart, "many consultants suffer a bit from megalomania. They think, now here I am advising people how to run a business. I should be able to run one myself if I can advise someone else. I don't think that's necessarily true.

"Consulting is a different type of work. There are a lot of people who don't get any fun out of consulting. Therefore they get out and go back to running businesses. The guy in consulting is running a business which is an operating job, but the nature of it is consulting, so he's a hybrid."

Many within the management consulting profession relish the challenge of being asked to describe the particular traits that go into the making of a successful consultant. According to one Kearney consultant with whom I spoke: "The consultant is a professional problem solver who likes solving problems for the thrill of it, for his own satisfaction. He likes to face variegated problems frequently. He's not the kind of guy who could sit for twenty years behind the same desk. Psychologically speaking, he probably fits into the psychotherapist-minister syndrome. He likes the feeling of omnipotence. He has the consultant mentality in that he recognizes if he's wrong he's blamed and if he's right he'll never get the credit. His joy comes from working out something to satisfy his own psychological needs. He's also a guy who is intensely interested—not compulsively though—in the reduction of waste. If he is a good consultant he *does* shave by the numbers. He lays out all his shaving tools in an efficient manner. He's a systematizer."

When I spoke with James L. Allen he talked at some length about what kind of person he thought made a good consultant. According to Allen: "Assuming that he has better than average brainpower and assuming a certain knowledge in some area or another, a potential consultant has to be a person who wants to be helpful to someone else, who likes to take on other people's problems so that he can solve them. It's the same sort of motivation that pulls people into the Peace Corps. You understand now, I'm not saying that all the people in the Peace Corps would make good consultants. But they want to be of service rather than think that their ideas should dominate others. The person who has to dominate makes the best leader of a corporation. He probably wouldn't make a good consultant."

"The consulting syndrome is a whole lot of things," claims Philip W. Shay, executive director of ACME. "The professional consultant must plan and organize much of his own work, must readily grasp and assume effective control of situations which are inherently unclear, and must be able to lead people over whom he exercises no authority. All of this requires a good analytical mind and substantial initiative, imagination, and responsibility. The consultant

"A Rare and Treasured Human Being"

must be sensitive to people and to their total situation. While possessing mental and social resilience and a sense of humor, he must have the bearing, personality, appearance, and personal habits that command the respect of chief executives and their associates at various levels. The client must feel confident that the consultant will serve him in accordance with the highest standards of competence, objectivity, and integrity."

Rudy Dallmeyer of Donald R. Booz and Associates says: "It takes a particular mix of abilities to be able to work as a consultant day after day—and be happy at it. The reasons are that among other things, you don't ever really become an executive. You're a professional man. It's like being a lawyer—or an architect. If you don't like being a lawyer, or an architect, or a doctor, you shouldn't be in consulting. Now people don't enter law with the idea of running a large organization, so a selective process is involved. But many people enter the consulting business because they want to be a power. They want to be a leader. They want to be at the top of the pyramid over a lot of people. And many of these individuals find that they're getting a big charge in what they're doing up to the point where they want to be a big business executive. Now if they want to be a big professional man they can stay in consulting and do it happily. But if they want to be a leader over two or three thousand men they're not going to do it in consulting.

"Furthermore, there's a constant pressure on consultants for professional performance. It's the same pressure that a surgeon faces. A surgeon may ask himself why does he have to rise at 5:45 in the morning to get over to the hospital to perform an operation at 8:15 A.M., and another at 8:45 A.M., and another at 10:00 A.M. I'm sure doctors say to themselves, here I am fifty-five years old and while I can do more sophisticated operations and faster ones, I'm on a treadmill. Now if you take that attitude you'll probably be a pretty poor doctor, and if you take that same attitude about consulting, you're a damn poor consultant. You have to constantly feel the old thrill of seeing some problem that you've solved seven times before come clear before your eyes. Somehow you have to rise to the occasion."

"To me consulting is neither glamorous nor non-glamorous," says Kenneth R. Andrews of the Harvard Business School. "It's like every other job. It's got its attractions and it's got its drudgery."

"The kind of man who will make a good management consultant is hard to find," says Edwin C. Johnson. "There's a certain something in his personal makeup, and it boils down to, a guy's got both savvy and a good physical presentation. He's got a good solid job record. Yet he's smooth and suave enough so he's not antagonistic. He's a people handler, but not necessarily a nice guy. He looks like a nice guy, but he's really hard as rocks underneath. He smiles while he's cutting someone's throat. But another thing: he's motivated by ambition, and if his own personal ambition also happens to further the firm's ambition, then it's great. He's great, and everybody thinks he's great."

9

The Mating Game

The single most pressing problem facing most management consulting firms during the sixties has been not a lack of business, but rather a lack of hired hands. "Our staff is so chargeable it's breaking at the seams," moans Richard Strubel of Fry Consultants. "Our greatest limitation, again and again, is our ability to hire and train outstanding people. If we have a good man we can keep him busy, but it's hard to find good men."

Without question consulting has become a high status job and tens of thousands of college graduates and young executives seek to enter the profession each year. The problem lies not so much in a lack of desire on the part of applicants, but rather a lack of talent. Like the medical profession, the consulting industry imposes necessary but incredibly high qualification standards on job candidates.

During 1965, for example, McKinsey & Company interviewed a total of 1,650 job applicants—and hired only forty. The number 1,650 represents only those whose resumes or letters of application survived the initial screening. Many hopeful applicants got only a polite "no thank you" and weren't invited in for an interview. McKinsey ran one blind ad in the *New York Times* and from a thousand replies failed to hire a single person. The firm bought a series of four ads in the New York and Chicago metropolitan editions of *Time* during the summer of 1966 at a cost of nearly $20,000. These ads drew only thirty-six responses from which the firm looked closely at three and hired none.* The frustrations felt by McKinsey in trying to locate job prospects to match their standards are felt in varying degrees by other management consulting firms. For the last five years Fry Consultants has interviewed between twenty and twenty-five applicants for every job offer they've made. The Chicago office of Cresap, McCormick and Paget examines between twelve and fifteen candidates for every one it sends to Dr. Charles McDermid for a psychological evaluation. Of every three McDermid sees, CMP may hire only one. Because of the expense, consulting firms take a close look at applicants before sending them to the psychologists. Even so, McKinsey & Company spends nearly $400,000 a year in psychological evaluation. The amount of money lost because of the time that partners devote to recruiting new employees is a major expense for most firms.

One problem faced by management consulting firms in filling staff positions is that in seeking individuals with

---

* Not everyone within the consulting profession thought the purpose of the ad was to attract job applicants. See page 230.

The Mating Game

three to five years' business experience on top of an M.B.A. degree, the firms must sift through the ranks of the already employed. The organizations most likely to harbor potential consultants may be either customers or potential customers. This may not bother a small firm with a limited number of clients, but a Booz-Allen must step gingerly.

Indeed, a certain number of company presidents actually fear (or say they fear) allowing consulting firms in the door because they don't want to lose their most talented employees to the consulting ranks. Undoubtedly many a consultant received his introduction to his profession by having a management consulting firm visit the company where he worked. He may have watched the consultants in operation, liked their style, noticed how the company president deferred to their judgment, and decided at that point to quit his job.

But when an employee of a client company approaches the consulting firm, he learns that as a matter of policy they will refuse to hire him. He has bumped against Article X of the ACME Code of Professional Ethics: "We will not make direct or indirect offers of employment to employees of clients. If we are approached by employees of clients regarding employment in our firm or in that of another client, we will make certain that we have our clients' consent before entering into any negotiations with such employees."

Thus the hopeful job applicant will be told he must quit work before the consulting firm will discuss employment. And considering the rejection rate of those who interview for consulting jobs, the risk on his part may be considerable, particularly since the consulting firm will not want to appear as having pirated away a client's employee. One individual I knew who worked as an engineer for a small company quit that company and accepted a job with a minor consulting firm. A year later he appeared on the staff of A. T. Kearney, the same firm that had his original employer as a steady client. When I asked him about this, he insisted that he hadn't left his first job with the intentions of eventually shifting to Kearney. Nevertheless, many of the people at his former company thought he did, and Kearney carefully refrained from reassigning him to that particular client even though the engineer still lived within a few miles of their factory.

McKinsey & Company traditionally has hired a large proportion of its staff directly out of business school (usually the Harvard Business School). Seemingly this would circumvent the problem of offending a client firm. In the past, however, the typical M.B.A. candidate had worked two or three years in industry before returning for his business degree. But in the sixties, students and consulting firms found themselves faced with another factor: the draft. Many students now choose to go directly into graduate business school after four years of college, thus the majority of those emerging at the end of the pipeline possess even less experience than McKinsey likes. "McKinsey used to say you had to be twenty-six to join their firm," one class of '67 Harvard Business School graduate told me. "But several of my classmates who were only twenty-three or twenty-four went with McKinsey."

The Mating Game

Outside of this one legitimate hunting ground, the college campus, management consulting firms seek prospective employees much in the way a woman seeks a husband. She would rather have the man do the proposing. Similarly, consulting firms would rather have prospective employees walk in their doors begging to be hired rather than have to do the begging themselves. A sound financial reason (which we will come to later) exists for this, but basically most firms are looking for men with desire and ambition in addition to analytical talents. Those who walk in advertising their talents (unless they are broke and out of a job) obviously show more desire and ambition than those who need to be coaxed. Not only that, but an individual who either writes to or walks into a specific firm and expresses an interest in working for *that* firm alone, "because I've heard a lot about your reputation," will probably be looked at much more closely than an individual of similar talents who merely answers a blind ad that could have been placed by *any* management consulting firm.

Take the case of a typical individual desiring a position as a management consultant. Assuming he isn't being recruited directly from a college campus, he probably will be in his late twenties or early thirties. Like most men his age he will be married with one or two children, but whereas in industry a happy married life (with a wife who mixes well with other company wives) is almost a prerequisite for advancement, he will discover the management consulting firm to be more interested in *him* than in his family. (In fact, once he gets the job he will discover long periods of time spent away from his family to be one of his major problems.)

The item that will concern the consulting firm the most will be their prospective employee's scholastic record—not necessarily whether he achieved A's and B's (although that too is important), but *what* school and *how many* degrees. Degrees from Ivy League universities impress partners of the Big Image consulting firms the most. The education a person obtains there may or may not be better than elsewhere, but members of the business establishment tend to come from these schools—and so do the consulting firm partners.

Partners smile on liberal arts degrees more than do other employers, since they are looking for people who can both think and communicate; but the person with a liberal arts degree should also have a master's degree (preferably in business administration) tacked on top of it. Engineering degrees, mathematics degrees (particularly since computers have come of age), and psychology degrees are highly valued by the firms—and always were—but because consulting firms have become more and more specialized they now thirst after previously unwanted skills. A capable individual with a degree in hospital administration, for example, would probably be hired the moment he walked in the door at Kearney or Booz-Allen. However, a person without an advanced degree of some sort (even if it is only in social thought) may find his chances of employment slim, in fact almost nonexistent. "The majority of the men we've hired during the past year have at least a master's degree," claims Kearney's Richard Lopata. "The few without an advanced degree were unusually qualified on the basis of experience and skill." One McKinsey principal with whom I talked, after admitting he had only a bachelor's degree, quickly explained: "I'm the exception that proves the rule."

The consulting firm will examine the prospective employee's previous job record closely, but again they're looking for patterns as much as for particular indications of brilliance. A person having worked first at a large corporation will have scored a plus, since most large corporations have extensive training programs for those employees they hire directly from college campuses. After two or three years with the big corporation the ideal consultant prospect will have shifted jobs, preferably to one or two smaller companies where his talents presumably will have pushed him into positions of immediate responsibility. While stability is a character trait smiled on by most people, this is not necessarily true with personnel directors. The individual, who after having worked for a single company, comes to a consulting firm and claims to have had five years of business experience, will be told quite frankly: "You don't have five years of business experience. You have *one* year of business experience multiplied five times." Consulting firms thus desire a certain amount of promiscuity on the part of their job candidates—as long as it is selective promiscuity.

The prospective job candidate's resume and/or application letter will also receive scrutiny as to its readability. An important skill desired by the Big Image consulting firms, and in fact *demanded* by them, is an ability to communicate both orally and in writing. An individual may be a superb thinker, but unless he can transfer his thinking into written or spoken terms so that the client company can benefit from his thinking he will be of little value to anyone.

Occasionally consulting firms carry specialists on their staffs (a computer scientist, for example), just as a pro football team will carry a field goal kicker, but these specialists have limited futures. To make partner you must be able to sell, and you sell by being a consultant and sitting across the desk or luncheon table from the client president. It is the quarterbacks not the field goal kickers who eventually make coaches in the National Football League.

Up until this point our prospective job candidate may have had no contact with the consulting firm for which he wants to work other than by mail or phone. Now the staff recruiter invites him to visit the office for the first face-to-face confrontation. The candidate will probably think of this staff recruiter as rather a formidable and impressive person, a symbol of authority and success. More than likely, however, the recruiter will not have worked for the consulting firm for more than a few years, and may already be reading want-ads himself.* However, the staff recruiter,

---

* One sure sign that you're going nowhere in a consulting firm is to be removed from client work and returned to the home office for some administrative task. "Fred, we're stretched a bit thin in the area of personnel. How would you like to switch over there for six months?" can be loosely

regardless of his lack of tenure, knows exactly the kind of man the partners want to hire: a cross between a missile scientist and a model for Brooks Brothers ads. "Let's admit it," one consultant said to me. "This business puts a premium on being a face man." As for mustaches or beards, you find them in the Peace Corps, not in Booz-Allen.

A former staff recruiter for Booz-Allen once described to me how a job candidate, an industrial engineer, narrowly missed elimination for lack of understanding of the rules of conformity. The engineer had visited the firm several times for interviews with various officers and had impressed everyone with his appearance and manner. For the final interview, however, the engineer appeared wearing non-matching double-breasted coat and trousers. (This was before double-breasted sports coats returned to popularity.) The staff recruiter blanched at the sight when he met the candidate in the lobby, anticipating rejection if any of the partners spotted him. "Fortunately, it was a hot summer day," explained the recruiter to me. "I suggested that he hang up his coat in the outer closet, and no one else that day saw him in anything but a short-sleeved shirt. After he had been hired we sat down and had a little talk about fashions."

Appearance is an important attribute for a consultant. The consultant has to command respect by the way he looks as well as by his ability. "We have no short, cross-eyed,

---

translated as: "Fred, you really botched the last two client assignments. How would you like to move inside where you can't do us any harm? We're getting rid of you in six months anyway."

bald-headed officers in this firm," one Booz-Allen employee informed me.

In examining the staffs of consulting firms, you probably will not encounter many with hooked noses or with a complexion any tanner than could be acquired during a winter at Delray Beach. Some years ago the staff recruiter for one ACME firm, reading the mailed application and resume of one promising job-seeker, invited him in for an interview. When the job-seeker walked in the door the recruiter discovered to his dismay that the man was Negro. He walked him back out the door as quickly and politely as possible.

This incident occurred in the mid-fifties, when a Negro college graduate had difficulty obtaining an executive position anywhere. Unfortunately, the recruiter failed to flag the folder of the applicant. His application and resume were filed bearing no reference to race. A year later, after demand for manpower had increased, his successor riffled through the files and uncovered the Negro job-seeker's original application. Impressed by his apparent qualifications, the new recruiter invited him back again to interview for a staff consulting position. The Negro got no further the second time than he had the first.

In the past, management consulting firms merely reflected the prevalent attitudes within the business establishment. But during the mid-sixties, partially spurred by a shortage of qualified manpower, most large corporations began actively to recruit Negro college graduates. The consulting firms still lag far behind. The ACME firm previously mentioned finally did hire a Negro in the late 1960's. He

The Mating Game

quit, so they had to hire another one. This tokenism seems particularly interesting when you consider that the Federal Government recently has shown a reluctance to do business with companies who do not practice equal employment. Several of the large consulting firms do considerable Government contract work.

Negroes alone haven't been excluded from the consulting ranks. "Consulting has become a very closed and WASP-ish field," Donald R. Booz admitted to me. "I went to an ACME meeting recently and I had never met as many WASP's before."* If we accept Marvin Bower's definition of consulting as a profession, certainly fewer Jews have entered it than the professions of medicine and law. When you mention this, however, someone always remembers that at least one Booz-Allen partner is Jewish. Then someone else will correct the first person, reminding him that that partner is only half-Jewish—like Barry Goldwater.

Most management consulting firms ask prospects on their first visit to take a test of an hour to ninety minutes' duration to test their general intelligence. Anyone failing to score a minimum number of points gets no further. The minimum is high enough to wash out the greater majority of applicants at this point. Assuming that the job candidate survives, his ordeal has only begun. The staff recruiter will call the candidate and suggest that he return for another visit "to meet some of the people he will be working with." The recruiter then may personally escort him from office to office introducing him to various members of the

* By WASP, of course, he refers to White Anglo-Saxon Protestant.

firm, usually starting with those at the lowest level. He may shake hands with twenty or thirty members of the firm. At least seven or eight will interview him, or talk with him at some length. They will ask questions and he in turn will be invited to ask questions of them. If he inquires about travel he will learn that a consultant spends a good share of his time away from home. "But you will always get home on weekends," he will be told. "That is always part of the agreement with the client company." His early inquiries about salary (if he dares voice them) will usually be answered only in general terms, but details will be given about bonuses and profit-sharing, the frosting on the consultants' cake. Although the staff members of the consulting firm are examining the job candidate to determine his acceptability, they also are trying to sell him on coming to work for their firm.

These interviews will last between a half hour to an hour apiece, and the candidate will probably go to lunch with three or four members of the firm including at least one partner. If he is smart he will not react too quickly when the waitress asks if anyone wants a drink before eating. The job candidate will ordinarily return to the consulting firm's offices two or three times for interviews. The firm may even choose to fly him to one of their offices in another city if they hope to relocate him there. Each time he will find himself being introduced to persons at higher and higher levels. Perhaps the single most desired characteristic in a new employee is an ability to work smoothly with the partners, so although they will accept recommendations from lesser men on their staffs it is these partners who serve as ultimate judges of a candidate's acceptability.

In many respects, applying for a job with a consulting firm is like trying to rush a fraternity. More often than not, the individual desiring to become a consultant will apply at several major consulting firms at once. When accepted by more than one he will select the best bid. (Being hired by McKinsey might be compared in many respects to pledging Sigma Chi.) The job candidate visits the consulting firm's offices, much as a rushee visits a fraternity smoker. His being invited back for another smoker, or a lunch, depends upon the impression he makes. After his visit the members of the staff may have their equivalent of a hash session to decide on his acceptability. A candidate might be rejected by a consulting firm for the same reasons that would lead to rejection by a fraternity. Sigma Chi still discriminates against Negroes, as do several other fraternities. Jews find themselves accepted almost on a quota basis, if even on that. Consulting firms are less impressed by athletic credentials than fraternities, however.

Consulting firms, similar to fraternities, have a "dork" system. If any partner, for any reason, consciously or unconsciously dislikes a candidate, he can dork him. All the brothers, or partners, will accept this. The job candidate will be thanked for his time but will not be asked to return. In fraternity lingo this is known as being "walked." Of course, at a college fraternity this mating game occurs only once, or maybe twice, a year. At management consulting firms the game operates continuously, all year long.

Even if he successfully has survived this gauntlet, the job candidate may have one more hurdle to clear: the psychological evaluation. Of the five Big Image management consulting firms, only Booz-Allen scorns the use of psychologists. Fry and Kearney have psychologists on their staffs to whose judgments they defer when accepting new employees. McKinsey and CMP hire outside firms, although not the same ones in the same cities. In Chicago McKinsey works with Rohrer Hibler & Replogle, while CMP utilizes the services of Management Psychologists, Inc. In San Francisco, however, McKinsey hires Dalaba Associates. In New York CMP works with James N. Farr Associates.

In Chicago CMP deals not so much with the McMurry Company as with its Dr. Charles McDermid. CMP followed McDermid from another psychological evaluation firm to his current executive vice-presidency with McMurry. James C. Worthy, a partner at CMP, explained to me that because McDermid had worked with them so often they felt he had developed an instinctive knowledge of who would succeed with the firm.

McDermid gives the prospective job candidate a four-hour evaluation, the first two hours devoted to an in-depth probing into the individual's past history. "The most important thing is a pattern of past achievement," says McDermid. "The fact that a baseball player over the past ten years has batted over .300 and averaged thirty-five home runs, makes you feel secure that he will do so again this year."

The Mating Game

McDermid also looks for signs of a person's being what he refers to as a "late bloomer." By this he means someone who, because of devoting himself to perhaps a large number of activities, failed to achieve significantly high grades in school, but who through drive and ambition has promoted himself into a series of increasingly important positions in the business world. McDermid also will check references to make certain a person's job record is as stated.

He devotes the last two hours to probing the person's personality. This will include three short tests of mental ability and two projective tests, frequently including the Rorschach test. He is seeking to determine the individual's (1) intellectual capacity, (2) emotional stability, (3) ability to form interpersonal relationships, and (4) future aspirations. All this will be balanced with his general impressions of the individual. "If he comes on too strong he may not be too successful operating as a consultant at CMP," says McDermid. "On the other hand that's exactly the kind of person that some of my other clients want."

McDermid then prepares a written report on the individual fitting him into one of three categories: (1) recommended for employment, (2) not recommended for employment, or (3) recommended for employment, but with reservations. CMP generally accepts all those in category one as well as many of those in category three. (This doesn't mean the candidate automatically joins CMP; he may decide to work for someone else.) McDermid has found that many of the ones recommended for employment with reservations later prove to be less successful as consultants. He says of CMP, however, "They're professionals. They know how to use my services better than any other client I have."

I asked McDermid what if an individual wanted only to become a consultant for a few years, to obtain sufficient experience to propel himself further upward in his business career; could he be detected? "A highly articulate con man probably can disguise his true motivations," admits the psychologist.

There are those within the business community who might consider "a highly articulate con man" to be a rather effective definition of a management consultant.

All during this complicated bidding-in process only one subject will have failed to have been explored in depth: the exact dollar amount the newly hired consultant will be paid for his services. If the candidate asks about salary one time, his question will easily be sidetracked by the staff recruiter, or answered only in vague and general terms. If he asks a second time, or still failing a satisfactory answer, a *third* time, and acts as though he expects the dollar figure to be clearly stated, the black ball may drop at that point. Partners in consulting firms like their young consultants to be ambitious; they don't like them to be pushy.

And, particularly, they don't like them to be expensive.

Thus the subject of money will not rise to dirty the air until the eleventh hour. After the preliminary meeting, the intelligence tests, the two or three days of interviews, the lunches with partners, the psychological evaluation, the reference checks, the travel expenses (all of which the candidate may rightly compute as having cost the hiring firm several thousand dollars), the candidate may consider his services extremely valuable. He may visualize himself as the highly skilled All-American quarterback who in offering his services to a professional team deserves a bonus. In truth, however, he is just another center lineman who probably will play only a few years with the taxi squad.

When the candidate finally hears the salary offered him, he may be shocked. Not only will the consulting firm probably offer only to match his present salary, but in some cases they may offer him _less_.

"By that time they've got it honed down perfectly," says Edwin C. Johnson. "They've raised the guy's interests so damned high that they've got him hooked. They are masters at getting him at the absolute lowest figure he would ever accept. The guys that end up joining a consulting firm are amazed how close they came to saying no." Of course, the job candidate operates at a distinct disadvantage in this mating game. Most likely he will only be applying for a consulting job once in his life. Those hiring him, however, have the advantage of having hired and interviewed dozens and sometimes hundreds of consultants.

The management consulting firms find it easy to rationalize the comparatively low starting salaries they offer new candidates. "We don't pay people more to come to work here than they made previously, for a good reason," says John Lutz III of McKinsey. "We don't want them to come to us just to make money." Lutz merely equaled his previous salary in moving into consulting—although his former employers tried to lure him back with a 25 per cent raise. In retrospect his decision to reject their offer proved wise. As a recently elected principal at McKinsey, his salary prospects have brightened considerably.

"The only way we can attract men is to offer them intangibles such as challenge," says Marvin Bower. "If a man wants to make more money he can leave us, but on the average our people make more money than those in industry."

Of course, starting salaries vary from firm to firm. In attracting new employees, management consulting firms find that two very attractive lures have nothing to do with challenge. For one thing, the climbing young executive may think that one or two years' experience with a Big Image consulting firm will brighten his resume when he seeks future jobs. Second, once a consultant has survived the first few years in one of the prestige firms, his salary will leapfrog his earning potential in industry. McKinsey and Booz-Allen offer both name and potential, thus can attract good men with relatively small starting salaries. Lesser known firms find they must pay more for comparable talent. Thus the bigger the image, the smaller the comparative salaries. One person who did recruiting for a competent but relatively unknown ACME firm told me he had to offer new men 15 to 20 per cent more than they made in industry. But because of the shortage of people during the sixties, even the so-called Big Image firms found their starting salaries inching upward. While recruiting at the Harvard Business School in 1969, McKinsey offered $18,000

The Mating Game

as a starting salary to at least one key graduate. "I've seen the resumes of several people who just left Booz-Allen," says one recruiter. "They're beginning to pay their people decent money now." Booz-Allen's salaries now could be called "competitive with industry"; but the point is, they probably work their men harder than in industry.

The increase in costs as represented by higher salaries has pained the partners of management consulting firms for an obvious, but perhaps little understood, reason. The money collected from clients gets divided roughly into thirds. One-third goes toward staff salaries. One-third goes into administrative expenses and overhead. The final third remains for the partner's kitty, the profit, which gets distributed through a complicated point system, mostly to the upper two levels of command in consulting firms, and particularly to the uppermost level. It is this third of the firm's gross billings that fills the pot at the end of the consultant's rainbow.

The average consultant may produce as much as $50,000 in billings for his firm during a year. (Of course, many will produce less.) Thus if the partners have to pay him much more than $17,000 in salary, his increased earnings (applying the $\frac{1}{3}$–$\frac{1}{3}$–$\frac{1}{3}$ ratio) must come out of the pot at the end of the rainbow. Ordinarily the consulting firms like to hire new men at less than a third of their billable rate and provide a cushion for nominal raises to the new employee for at least the first two or three years of his consulting career that will not shave the profit ratio out of line.

The ideal individual that management consulting firms

seek in filling their staffs is thus: a man with personality, an attractive appearance, a graduate degree, several years' business experience, great analytical abilities, and who (through no fault of his own) is making relatively little money in comparison to his qualifications. Otherwise he may not be able to afford to work at a bottom-rung consultant's starting salary.

Nevertheless, the pot at the end of the rainbow beckons. Although starting salaries for consultants seem relatively low, the promotable man will soon reach salary heights that otherwise would seem unattainable in industry for a man his age. A consultant who is particularly effective and who starts young can be earning $40,000 a year around the age of thirty. The junior partners in the major consulting firms earn salaries of $100,000—and often before they reach forty. Estimates of the salaries of Marvin Bower and James L. Allen in *Fortune* and *Business Week* have ranged between $250,000 and $300,000. These figures probably are conservative. One former Booz-Allen consultant told me he believed Allen's earnings to be close to $500,000 a year, and even *he* may be low. Allen's billing rate reportedly stands at $500 an hour—in fact, $500 an idea.

It is this expectation of future riches, plus the belief that several years' experience with a good consulting firm advances a man's career, that attracts bright young men to the management consulting profession. As we shall see, both of these two reasons are illusory.

10

———

Like Ships Passing in the Night

It is a strange fact of life that many otherwise level-headed executives look upon management consultants as leading a glamorous, exciting, almost James Bondish existence. The idea of the square-jawed consultant, who, briefcase in hand, strides onto the first-class section of a jet plane and flies off to some distant city, where he will use his vast analytical powers to push a large corporation several notches upward on the *Fortune* 500 list, appeals to many desk-bound executives. In researching this book I talked to numerous individuals within business and industry who knew consultants either by reputation or from brief contact. A considerable number admitted that, had the opportunity occurred, they might have enjoyed the experience of working for a management consulting firm. It's like the baseball fan who dreams of pitching in the major leagues. In addition, many executives think of consulting as a logical means of advancing a promising business career.

But for every Denny McLain, several hundred pitchers spend most of their baseball careers shuffling from Peoria to Birmingham. The seemingly glamorous job of doctor to management suffers from many drawbacks unrecognized by the average worshipful executive. Consider, for example, the problem of travel.

As part of its continuous effort to attract business school graduates into the consultant ranks, McKinsey & Company several years ago produced a record entitled "Career Opportunities in a New Profession." The LP record, which the firm has distributed to college radio stations, features two consultants talking informally with three university students—one from Harvard, one from New York University, and one from the University of Chicago—about consulting as a career. Richard F. Neuschel, a director, and James T. Bartlett, an associate, represented McKinsey. Midway through the interview the Harvard student asked about the amount of travel involved in consulting.

Neuschel responded to the question: "The amount of travel varies enormously from near zero, if one is serving a client or clients in his home-based city, to fairly extensive travel. We have a policy of always bringing our men home to their families on weekends unless they are so far that the amount of travel would make this impractical, and then we arrange for them to come home every other weekend."

"Let me add just one point to that," commented Bartlett. "It's been our experience that if an individual has the interest and the skills and is dedicated to the professional life, he will not find the travel that he is required to do a real problem for him."

This record received distribution only among college students through their radio stations. If it had been mailed to ex-consultants (and present ones), the resulting moans of dismay might have reverberated loud enough to shatter windows from New York to the firm's offices in Melbourne, Australia. The major reason why men leave the consulting field is travel: their apparent unwillingness to spend most of their time in some city other than their home. "The average amount of traveling a consultant does is no more than that done by the average member of middle or top management in corporations," insists Philip W. Shay, executive director of ACME, but many would challenge that statement.

"At Booz-Allen we were told that 50 per cent of the work involved travel," Greg Tuttle, now an association executive, explained to me. "What they really meant was that 50 per cent of the staff travels *all* of the time and 50 per cent travels none of the time. I was among the 50 per cent that traveled all of the time." Tuttle worked out of Booz-Allen's Chicago office and on one assignment spent nine consecutive months in Buffalo, New York, getting home only on weekends. He remained at Booz-Allen only two years.

Tuttle worked for Booz-Allen in the early fifties and traveled from Buffalo to Chicago each weekend by train.

Advances in jet transportation have eased the consultant's burden somewhat—or so they rationalize. "A lot of jets leave O'Hare Field at six on Monday morning," Richard Strubel, a managing principal with Fry, once informed me. As a middle-level consultant with seniority, he spent considerable time near home. But on one assignment he worked three months surveying administrative functions at swiftly expanding Southern Illinois University. The only practical way to reach Carbondale, Illinois, in time for work on Monday morning was to catch a four o'clock train from Chicago's Union Station on Sunday afternoon.

"I don't mind travel per se," said Strubel. "I like to stay at the Waldorf and dine well. But I don't like to be away from my family." Strubel later left Fry after five years' service for a position with a large conglomerate.

Not all assignments find a consultant rooming at the Waldorf. Nor does the consultant always find himself able to arrive at one motel on a Sunday night or Monday morning and neatly unpack his suitcase for a five-day stay. Most clients large enough to justify paying the services of a management consultant have more than one plant or office. The consultant often must hop from city to city—either by car, train, or plane—to visit the client company's many branch or divisional offices.

While interviewing one consultant during an apparently rare visit by him to his home office, I overheard him mention during a telephone conversation that he had flown on twelve airplanes the previous week. He said it matter-of-factly, as though it happened all the time. Another con-

Like Ships Passing in the Night

sultant who lived near me and whom I interviewed at home one Saturday afternoon outlined his schedule for the next week. On Monday he would travel to Kansas City and from there to Birmingham, Alabama. On Wednesday he would return to his home office in Chicago. Thursday he would travel to Galesburg, Illinois, and on Friday back to Chicago. He recently had left A. T. Kearney & Company to become a principal of a medium-sized firm, thus traveling only about 50 per cent of the time as compared with 90 per cent previously. While he was at Kearney, I had spent several months trying to arrange a mutually agreeable time for an interview and had made numerous phone calls to his home. I abandoned trying to reach him on Friday evenings because invariably his wife would tell me he wasn't expected home until Saturday noon. But maybe he already had arrived home and she was guarding one of the few times they could be alone. Eventually he quit consulting for a more stationary job with a Chicago bank.

"It wears you down," admits Bruce McLagan. "After a while you wish you never saw another airport. Over a long period of time you get hardened to travel. That's not good either. Some men wake up one day and find it no longer makes any difference—to their families or to them."

For someone who dislikes travel, Chicago undoubtedly rates as the worst location. New York, because of the many corporate headquarters located within Manhattan, presents innumerable opportunities for consultants to work within commuting distance of their front lawns. Los Angeles is a megalopolis and so, to a certain extent, is San

Francisco. Offices in cities such as Washington, Dallas, or Atlanta often exist mainly to service business within those particular cities. But Chicago sits dead center amid many important industrial cities including Milwaukee, Minneapolis, Kansas City, St. Louis, Detroit, and Cincinnati. The majority of the better-known consulting firms began in Chicago, and they continue to maintain large headquarters offices in that city. With excellent transportation in and out of Chicago, partners have little incentive to open additional nearby branch offices merely for the pleasure of the junior members on their staffs.

Thus, the average consultant spends a good share of his time away from his desk. In fact, he may not even have a desk. When he needs a desk one will be assigned him, but as soon as he leaves on another long, out-of-town trip he will lose it to the next consultant through the door. Sometimes he might feel lucky to obtain even a chair in the library. At specific times of the year when staff meetings require all consultants in the field to congregate on headquarters, members of the firm may find themselves standing in the aisles. "It's a problem," admits one member of Booz-Allen, "to provide enough space for everyone when they're in, yet not have the entire place look empty the rest of the year."

Because staff members come and go like ships passing in the night, many consultants, particularly on the junior level, may fail to meet others working for their firm, even if the firm is relatively small. One Kearney consultant told a tale of flying in a jet and starting a conversation with his seatmate. After several minutes' discussion, he discovered his seatmate was a management consultant. The Kearney consultant's interest perked up and he asked his seatmate the name of his firm. It turned out they both worked for A. T. Kearney!

For the individual who enjoys the challenge of consulting but dislikes its peripatetic aspects, one solution may be to found his own firm. A desire to spend more nights at home prompted Bruce McLagan to do just that. Victor Lennon and Sam Rose were similarly motivated. "I used to be in consulting with another firm," Sam Rose explained to me. "I traveled almost constantly and I was sick of it. So I started my own firm, planning to concentrate primarily on the greater Chicago area." That was in 1955, but reputations spread fast in the business world and success has certain disadvantages. Lennon/Rose and Company, now expanded to ten professionals, finds itself called upon by companies from coast to coast and overseas.

If the consultant doesn't sicken of the travel, his wife may. "We recently lost a man because of travel," I was told at Fry. "He said his wife couldn't take it any more."

One young consultant with whom I spoke had graduated from Harvard, joined Fry, and gotten married almost simultaneously. "We had a one-weekend honeymoon," he said. "That set the tone for our entire marriage."

John Zeisler, now an investment banker, told me of an experience he had while working for Booz-Allen on a survey at the Johnson Wax Company in Racine, Wisconsin. On Friday afternoon he called his wife to tell her what time he planned to arrive home. Another consultant, whom we'll call Fred, planned to remain in Racine until Saturday night even though his wife had been planning a birthday party for him. Fred, either being busy or a coward, asked Zeisler to relay this little bit of news. "Would you call Fred's wife and tell her he has to stay over an extra day?" Zeisler informed his wife.

A half hour later Zeisler's wife called, after having talked to the spouse of Fred. "Tell Fred that if he doesn't get home tonight his wife plans to divorce him," she announced. Zeisler admitted that the wives of all consultants complain bitterly.

"Most of the wives of people in this field are a pretty unhappy bunch," a former Kearney consultant told me; then added, "now don't quote me on this for Christ's sake. I think a lot of consultants have what otherwise would be an unsatisfactory marriage. They want to be out of the old lady's hair to avoid abrasiveness. They have unhappy home lives, so staying away from home is a way of adjustment—a form of token separation. The wives of consultants can be a shaky lot."

I heard of another individual who in joining a consulting firm made only one request—that he be kept on the road five days a week. Management consulting exists as a rare area in business where a divorce, or an unhappy home life, does not impede a man's career. In fact, if you want to make partner, it may help not to want to come home every night.

Certainly success in management consulting depends on a willingness to abandon all claims to your own time.

Like Ships Passing in the Night

"It's not a nine to five job," says McKinsey's John Lutz III. "You can't be successful at anything less than nine to seven, and that includes lunch." At McKinsey it also includes Saturday meetings at least nine times a year.

The consultant away from home may find himself a captive in his own motel room. He and other members of his consulting team (if he is lucky enough to have others with him) may find that they can waste only so much time dawdling over dinner. After a while he will have seen every movie in town. Soon he may feel that the television set has begun to stare back. One individual with whom I spoke recalled one assignment he had while working for the Alexander Proudfoot Company. "We were staying at a Holiday Inn in Seattle," he said. "There were between ten and twenty in our crew. It was like basic training. First, we were restricted from using the bar in the motel. Then, they were touchy about the rental cars, so we were without transportation. Once every month everybody in the firm, between three and four hundred people from all over the country, would gather in one location for a meeting. We'd leave Seattle in the early afternoon, arrive in New York around seven, have the meeting, and catch a plane returning to Seattle after ten that night. Then we'd be expected to be back on the job the next morning. A lot of guys couldn't take it. People were leaving at the rate of one a week." The consultant I spoke with lasted with Proudfoot only six months.

"Sometimes while on the road I'll stop in a cocktail lounge," a Fry consultant told me. "Often I meet a lot of salesmen. The first question is, 'What's your job?' Once I've established myself as a consultant it gives the person a go signal to talk about his business. You've been interviewing people all day and listening to their problems. So you sit down at night to have a drink and discover you have to listen some more."

A few consultants may attempt other diversions. One company president, leaving the office at five one evening, smiled at noticing his consultant working hard. At home, however, he discovered he had forgotten an important document. After dinner the president returned to his inner office and found the consultant compromising his secretary, or vice versa. The president fired the secretary and fired the consultant, but being a practical man, continued to work with the consulting firm.

In discussing management consulting with psychologist Dr. Charles McDermid, he told me that probably only a relatively small percentage of consultants become alcoholics. He said that when on the road consultants probably would be less inclined toward sexual adventures than the average traveling salesman. Consultants may ignore sex and liquor because their work is self-fulfilling. The challenge involved in each assignment often will cause them to carry their work with them back to the motel room. They may work fourteen to sixteen hours a day partly out of boredom, but mostly out of a general fascination with their work. McDermid claims this is true whether the consultant is on the road (and thus theoretically a captive of the client) or at home.

Like Ships Passing in the Night

While not suffering from alcoholism consultants may be prone to another disease. One candy company president with whom I spoke, a former Booz-Allen man, felt consulting to be an ulcer mill. He said: "It didn't give me an ulcer, but a lot of the others were getting them. The guys that were bucking for partner were going day and night."

An article in *Dun's Review* quoted one consultant as saying: "You work hard including Saturdays and Sundays, and get poor pay. But you still keep reaching for that carrot. The ones who make it to the top are usually crackerjack types. Many of them join the company at something like thirty-two and by the time they are thirty-eight or thirty-nine they are getting big money. By then, they're so tough they don't even get ulcers. But most men simply can't take it."

One ex-consultant from McKinsey told me of the struggle one member of that firm had to become a partner. For every year it took him, there were at least two occasions where he would work himself to the absolute limit of his physical and mental abilities. "There are several reasons why the pressure is so intense," explains Rudy Dallmeyer. "First of all, you're constantly trying to provide things that companies can't do for themselves. This means that you're standing on tiptoe all the time. Nobody wants to hire a consultant who can't provide something he can't do himself.

"Secondly, I suppose it's true that there is literally no limit to what you can and should try to give a client. There's no point where you can stand back and say, 'That's it. It's done. Perfect.' We never wrote a perfect report. Nobody's going to be able to pay us enough to write a perfect report or study, because we can always refine it by shades of differences, provide more alternatives, etc. But within the budget we're allowed we just drive like hell. There are some who can do this and some who can't. The pressure's on all the time. You sit down for two hours and the competition has overtaken you."

Working as a consultant can be an exhilarating experience, but it is somewhat akin to being an artificial-insemination donor. There's a certain excitement involved, but in most instances you never participate in the end result. The consultant may become thoroughly involved in the day-by-day operations of a client company. He may get to know intimately many of its executives. For weeks and months he will accompany them to lunch and listen to their problems. After a certain time he may even consider himself one of them rather than an outsider. Eventually a day will come when the consultant presents his report to the company president and walks out the door. By the time his suggestions have been fully adopted, he may be nine months and a half dozen assignments down the road. He may hear about the results of his work (or may notice that the company's profits have increased), but he rarely will implement his own suggestions fully.

Or in some instances his work may end in frustration as the client president ignores the consultant's advice, or accepts it only in part. "I've got one job I'm still irritated about," one Fry consultant told me. "We worked on it six months ago and our client accepted most of our recommendations. But there was one they wouldn't buy, one out of fifty—and this still concerns me. I know they're going to have to buy it eventually because we have the facts on our side, but it really gripes me.

"This is a frustrating aspect of our business," he continued. "You work extremely hard doing something creative, but then you can't bang your fist down on the desk and have it done by fiat. The client starts digging in his heels. You cajole. You try to bring him around. Fortunately this is a rare occurrence. Most recommendations get implemented."

However, the principal frustration among those who enter the management consulting ranks may be related to money: the failure of the majority to reach the pot at the end of the rainbow. A young executive often will accept a relatively low starting salary under the premise (and often the promise) that within a few years, when he becomes eligible for bonuses and profit-sharing, his salary will increase even faster than the national debt. Then at the end of a few years the rainbow begins to fade and the pot gets snatched away. To dip into this pot a consultant must remain with a firm a minimum of two to three years. Most don't. Men flee from consulting because of the hardships of travel or because of the killing pace, but even if they don't leave they may be pushed out the door. "Let's be honest," one former McKinsey man told me. "I was told to leave. Not many leave McKinsey because they see something better."

McKinsey claims to have an annual turnover of 15 per cent. This would indicate that their average staffman lasts six years which, even including the partners, sounds rather low. The greater majority of associates will never rise to become principals, much less director. Most will be turned away before their third, frequently before their second, anniversary. At Booz-Allen the mortality rate, if anything, is higher. "You might say that we have a revolving door policy at this firm," is the way one Booz-Allen consultant expressed it to me.

James L. Allen also commented on the high turnover in consulting when I spoke with him. "We're obviously not running this firm as an educational institution," said the Booz-Allen chairman, "but we do know that we find some people who are not going as far up as we want them to in this business. When we see this occur we sit down and talk it over, and their careers are readjusted." Allen mentioned having just talked to one individual ("one of our bright young men") who had worked for the firm five years and was "readjusted."

McKinsey refers to its process of readjusting careers as an "up or out" policy. Unless an individual makes steady progress with the firm and shows himself capable of assuming increasingly more difficult assignments he will be invited to leave. When I spoke with Everett Smith in McKinsey's New York headquarters he told me that earlier that morning he and the other partners had disqualified two men and qualified one. "The two will be sent along right away," he said. "They're very conscious of it. Advance-

ment or not comes on their anniversary date, and we don't
try to play any secrets."

The critical point for the young McKinsey associate is
the second anniversary of his joining the firm. On that date
he either will, or will not, be elected to the bonus roll,
which means that not only have his salary prospects significantly brightened, but he has been allotted a position
on the escalator moving upward. McKinsey men sometimes
make book on who will, and who will not, feel the golden
touch. Occasionally a decision may be deferred until an
individual's third anniversary. Although the new bonus-
roll member will make more money, he will retain his title
as associate. After he has worked for the firm between six
to eight years, another critical anniversary arrives for the
McKinsey man. At that point, if he survives, he will be
elected to the management group and given the title of
principal.

At Booz-Allen the crises appear at approximately equal
intervals, but the signposts differ. When after two to three
years the young Booz-Allen staffman achieves beatification,
he changes his title from consultant to associate. At approximately the point in time where the McKinsey associate
becomes a principal, the Booz-Allen associate becomes a
vice-president. He also reaches a financial crisis since he
is expected to invest in the firm as a partner. Booz-Allen has
a standard arrangement with a local bank to provide sizable
loans for their men who reach the partnership level. Within
a few years the vice-president will easily earn enough to
repay his loan, but at this one point in his career when he

finally achieves success, he finds himself deeply in debt and often drives a used car. As for the bank's granting him the loan, it is somewhat like investing in a newly uncovered oil well.

Those who reach the rank of principal or vice-president discover they have no sinecure. "We don't want a fellow in here at fifty who's not going to become a director," explains Everett Smith. "He's not going to be happy and neither will we. I can remember being concerned over our turnover. Still, if we want to maintain our standards we would be lowering quality if we didn't have turnover. If a person is not a howling success we feel it's not fair for him to stay, so we have a constant set of hurdles. We constantly try to upgrade our staff. The only other asset we have is the furniture and the drapes."

In recent years, however, McKinsey has found it expedient to, if not change, at least modify its standard "up or out" policy simply to meet the present skyrocketing demand for the firm's services. "The biggest restraint on our growth is our ability to recruit competent new men," says McKinsey's John Lutz III. "We can't afford to lose people. So now we're less cavalier about putting our men into a sink-or-swim situation. We now have to concentrate on those who might swim with a bit of help."

Lutz added, "At the same time it's still survival of the fittest."

Survival of those able only to dogpaddle may be contingent on the demand for consultant services. "I can remember sitting around in the Booz-Allen library waiting

Like Ships Passing in the Night

for an assignment," says John Zeisler. "You're an overhead. Your salary has to be paid."

In the fifties, one group of men at Booz-Allen found themselves plateaued at a level immediately below the vice-presidents. It became obvious to them, and to the firm, that they would rise no higher. In most major consulting firms, but particularly at Booz-Allen, a man's value at the upper levels is measured not only by the quality of his performance but by the amount of business he brings in the front door. Few individuals make partner at Booz-Allen unless, in addition to their analytical skills, they are able to sell. In addition, through no fault of their own, this particular group had entered the firm at a higher than average age, thus they found themselves competing for partnership positions with men three and four years younger. "If you have a choice between a .300 hitter who is twenty and one who is thirty-five, you go with the rookie," says Edwin C. Johnson.

To preserve the particular talents of this group of men, a special level of "senior associate" was created within the firm. They were assured of tenure for life. This made sense during a period of economic prosperity when demand for consulting services remained high. But the American economy moves in waves. Two years later practically every senior associate got fired. The polite expression around Booz-Allen was that they had "topped out."

There are certain areas within a firm such as Booz-Allen where it becomes easier to "top out" than others. Any specialist is vulnerable since he may travel only as high as

his specialty will carry him. Those within executive search
also are vulnerable since the majority of their time is devoted to consulting with those outside the client firm (job
candidates) rather than those on the inside. EDP specialists
are vulnerable since they work with machines and the most
prized skill in any consulting firm is an ability to work with
people. Perhaps the most vulnerable position is on the
administrative staff, yet the administrative staffs of consulting firms necessarily are swelling as the firms grow in
size and become more complex internally. Any non-
consultant finds his route to the top blocked by the unwritten rule in most firms that even the most senior partners
in the firm continue to consult. Thus occupying a non-
consultant position with a consulting firm might be compared to being a white accountant for *Ebony* magazine.
Supply officers don't become generals. It might be worth
noting that one of the established steps practiced by consultants in reorganization studies is first to remove all
dead-end jobs, so that theoretically everyone in a company
has the opportunity to climb to the top.

While partners in management consulting firms excuse
large turnover as their only means of maintaining quality,
the question might be asked: do they mean quality for the
client or the quality of their own profits? This returns us
to the ⅓–⅓–⅓ billing ratio of staff salaries to overhead to
profits mentioned in the last chapter. Assuming overhead
to be more or less a fixed cost, as staff salaries go up, profits
go down. Since the supposed value of a management con-

Like Ships Passing in the Night

sultant is not his experience but his analytical powers, economics dictates that it is better to hire the analytical powers of a man in his twenties for $15,000 a year than a man in his thirties or forties for $30,000 a year.

The consulting firm thus utilizes the services of the young man to the point where his salary begins to nudge past the one-third point. They then replace him with a younger man at a lower salary and, with a pat on the behind, usher their graduate consultant back into the world of legitimate business, hoping they have treated him with sufficient gentleness so that if he ever rises to a position where he can hire a consulting firm he will remember his alma mater.

The former Proudfoot consultant who complained about being cooped up in a Seattle motel believed that much of what he called harassment to be part of a calculated policy of operating with young, and therefore low-salary, employees. He told me that Proudfoot consultants began at $105 a week starting salary, moved up to $155 a week after thirteen weeks, then reached $180 between six and nine months. Proudfoot classified ads promise salaries of $25,000 within a few years, but of course if an employee quits within two years he never will reach that level. The consulting firm meanwhile reportedly bills clients $800 a week per consultant. One former officer of the firm indicated to me that Alexander Proudfoot,* founder of the company

* Proudfoot, who recently sold his interest in his company and retired, played football under Amos Alonzo Stagg at the University of Chicago dur-

and a former George S. May employee, believed that only
one out of every ten men hired could fit into the operation
and in order to uncover talent, the company had to maintain a constant turnover. The May Company also functioned with a large turnover of employees.

The interim consultant often realizes that he has been
used, but he may not necessarily resent it. He may feel
honored to have been allowed to function as a management consultant for a few years. He also may be sufficiently
tired from the travel and long hours to rationalize his
dismissal as a welcome change. His friends, of course, will
be told he quit for those reasons.

But apart from the rationalizations, many ambitious
executives enter consulting firms consciously plotting to
use *them!*

Partly this is because of the graduate-school atmosphere
of most consulting firms, an atmosphere carefully culti-
vated by the partners. Where else, they say, can a bright
young man learn as much about business as in consulting?
And they are right. The average consultant probably will
learn more in two years with a consulting firm than he
could in two decades in business. Certainly he will ac-
cumulate much more knowledge than during his two
years in business school. Being able to list management
consulting experience on your job record (hint the firm

---

ing the early 1920s. Unlike George S. May, he and his company have
shunned publicity. One former employee said that during the time he
worked for Proudfoot he never even saw a company letterhead. All com-
municating was done orally, so he claimed.

recruiters) is the equivalent of having an additional business degree.

The calculating bright young man thus will chart a few years in consulting as part of his plan to succeed in business by really trying. The chart goes something like this:

1. Four years of college at some university with a large business alumni group, but not Harvard.
2. Two years in the training program of a large corporation, such as General Electric. (A second company may be added here as an option after the corporation experience.)
3. Two years at the Harvard Business School.
4. Two to five years of additional business experience with two or three companies, at least one of them relatively small.
5. No less than eighteen (but no more than thirty) months with Booz, Allen & Hamilton. Emerge at the age of thirty-two having resisted offers to remain with the firm.
6. Four to six years with one or two companies in an area of business that will have been carefully selected while working as a consultant.
7. Success!

There are numerous other routes to the top of the ladder, but that one will work as good as any. If the calculating bright young man has charted his course properly, the Jaycees will have named him one of their "Outstanding Young Men of America" before age thirty-five and he will have been elected to membership in the Young Presidents' Organization before age forty. For the next twenty-five years prior to retirement he should have nothing to worry about—except mergers, or hiring a consulting firm that might recommend his replacement.

But as any bookie or stockbroker can tell you, charts do not always work. One person I know planned a career in investment banking after having obtained a law degree. He decided that two years as a management consultant would qualify him better as an investor—and he may have been right. Booz-Allen hired him. But after working only a short time on client assignments, he got transferred into executive search, a sort of limbo within Booz-Allen sometimes used to hide either those too incompetent or too outspoken to work inside client companies. A year and a half later he walked through the revolving door experienced only in the area of executive search, which is something like coming out of college with a degree in ornithology. After several years and several additional false starts this individual finally found a job in investment banking.

Many ambitious men approach a consulting career hoping to use it as a listening post for obtaining a better position. They hope that by displaying their talents in a variety of marketplaces they may receive job offers from those with whom they consult. The first shock comes when, on the

Like Ships Passing in the Night

day of their final job interview, they discover they must sign a contract that prohibits them from soliciting a job from a client. They have encountered Article XI of the ACME Code of Professional Ethics: "We will make certain that the members of our professional staff, in order to insure their continuing objectivity, shall under no circumstances use a consulting engagement as a means of seeking new employment for themselves."

Anyone discovered in the act of soliciting a job with a client receives a dishonorable discharge almost immediately. One former Booz-Allen consultant told me the story of a staff member with a wealthy parent. While working on an assignment with a mattress company he began to examine the possibilities of his family's buying that company. "The news came out one morning," related the consultant. "He was gone by noon."

If a client president desires to hire a consultant, the firm partners probably will attempt to discourage him. In a cover story on Booz, Allen & Hamilton in its November 15, 1967, issue, *Forbes* magazine discussed this: "A top Booz-Allen officer is likely to call the client and assure him that the consultant is not nearly so capable as the client thinks. 'The client may have misjudged the applicability of the man,' [Booz-Allen president Charles P.] Bowen puts it. 'He will expect from the individual what really the team has been delivering.'" If the client insists, the consulting firm may eventually acquiesce—particularly if it is someone they were planning on firing anyway. A consultant occasionally steps into a better job with a client company, but the person who enters consulting anticipating such a bonanza probably will be disappointed.

The interim consultant also may be disappointed when, after accumulating his planned several years' experience, he attempts to return to industry. He may discover that rather than stepping upward into a more important job, he will need to make a lateral move. In many instances he may find himself stepping downward. Realizing that many executives think of interim consulting as one means of advancing a business career, I questioned numerous employment agency counselors as to whether or not this was true. Most had a low opinion of consulting as a stepping-stone profession. According to one counselor at Cadillac Associates: "We find that anyone who entered consulting because of either choice or necessity has taken the initial step down to oblivion."

He may have been overstating his case (and may have known mostly consultants from non-prestige firms), but certainly a person with ambitions in business cannot afford to remain a consultant too long. Two years is about right. Three years may be pushing his luck. In most instances the partners will take the choice out of his hands, but the consultant who survives the initial cut, becomes an associate, but fails to make vice-president a half dozen years later may be in trouble. He will find himself thrown back to the business world in his late thirties without a salable specialty. His only choice may be to return to consulting with a lesser known firm than the one he had left. Vice-presidents have their careers "readjusted" too. When they leave consulting they may be spoiled for ordinary work because of their relatively advanced age, their high salaries, and their total lack of experience due to their having operated as tellers instead of doers.

"There are many consultants I wouldn't begin to recommend for a job in industry," says Rudy Dallmeyer. "Often they are critical—highly critical—and not very constructive. Often they are looking for some kind of golden sinecure. Many good consultants can't fit well into a company. Many are such good staffmen that if they go into a company at a line position they just don't fit."

A recent issue of *Forbes* contained separate articles on two organizations whose earnings and stock prices had just dipped catastrophically. By coincidence, one firm was managed by a Booz-Allen alumnus, the other by an ex-McKinsey man. Dallmeyer claims that often there is no correlation between success (or lack of success) in consulting and success in the regular business world. "Many corporation presidents were not notably successful as consultants," he says. "A few spent rather short terms in consulting. They were action-oriented, often impatient and sometimes inclined to shoot from the hip. That last can be okay if you are the final judge and can cover or explain away your mistakes, but it's dangerous for anyone as much on record and on view as a consultant."

Personnel managers often consider former career consultants as unstable individuals and may avoid hiring otherwise qualified men for fear that they will jump back into consulting should they become dissatisfied. And consultants become dissatisfied easily. Their analytical skills will have become so finely honed during their years in consulting that they will readily recognize problems within their new company—but they may not be in a position to suggest improvements. In their previous job they will have worked closely with company presidents and board chairmen. In their new job if the president wants a problem solved he probably will not turn to them—he'll go outside and hire a consultant. Where previously they could perch on a cloud and say what *should* be done, they now will have arrived at a level where they can see why it *can't* be done.

While visiting Boston I spoke with a former consultant who, in his second or third job after leaving McKinsey, discovered the vice-president above him to be incompetent and thus contributing to the company's downfall. He walked into the president's office and informed him of the fact. His reward was two weeks' severance pay. Several years later the company went bankrupt and the bank examiners who scrutinized the ruins agreed with the former McKinsey consultant's analysis.

A person leaving consulting often will hopscotch from company to company before eventually settling into a permanent position. Only if he patiently waits another eight or ten years will he progress to a point on the executive pyramid where he can make full use of his previously won experience. Former consultants, like bull elephants, probably don't reach full maturity until their skin begins to wrinkle.

"When I first started in consulting I thought the experience I was obtaining was God's greatest thing," says William Higgs, an investment publisher. "When I returned to industry in an operating-line capacity, I realized that consultants do not have to come to grips with day-to-day operating problems. It's quite different to make a recommendation and to put that recommendation into effect. There's a wide gap separating the consultant from the businessman unless you happen to be a John Burns and re-enter the business world as president or board chairman. After you're in consulting awhile you lose perspective of all the grubby details required to make a business operate successfully."

In making his statement Higgs had referred to John Burns, who moved from a high partnership in Booz-Allen to the presidency of RCA in the late fifties. But within a few years Burns clashed with the Sarnoffs and left. Mark Cresap experienced similar difficulties when he left the firm he helped found to become president of Westinghouse.

The Big Image consulting firms can point to a seemingly impressive list of their alumni at high levels in business, but on the whole these are extremely skilled and talented individuals who probably would have reached these levels without having consultant credentials. A determined individual can occasionally use employment with a consulting firm to help further a business career, but consulting experience is no substitute for basic talent and a desire to use it. "Some people might think of consulting as being the best training ground for the President of General Motors," says one McKinsey staffman. "But I suspect that the kind of fellow who has his eyes on that spot might just as easily join General Motors to begin with."

11

The Marines Have Landed

According to one consultant with whom I spoke: "My own personal view of consulting is that it is a business. It wasn't recognized as a business too many years ago, but it's a business, and it's like anything else. It has its basic talent requirements, and the techniques that are used are just like you're selling soap."

The partners of most management consulting firms will probably cringe at the comparison of them to soap salesmen—even *soft*-soap salesmen. Nevertheless, very few individuals ever reach the upper levels in the world of management consulting unless they possess the one most important talent: the ability to sell. Their sales pitch, of course, needs to be muted carefully to fit beneath the blanket of the ACME Code of Professional Ethics.

The ACME code resembles in many passages a cross between the Boy Scout oath and the Beatitudes. Only on occasion does it descend briefly to earth and its statement on advertising occupies a position in space somewhere just short of the moon. "We will publicize our firm or services only in a manner upholding the dignity of the profession," begins Article III of the code. Though the language may lack precision, the partner in every ACME firm retains a clearly defined picture of how to maintain the profession's dignity. Thus there was a "big stink in the industry" (so said one of the principals of an ACME firm) over a series of four ads in *Time* purchased some years ago by McKinsey & Company.

"What does it take to succeed with McKinsey?" asked the headline in a full-page ad that ran in *Time's* June 17, 1966, issue.

The answer came in one of the paragraphs below: "Outstanding mental equipment finely honed by a first-rate education, coupled with the imagination needed to solve complex problems; the self-confidence, skill in expression, and sensitivity to other people that lead to high personal effectiveness; and, of course, good character and high standards."

Theoretically, the ads were designed to attract young men who might want to come to work for McKinsey. Actually, they provided a subtle pitch to potential clients. "They were very clever ads," Fry's John W. Mitchell admitted somewhat wryly to me. "They did a good job institutionally of saying what a nice firm McKinsey was." McKinsey thus had quarterbacked a well-executed end run around the unspoken provisions of the ACME code,

The Marines Have Landed

which seemingly would prohibit its members from making a straight pitch in a national magazine.

In choosing this advertising path McKinsey inadvertently may have administered a glove-handed slap at several of its association brothers. A few years before two factions had developed within ACME over whether or not to sponsor a series of institutional advertisements promoting the association's image. One faction (primarily the lesser-known association members) believed in actively promoting the ACME label as a sign of respectability and as a means for businessmen to identify blue-ribbon consultants. The other faction (with McKinsey prominent) felt that should institutional advertising receive sanction, each firm should promote itself, not the association. Of course, McKinsey already had an established name with or without the association. In approving ads promoting ACME, McKinsey would merely provide a means by which lesser-known firms might challenge their leadership. Hertz Rent-A-Car doesn't suggest that you be put in any other driver's seat except the one provided by Hertz. The question of institutional advertising for the association was referred back to committee, wherein it sank rapidly from sight.

McKinsey also advertises frequently in German newspapers to attract men to join its Düsseldorf staff, but with apparent undertones of appeal to German businessmen. "Obviously it's a sales ad," one German businessman told me. "If so it's a very bad ad. They describe a person they want to hire as such a top-notch man that he would have to be hired away from some potential client. The German firms may resent this."

Other firms outside the pale of ACME feel no obligation to subscribe to its code of ethics, either written or unwritten. Only a few months after the McKinsey *Time* series, an advertisement in the *Wall Street Journal* asked the reader to consider the George S. May consultant, a man reported to be well educated, broadly experienced, and enthusiastic about solving business problems. If the businessman shopping for a consultant used only paid advertisements, he would have difficulty differentiating a May man from a McKinsey man. May's ad had been directed quite openly to potential clients, but some might question how successful any such campaign could be.

"We don't do a lot of advertising," Little's Reid Weedon told me, "but it's because we think it doesn't particularly help our business, not because of any guilt complex. If I thought I'd get a payoff out of a general advertising campaign, I'd run a general advertising campaign."

Because the nature of consulting is so amorphous, direct advertising often will not work effectively. Management consulting is too complex an art to be explained effectively in the limited space of an advertisement. About all a consulting firm can talk about effectively is the extremely high competence of its personnel. The effect might be somewhat similar to the Roman Catholic Church's taking two pages in *Life* to advertise God. The person most likely to respond to a direct sales pitch probably isn't a president

The Marines Have Landed

of a *Fortune* 500 corporation. About all the consulting firm or individual consultant can do is try to keep its, or his, name before the business public and hope that when a sudden need for consulting services arises, that name will be remembered. Thus, selling consulting services *is* like selling soap.

Many subtle ways exist by which a management consulting firm can present its name to the business public. The first move a new consultant makes, even before painting his name on the door, is to reach for his Christmas card list. "I sent out 2,500 announcements," I was told by William Cousins of Cousins & Preble, a relatively new recruiting firm. "Two thousand went to my acquaintances and five hundred went to those of my partner. It's advertising, but in a rather sophisticated and accepted way."

Consultants mail business announcements with the frequency of Irishmen mailing birth announcements. If a consulting firm moves into new offices it provides an excuse for a new mailing. If it adds a new partner it provides an additional excuse. These announcements normally arrive finely engraved, on stiff white paper, with a tissue paper that flutters out when you open the envelope. When you receive one in the mail you think for a moment that you are being invited to a wedding. For example, one typical announcement received by an acquaintance:

WE ARE PLEASED TO ANNOUNCE THAT
HARVEY N. SHYCON
HAS JOINED US AS A

VICE-PRESIDENT

BASED IN OUR NEW YORK OFFICE

BOOZ·ALLEN & HAMILTON INC.

Management Consultants

NEW YORK   WASHINGTON   CLEVELAND

DETROIT   CHICAGO   DALLAS

LOS ANGELES   SAN FRANCISCO

LONDON   DÜSSELDORF

When you receive such an announcement in the mail you almost feel obligated to send a gift.

But announcements apparently bring results. According to Philip C. Martin, another executive recruiter: "After I send out engraved announcements, for the next two months I get a flood of phone calls. Then they start to taper off. I figure that to keep in the forefront and obtain publicity, I should send out something at least every six months."

A consultant can also maintain the dignity of his profession if he: *a*) purchases an inch-high "tombstone" ad on the back page of the *Wall Street Journal, b*) places his name in bold print in the classified telephone directory, and *c*) receives mention in various directories and catalogs of consultants that receive circulation from time to time. ACME mails a directory of its members to anyone expressing an interest in seeing it. One reference volume published by Cornell University lists 2,612 consulting firms, their addresses, their principals, and their specialties.

The Marines Have Landed

However, those company presidents who need to search in a directory for the name of a consulting firm probably won't be hiring McKinsey or Booz-Allen. Each year the bigger consulting firms issue a number of publications directed toward businessmen and business libraries. Marvin Bower recently wrote a book entitled *The Will to Manage* and McKinsey director Arch Patton has written *Men, Money, and Motivation* (reissued later in a paperback retitled *What's an Executive Worth?*). Partly because of that book Patton has become the man that corporate presidents think of first when desiring an executive compensation study. The firm also publishes *The McKinsey Quarterly,* a kind of *Kenyon Review* for executives. Its table of contents contains a description of the publication as "a review of top-management problems, published to keep McKinsey & Company consultants here and abroad informed on topics of common professional concern." Though theoretically for internal use, a few copies of each issue manage to fall into the hands of the right businessmen. Members of the McKinsey staff also write about a dozen magazine articles a year, a productivity that probably does not meet the demand by editors of business publications. The firm doesn't produce promotional literature as such, preferring to reply to each inquiry concerning its services on a personal basis rather than send pamphlets through the mail. Still, it is difficult to walk into any consulting firm and ask for information about its services without leaving with your attaché case overburdened with literature.

Several management consulting firms (Kearney and Booz-Allen among them) organize management seminars for executives at various levels and in various fields. In one fairly typical example, Booz-Allen sponsored a seminar entitled "Emerging Operations Management Concepts" at Chicago's Pick-Congress hotel. The seminar featured ten discussion leaders, all but three of them from the Booz-Allen staff. From the size of the registration fee ($250), the seminar obviously was not designed to lose money, but perhaps one of its main functions was to remind those executives who attended that there is a management consulting firm named Booz, Allen & Hamilton that someday might be able to help them with their problems.

Most of the larger consulting firms have at least one specialist on their staff assigned to the task of preparing articles and polishing the speeches of members of the firm who will appear in public (and removing from those speeches anything controversial that might make anyone angry). I mentioned earlier that I had encountered a Booz-Allen vice-president serving as a speaker at a paper-box convention. He was on display primarily to influence the businessmen at the convention to think of Booz-Allen the next time they needed a consultant. The previous day an Arthur D. Little spokesman also had addressed the convention. I lunched with him and learned how his firm consciously develops its staffmen into effective public speakers, testing them first before small business luncheons before serving them as the pièce de résistance at a large convention. All speaking engagements are part of a conscious selling effort. *Fortune* magazine recognized this when it said: "Executive seminars, articles in business reviews, lectures at the business schools—these constitute a kind of intellectual gymnasium where consultants do backflips and daredevil stunts to attract new customers." And *Forbes* magazine added in its story on Booz-Allen: "Senior (consultants), for all their polish and good breeding, are salesmen who would put a used-car dealer to shame."

Those consultants possessed of gymnastic talents find their paychecks swelled considerably at the end of the fiscal year. Rewards come in the form of magnified bonuses that may run from $500 to $8,000 a year—or even higher! Kearney refers to this as "discretionary bonus." At McKinsey they call it "productivity pay," or "performance bonus," and it may account for between 10 to 50 per cent of a person's salary. Because the size of this bonus serves as considerable incentive (particularly to consultants capable of attracting and holding clients), it might be worthwhile examining how at least one consulting firm, Fry Consultants, lavishes extra rewards on its most productive men.

Fry splits its reward into three different portions. The first is what men on the staff refer to as the "warm body bonus." Anyone, so to speak, alive at the end of the year receives the equivalent of a half month's salary. "Spread out over a year it wouldn't seem like much," said the Fry consultant, who explained the system to me. "Coming in one lump sum at Christmas time, it's a nice gesture."

The second portion consists of profit-sharing in which every employee with the firm long enough to qualify participates in direct proportion to the size of his base salary and his seniority. As we have already noted in an earlier chapter, it takes the typical new consultant between two to three years to qualify for bonuses.

The most significant reward feature (at Fry and Booz-Allen as well as at most other firms) consists of an additional incentive bonus, figured on a point-scoring basis. Any effort a consultant makes that contributes to the profitability of his firm will be evaluated and rewarded by a certain number of points, and those points eventually will get translated into dollars. There are five (not necessarily equal) areas in which points can be scored:

1. *Service improvement.* Consulting firms figuratively, if not actually, have suggestion boxes similar to those of most businesses. If a staff member should "develop a new method or technique which contributes to the improvement or expansion of services offered to clients," he would receive points.

2. *Articles.* Points also get awarded for articles written by staff members which, because of their publication in general media, may attract clients to the firm. The more significant the magazine, the more points a staff member receives. Articles published in the *Harvard Business Review* make partners extremely happy. Should any consultant ever hit *Fortune*, the coffers of his firm undoubtedly will empty into his pockets.

3. *Speeches.* As with articles, speeches before management groups also enhance the firm's image, and the more significant the speech, or group to whom it is given, the higher the number of points. "Most of these speeches are given at night so a person should receive extra compensation," explains the Fry consultant.

4. *Chargeability.* A person spending all his time on client assignments obtains more points than one sitting in the library (where presumably he has time to write speeches or articles or fill the suggestion box). The chargeability ratio depends on what percentage of a consultant's time can be charged to client (billable time) versus the percentage charged to the consulting firm (overhead time). In fact as well as theory, a person affects his chargeability by his skills. The partners or principals in charge of picking consulting teams for assignments will normally select the most competent men. In times of high demand for consulting services, however, almost every member of the firm will have a high chargeability ratio.

5. *Business development.* When a consultant speaks about "business development," he really means the ability to sell. The consultant capable of attracting business obtains a significantly greater number of points (and thus a larger reward) than for any other activity. The bonus points awarded for the first four items on the scale (service improvement, articles, speeches, and chargeability) might amount to 5–10 per cent of a person's salary. The bonus awarded for business development is open-ended and can be a significant element of total compensation. According to the Fry spokesman: "We can say to our people, if you want to get ahead you have to establish yourself as a top consultant. This will be reflected in your chargeability. If you show you can develop business you will really further yourself in Fry."

Thus not only will the number of points awarded determine who will obtain the largest salaries at the end of each year, but a person's promotion will also be affected. The lowest-level consultants probably have few direct opportunities to attract business. They may be promoted to associate or principal after two or three years because of their consulting skills or potential. But few associates will reach the level of vice-president or partner without proving their ability to sell. "A person can be an absolutely crackerjack consultant," one staff member at Booz-Allen told me, "but unless he brings business in the front door he's not going anywhere." One might question the ethics of a profession where the ability to bring in business counts equal to, or more than, the ability to do good work. In some firms, of course, the point system will be weighted more heavily toward soliciting business than in others.

It might be argued that the best means of attracting new business is to do the most effective job possible on each assignment, hoping that your satisfied customers will refer you to others in need of consulting help. To a certain extent this does happen. But a fair amount of business "happens" because of partners' going to lunch with the best people, living in the right suburb, and belonging to the proper

The Marines Have Landed

country club. In this respect Booz-Allen has perhaps the most sophisticated system of maintaining close acquaintances with individuals who can bring them business. These are known as "marines."

No one willing to say so remembers the exact origin of the term "marine." Edwin G. Booz supposedly originated the term as descriptive of those friends of the firm most likely to send business their way. Sewell Avery was a marine; so was Frank Knox. "The marines have landed and the situation is well in hand," might be one means of explaining the term's origin.

It will probably come as a surprise to anyone acquainted with a Booz-Allen employee that his name most likely will be contained on a file card somewhere in its headquarters. Booz-Allen quite definitely is watching you! Anyone first coming to work for the firm fills out an "executive acquaintance" list. These are not just casual acquaintances, but individuals, usually with some business connections, with whom the new employee may have worked, attended school, or known for any other reason. If you are an executive and on a Booz-Allen consultant's Christmas list, your name probably will be found in that firm's files. Several file clerks maintain this massive list, keeping it up to date by clipping notices of promotions and job changes from business magazines and newspapers. This massive Who's Who of Booz-Allen friends within industry becomes an extremely valuable tool, not only for maintaining business contacts, but especially for use by the firm's executive recruiters in trying to obtain leads of available executives.

As the Booz-Allen consultant advances within the hierarchy of his firm, the names of his most significant and influential friends will be separated from his executive-acquaintance list and designated as "marines." Most marines are either executives at an extremely high level within industry or individuals on the outside—attorneys, bankers, brokers—to whom businessmen turn for advice when seeking consulting aid. The card containing the name of the marine will also include his address, phone number (business and home), position within his company, plus any significant information as to why or how he might aid the firm. The file containing all these names is cross-indexed so that a staff member can easily determine the number of friends that Booz-Allen has within, say, Abbott Laboratories or Borg-Warner. Most important, each marine's card will contain the name of the particular partner (or partners) who has first claim on him. No member of Booz-Allen will approach another partner's marine for any reason without first checking with that partner. It's part of the etiquette of the game.

Such a classification system of executive acquaintances is given varying degrees of attention by all consulting firms. A hustling consultant attempts to expand continuously the number of individuals who can bring his firm business. One principal at Kearney told me he had developed three business leads simply by talking to people who sat next to him on jet planes. Of course, he probably carefully selects his seat partners.

The Kearney principal told me he always traveled tourist

The Marines Have Landed

class under the theory that so did most businessmen. Within recent years Booz-Allen upgraded the travel arrangements of its consultants, moving them up with the first-class passengers under the theory perhaps that most *top* businessmen travel there. This reflects less of a munificent attitude on Booz-Allen's part than you might suspect, since client firms pay most travel expenses. The question might be raised, however, that if Kearney travels tourist, and Booz-Allen travels first-class, how does McKinsey fly?

For those individuals who leave the major firms to open offices of their own, the fact that they may have worked for McKinsey or Booz-Allen may provide them with valuable contacts. Because of its size as well as its high turnover rate, Booz-Allen particularly has alumni scattered throughout industry, many of them at high levels.

One former Booz-Allen man, now an executive recruiter, admitted to me how he openly traded on his alumni credentials in soliciting new business. He described attending a luncheon at which another Booz-Allen alumnus, the president of a major pharmaceutical company, had sat at the head table. As soon as the final speech had ended the recruiter popped off his seat and flew like an arrow toward the pharmaceutical president. "How are you?" said our recruiter, calling the president by his first name, shaking hands and at the same time introducing himself as a fellow Booz-Allen alumnus. In the space of a few minutes of small talk the recruiter swung the conversation to a point where the president, to be polite, had to ask him, what was he doing now? Executive recruiting, of course. Before moving away, the president requested a business card and said he might give him a call.

Another individual management consultant, who only recently had opened his own office, told me quite frankly that he got most of his business because he: *a*) had worked for McKinsey, and *b*) had gone to the Harvard Business School, and was highly regarded at both places.

Most of the so-called reputable management consultants deny categorically any suggestion that they might approach a company with the proposal that they do some work for them. They indicate in interviews with the press that such unethical approaches are only made by the "notorious firms," which in keeping with the profession's tone of dignity are rarely mentioned by name.

Nevertheless, the ability to sell business has become a well-established criteria for success within the bluest of the blue-ribbon firms in the ACME directory, although a few consulting firms have begun to experience mixed feelings about this fact. "It used to be that you had to write articles, or make speeches, or make a personal name for yourself to succeed," says McKinsey's John Lutz III. "But very few people are good in everything. If the only people who move up in your firm are good business-getters, you might not have the best collection of problem solvers."

Many people who buy consulting services feel more or less the same way. One company president told me: "Right or wrong, some consultants sell to corporations by sending in men whose major qualification is that they make a ton of money."

The Marines Have Landed

One other facet of how consultants obtain business is worth at least a passing glance. In his *Fortune* article "The Men Who Came to Dinner," Walter Guzzardi, Jr., said: "The best of the management consultants scorn the hard sell as unnecessary and ineffective; he scoffs at the standard soft sell as unimaginative and unworthy. True to the traditions of his craft, the big-time management consultant has invented something new: the self-perpetuating sell."

Most partners of the Big Image firms will point out, and rightfully so, that the contracts they sign with businessmen contain no long-term obligations. They are retained on more or less a weekly basis and the client may usher them out the door at any minute and stop paying fees as of that minute. Of course, George S. May operates in a similar manner. But rare is the client who having commissioned a major study will call a halt without receiving the final report. Beyond that, the ethical question might be raised: how much consulting work serves as a lead-on to a continuing relationship? "The first job is great," one Fry consultant told me in an unguarded moment, "but the name of the game is when you do job number fifty-three."

One way to reach job fifty-three is by performing work of such superb quality that the client company will want the consultant to return. Fry does well in this respect, and so do most of the Big Image firms, but even the best of them stand accused of being men who came to dinner. According to Owen A. Zapel, a Chicago art executive: "My own feeling is that a management consultant is no different than anyone else. He wants to perpetuate himself."

"Consulting firms tend to find other areas to explore," an industrial engineer told me. "We're in the position now of telling our consultants the dinner party's over." The engineer had no complaint about the consulting firm (which happened to be Kearney) and he understood the reasons for their explorations. "We have to sell in our business too," he said.

One of the most successful salesmen of consulting services, of course, was George S. May. Countless other firms have been founded by former May employees who have utilized May selling techniques. One of the most successful ones at the present time is the Alexander Proudfoot Company, which specializes in a business technique known as "short interval scheduling," originally developed by mail-order houses to speed orders through their plants. Alexander Proudfoot worked for May from May 1933 to February 1946, when he was chief sales manager. He then founded his own company, which by 1954 could report annual billings of $500,000. Within a dozen years, however, Proudfoot's business skyrocketed to $15 million annually. A former officer of the firm explained why to me in a memo: "Important facet of rapid growth is the abilities of supervisors to expand initial assignment into many others. Company has not only the ability to produce tangible results, but has refined the technique of expanding into several simultaneous projects. This of course is an ability which measures the effectiveness of supervision. At times the percentage of billings acquired after the initial sale has been fantastic. This is accomplished by a practical approach and

The Marines Have Landed

an intolerance by A.P. management so far as failure to carry out assignments as sold. Added to this is the 'brass' to ask for projects two, three, four, etc., before project one has produced dramatic results."

There are several dangers in prolonging the dinner party. One danger is that a small or specialist consulting firm may get lured into accepting business outside its competence. One Weyerhaeuser executive I met at a convention told me of a consulting firm that had done some excellent work for his corporation, "but then they had bitten off another piece of work about which they didn't know a single thing, and it had blown up in their faces."

"The smart companies don't like to say they got stung," says R. C. Trundle, president of Trundle Consultants, Inc., "but they don't hire consultants after that."

In theory at least, most of the Big Image ACME firms should not have to worry about overextending themselves. Being generalists, and having large numbers of various talented people with whom they can staff a consulting team, they should be able to solve almost any problem thrown at them. And that's one of their principal sales pitches. But dangers exist in this area too. "One trouble with the consulting firms," claims John Deardon of the Harvard Business School, "is that the quality of people varies widely within even some of the best firms, from people who are very good to those who don't know what they're doing."

All firms preach quality control, and most practice it. No management consulting firm consciously sets out to do a bad job. Even the so-called notorious firms want, within certain limits, to serve their clients to the best of their abilities. "You can certainly oversell your services," says Deardon, "and at some of the consulting firms a man's promotion depends on how many clients he can bring in. Now to the extent that he brings clients in because he's doing a good job, this is fine. But a lot of consultants have oversold themselves in that they're constantly looking for new things to do. There are a hell of a lot of things that a consultant can do better than staff members within a client company, but maybe these things are so expensive that it's not worth the money and time to do them."

Perhaps the greatest danger in the self-perpetuating sell, however, is that a consulting firm may soon become so much a part of the establishment that one of the prime reasons for its being hired—objectivity—soon vanishes. When business professor Charles L. Quittmeyer surveyed a number of executives concerning their attitudes toward consulting, he reported one as saying: "Our dissatisfaction is, to a degree, based upon the impression that the consulting firms we have worked with seem to color their recommendations to support the position they felt the client wanted them to take, thus losing the objective approach for which their services were hired."

What this boils down to is that a good consultant has to be prepared to tell his client to go to hell!

12

The Business of Hiring the Boss

Most major management consulting firms, in addition to offering generalized problem-solving talents, perform as specialists in many other areas of business. The small specialty firms normally concentrate in one or several areas touched by the major firms—or in some instances offer services that even a Booz-Allen can't, or won't, match. Cornell University's reference volume entitled *Consultants and Consulting Organizations* divides management consulting into 136 different disciplines, from accounting and auditing to warehousing, and includes such areas as employee surveys, office layouts, pension planning, and sales training. Among the major management consulting firms, Booz-Allen covers sixty-four, or nearly half, of these disciplines, McKinsey covers thirty-seven, and both Fry and Kearney claim fifty-eight (although not the same fifty-eight). It would be wrong, however, to confuse the number of disciplines with size. CMP lists seventy-four disciplines, ten more than the much larger Booz-Allen. Donald R. Booz & Associates, whose position in ACME remains as secure as any of the above-mentioned firms, conservatively quotes only five exceptionally broad skills: financial management, management (general), marketing, production management, and sales management.

Of the 136 disciplines, probably the most visible, the most controversial, and the least understood is what some people have called the "black art of executive recruiting." The Cornell volume lists 482 executive recruiting offices within the United States. Many firms who claim the title "executive recruiters" (or "executive search consultants") do so for reasons of prestige and are merely glorified employment agencies. Probably fewer than one hundred *true* executive search firms exist. These would include the twenty members of the Association of Executive Recruiting Consultants plus maybe double that number of firms or individuals who operate under similar ethical standards.* Without question, however, the recruiter is the glamour boy of the management consulting profession.

Executive recruiters, to their horror, have accumulated a string of uncomplimentary nicknames. They have been called flesh-peddlers, personnel pirates, raiders, body thieves, and head hunters. More accurately, they are management consultants who specialize in locating qualified men and convincing them to quit and go to work for some-

---

* Some of the better known search firms include Ward Howell Associates, Inc., Spencer Stuart & Associates, Inc., Handy Associates, Incorporated, Boyden Associates, and Heidrick & Struggles.

The Business of Hiring the Boss

one else. The executive recruiter is a man feared and sometimes hated by top corporation presidents, who resent seeing their top executives pirated for some other corporation. He is a man anticipated and sometimes courted by rising young executives for whom a call from a recruiter may mean a new and more responsible job accompanied by a considerable jump in salary.

Even more than most management consulting firms, the executive recruiter operates under a cloak of almost total secrecy. It is precisely this reason why his services are valued by corporate presidents. "When you start moving at executive levels, it's a small world," Robert Madigan of William H. Clark Associates once told me. "Presidents can't go blundering around themselves without making a lot of noise." Thus the executive recruiter often moves in a shadow world of disguised phone calls, unmarked envelopes marked "personal and confidential," and furtive meetings in airline terminals and restaurants. Some recruiters maintain apartments near their offices where they can meet quietly with prospective job candidates. Good reason exists for this. A corporate head who discovered one of his bright young men flirting with a recruiter might fire him before he got a chance to quit. Yet that seemingly tapped man might merely be one of maybe a hundred men called on one particular search.

The average search lasts two or three months; some last longer. "All we can guarantee you is our confidence," the recruiter normally will begin when first contacting a prospective job candidate. And often that is all the candidate will get. He may be approached for a $35,000 job, quizzed at length over the telephone, invited to the recruiter's office for an expense-paid face-to-face interview, quizzed and briefed over the phone again, invited for another trip to the headquarters of the hiring corporation (which often is identified only after weeks of negotiation), and then dropped like a bride who has just flunked her Wassermann test. Yet so skillful are the practitioners of the art of executive recruiting that the rejected candidate goes home with little rancor, proud and exalted at having gotten as far as he did. Three months later that same recruiter will fearlessly call again for information on people in the former candidate's industry for another search and the individual will spill his guts into the telephone. For those few men who do obtain new positions through the medium of executive search, it is somewhat like being canonized by the Church.

Although few executive recruiters would be tactless enough to admit for publication that they think themselves a notch or two higher than the average McKinsey or Booz-Allen consultant, most recruiters seem at least subconsciously aware of their own stature in the consultant hierarchy. For one thing they deal with the world's most important commodity: people. When a management consultant completes a marketing or organization study, frequently nothing visible happens. It may be possible to measure the results of his work four or five years later in a company's profit or loss statements, but maybe not even then. When a recruiter completes an assignment, however, a highly visible man will have switched jobs. Recruiters, because they deal with the careers of live people rather than with charts or abstract figures, obtain publicity in newspapers, magazines, and now in this book, undoubtedly out of proportion to the share they get of Big Business' consulting dollar. Yet the executive recruiter may influence the economy more than any other consultant. According to Kearney's Richard E. Petersen: "The single outstanding problem of top management is the selection of its succession. I've been in company after company where this problem has not been faced up to."

Ideally, companies like to pyramid executive talent by plucking bright young men off college campuses and offering them a steady series of promotions inside the organization. The development of good organization men by this method sounds most efficient, but in actual practice it frequently fails to succeed. Because of the tremendous upsurge in the world economy, the pyramid base of ten or twenty years ago has often proved insufficient for top-management needs today. The creation of new companies and even entire new industries has increased the demand for executives. Corporations the size of General Motors or General Electric can afford to maintain large pools of executive talent. The average middle-sized corporation cannot, thus must go more frequently outside to fill vacancies. Also, not all the bright young men with the talents to become president want to work all their lives for one company and spend most of their time sitting on the bench.

They may shorten the route to the top by jumping from one company to another.

In one American Management Association survey, 64 per cent of all firms queried said they expected to need to obtain executives from outside sources. Another 35 per cent estimated a fifty-fifty chance that such might be the case. In another survey of 516 major companies, 242 listed new chief executives during the past six years—a turnover in top management of 47 per cent. When I interviewed executive recruiter Ward Howell in New York in January 1967, he told me that week his recruiting firm was searching for four presidents for four large companies.[*]

A rather subtle difference exists between executive search firms and other organizations in the personnel field. "Even our own families don't understand us," claims Edwin C. Johnson. "They think we're mostly glorified employment agencies." Most employment agencies, which are regulated as to the size of the fees they can charge, either openly or covertly dislike executive recruiters because of the high fees the latter command. Basically a recruiter is approached by the *corporation* to find the man. He will get paid whether he locates anyone or not and sometimes will advise the client merely to promote somebody from within. The employment agency more often is approached by the *man*

[*] In an October 13, 1967, article on recruiter Sidney M. Boyden, *Time* listed a number of presidents and chairmen he had recruited: Virgil Boyd of Chrysler, Arthur Larkin, Jr., of General Foods, Stuart Silloway of Investors Diversified Services, John L. Gushman of Anchor Hocking Glass, A. King McCord of Westinghouse Air Brake, Harold S. Geneen of ITT, and Robert O. Fickes of Philco-Ford.

The Business of Hiring the Boss

to find the corporation. They get paid on a contingency basis, that is, when they fill a job, and often (but less and less in the tight job market of today) by the man who gets the job. In actual practice, however, this distinction often becomes fuzzy since many top-level employment agencies will operate like recruiters, searching for men outside their own list of prospective job-hunters.* No *ethical* recruiter, however, will take a man and try to find him a job. "If Jesus Christ himself walked in here," one recruiter once told me, "we wouldn't pick up the phone and call one of our clients."

For his work in locating a new employee the executive recruiter normally charges 25 per cent of the yearly salary of the individual hired. Since the top recruiters seldom touch a job-hunt that involves less than a $15,000 salary, their fees can be sizable. R. J. Wytmar, president of Maichle & Wytmar, Inc., estimates that 60 per cent of his firm's searches fall within the $20–35,000 range. Fifteen per cent lie between $15,000 and $20,000, with the remainder over $35,000. The median search conducted by Ward Howell in 1968 was for a $42,500 position which thus resulted in an average fee of over $10,000. Howell has fifteen professional staffmen in his offices in New York and London with each one capable of completing anywhere from ten to twenty searches a year and thus generating nearly two million dollars in billings for the firm a year. Boyden Associates contains thirty staffmen who,

---

* Employment agencies often masquerade as "executive search firms," reaching for the recent high prestige of recruiters, as do many job counselors who for a fee advise a man *how* to get a job but offer no guarantee that he will obtain one.

according to a 1967 article in *Time,* account for annual billings in the neighborhood of five million. Simple arithmetic would indicate that the average Boyden associate generates roughly $167,000 in billings, or two to three times the billing power of the typical member of a management consulting firm. Although the top recruiters don't rival James Allen or Marvin Bower in terms of annual income, they probably out-earn the average consulting firm partner, and particularly partners at consulting firms their size. In addition, their staffmen make more money than a consultant at the same relative level. Not only because of its high billing structure but also because of somewhat lower overhead (the main tool of the recruiter being a telephone, which gets billed to the client), recruiting is by far the most profitable consulting specialty.

Most executive recruiting firms tend to be small, with even the members of the Association of Executive Recruiting Consultants (the recruiters' equivalent of ACME) probably averaging only four or five professionals. Chicago-based Heidrick & Struggles equals Ward Howell in size with a dozen professionals in four offices. Spencer Stuart & Associates of Chicago, New York, and Westport, Conn., probably ranks as the largest recruiting firm. Stuart employs over fifty staffmen with about one-third of his firm's business conducted at overseas offices in Frankfurt, London, Paris, Zurich, and Madrid. Unlike a few other recruiters Stuart does not overlap back into the area of general management consulting but does provide top-level counsel on executive development and compensation. He broadly defines his firm's specialty as "consultant to corporate clients in the attraction and the effective utilization of managerial talent." A subsidiary firm of Stuart's called Management Formation, Inc., now in its third year and headed by Ulric Haynes, Jr., consults with business and government on minority group policy and programs and specializes in recruiting minority group executives, particularly Negroes. With its headquarters in Manhattan, MFI has a staff of five professionals (four are black) and recently opened a branch office in Chicago.

Most recruiters received their introduction to executive search by originally working as consultants. Gardner Heidrick once worked at Booz-Allen. Spencer Stuart worked at Booz-Allen and later for Heidrick & Struggles. Ward Howell originally worked for McKinsey and founded his own firm in November 1951 after McKinsey had decided recruiting was not a proper activity for a general management consulting firm.

McKinsey's main objection was that in recommending a change in personnel to a client on a regular consulting assignment they could be accused of sticking their hands in his pocket for additional business. "We decided this wasn't a professional activity," McKinsey's Everett Smith told me. "So we decided to get out of recruiting. It was one of the happiest decisions we ever made." The partners at Booz-Allen, however, see no conflict of interest between consulting and executive recruiting which (according to some sources) now accounts for an estimated 15 per cent of Booz-Allen's gross billings.

Most other management consulting firms also do executive recruiting. Not all firms approach this task as enthusi-
astically as Booz-Allen. For example, CMP avoids isolated
search engagements. "We don't consider ourselves executive searchers," says James C. Worthy. "We do it only incidental to the client engagement." Kearney's philosophy of
recruiting is somewhat similar to CMP. Among the accountants, Peat, Marwick, Mitchell & Co. has an active
recruiting division, whereas the more conservative Arthur
Andersen & Company has none. Haskins & Sells early in
1967 began to do recruiting, reportedly just to service its
audit clients. "It's a black and white proposition. You either
do or don't," says Reid Weedon, of Arthur D. Little, a firm
which doesn't. "It's a kind of difference pretty well understood by those in the business, and I think not so well understood by the prospective client."

Executive recruiting firms have remained small for some
very good reasons, one being that no successful means
exists by which a search can be mass-produced. Each
search requires a personalized and confidential approach.
"One person has to see everybody," is the way one recruiter
put it. "He has to have the yardstick in his head." Even
more than general consulting, recruiting is a quality rather
than quantity operation: the fees are large and the number
of assignments few. The clientele resembles that of the
management consulting firms in that, speaking in comparative terms, it fails to contain either the largest or the small-
est companies. The corporate giants frequently have extensive personnel departments in addition to a larger

reserve of home-bred talent from which to draw executives. There is less excuse for them to hire a recruiter although sometimes they do.*

Small companies simply can't afford the recruiters' large fees—at least not on a regular basis. The typical user of recruiters is a company large enough to be at least within range of *Fortune*'s 500 list but whose management pool is small enough so that when an opening occurs at or near the top they often have to look outside to fill it. Although exceptions do occur, the average company using recruiters may need them only two or three times a year, if that often. Compared with the number of people who change jobs on their own or through employment agencies each year, the total placed by executive recruiters represents an extremely small fraction.

One additional reason why recruiters have remained small is their obvious reluctance to search through client companies while working for other clients. The AERC code of ethics prohibits its members from searching within a former client within two years after completing an assignment—and some firms claim *never* to raid a former client. Obviously if you were searching in the automotive industry and could not touch Ford or General Motors your value as a recruiter would be limited.

All management consultants recoil at the thought of discussing their client assignments and are sensitive about their image; this is true with executive recruiters, but with

---

* According to AERC, two-thirds or more of all companies on *Fortune*'s 500 list are users of executive recruiters.

some subtle differences. A company president who might not wish to admit that he needed the help of an outsider for an organization study will certainly shy away from discussing his having hired a recruiter to lure an already employed individual away from one of his competitors. Recruiters rarely consider unemployed men. They instead sift through the ranks of the seemingly happily employed and, after they have completed their assignment, sometimes leave a nasty taste in the mouths of those from whom the executive has been "recruited," or pirated. Of course, the recruiters point out with much truth, if an individual is happily employed he will not want to leave. Obviously an executive does not hop from one job to another unless he gains something, usually more money, but more often, escape from a dead-end position.

Fortune and other magazines have written what many recruiters consider to be undignified articles about them. The recruiters cringe at being referred to as flesh-peddlers. Many recruiters, however, are probably more open in their attitude toward pursuing publicity (or at least not getting out of its way) than the average consulting firm partner. "Max Gunther wrote an article about me for *True*," Ward Howell told me, smiling as he did so. "Max had me roaming around the warehouse district staring into dark windows like a detective. It shocked some of our competitors. But it brought in business."

Part of the reason for the spectacular growth (and acceptance) of the relatively young executive recruiting profession has been the large amount of publicity—both favorable and unfavorable—it has received. The seemingly more open-minded attitude toward publicity on the part of many executive search men is partly because in their profession the founding fathers are still active. Entrepreneurs, by the very nature that caused them to found their own firms, tend to be more colorful, outgoing, and outspoken than the organization men who succeed them.

In addition, one particularly subtle difference between the consultant and the recruiter breeds more confidence in the latter. The consultant more frequently enters a company as a supplicant, begging information and cooperation from those who employ him. The recruiter also begins his assignment in the kneeling position, but then returns outside where he assumes the dominant position before those he would recruit. He is a person with a great favor, i.e., a better paying job, to dispense to those who meet his standards. When he returns to the client it is to throw before him a list of his hand-picked candidates about whom he can say with confidence: "These are the three best men in the world."

Almost any recruiter will admit, however, that there is nothing occult in his method of operation. "We're simply intelligence gatherers," explains R. J. Wytmar. The recruiter's chief weapon is not his engaging smile but his telephone. Experience tells a recruiter what companies, and what positions at those companies, most likely will produce individuals who will qualify for the job he is trying to fill.

After that it becomes simply a matter of picking up the telephone and determining who occupies those positions and how well they perform their job.

"It's a job of gumshoeing around," says E. B. Sollis, president of Spencer Stuart & Associates. "We find out who's who—the ones in the right jobs at the right companies." According to Edwin C. Johnson: "Nine-tenths of this business is stupid library research. A lot of searches can be run right out of a business reference library." At least one New York recruiting firm—Manpower Survey & Research, headed by Charles L. Fields—will contract to do only the preliminary research work of locating the thirty or forty men throughout the country who, because of their position, might qualify for the job in question. Most recruiters, however, prune this total down to the three or four men not only most qualified for the job but who also are interested in it. Because of this total service, quite obviously, they charge higher fees.

Normally when an executive recruiter receives an assignment he will take what some people might consider excessive pains to develop job specifications for the person being sought. "You can't hire an executive in a vacuum," I was told at Booz-Allen. "You have to know the company, the personalities, the sacred cows. You have to do a preliminary study to see what the company really needs and it must be done in sufficient depth."

Spencer Stuart, when assigned to a search, will normally send one, and often two, of his staff members to the client company to interview anywhere from five to ten of the

The Business of Hiring the Boss

executives who will be working with the prospective employee. Edwin C. Johnson tape records his interviews with the client and at various times during a search replays the tape to guarantee he still understands the job specifications. After preliminary client discussions Ward Howell drafts a list of specifications then makes certain every executive who will be involved with the new employee reads and initials it. Often personality as well as talent may be a determining factor in an individual's acceptability. "A man can be an astounding success in environment A and a complete bust in environment B," says E. B. Sollis. "Our job is to match personality with environment."

Occasionally an executive recruiter must rely on a certain amount of extrasensory perception in determining the kind of man a client president will *not* hire. One recruiter told me of a search he conducted for a president of a subsidiary bank in a very rich community, largely Protestant and dominated by the paper marketing industry. The bank executives thought *only* a Protestant would succeed in that job although tact prohibited them from saying so. And apparently not just *any* Protestant would do, since one prospect uncovered by the recruiter was rejected because he was a Christian Scientist and thus presumed to be too dogmatic. "The number of Jewish people we've recruited is pretty few," admitted another recruiter. The executive recruiter might be compared to the real estate broker who makes certain the right people get steered to the right neighborhoods.

Once the recruiter has thoroughly defined the job specifications (and by means of research located the most likely candidates), he then will contact them by telephone. "Everyone may say that this person is locked into his job and won't move, but you'll never know unless you ask. The guy can be just as ripe as an apple in the fall."

In locating a single executive a recruiter normally will contact anywhere from two to three hundred candidates. He may meet between twenty and thirty of these either in his own office or on trips around the country. This will permit him to recommend anywhere from three to six of the best qualified and most willing to the client, who will discard all but one. A recruiter will spend about a week drawing up specifications and four to five weeks in the actual search to determine the three to six candidates he will present to the client. Another month and a half may elapse while the client makes final interviews, often with the recruiter at his elbow. By the time one man emerges victorious, approximately three months will have passed. According to R. J. Wytmar, 80 per cent of all searches last approximately this long with a few being completed faster and a few slower. Recruiters note that when a search drags past three months the trail gets cold, the client gets antsy, and the recruiter gets nervous because in most instances he will be losing money.

Sometimes a client will cancel an assignment before it is completed. Ward Howell told me of one assignment he had for a large chemical company whose top three ranking officers consisted of a chairman of the executive committee, a president, and an executive vice-president, who at age forty-two felt confident of moving eventually into the president's position. Howell had to locate another executive vice-president to compete with the incumbent. He eventually presented four men, two of them he described to me as "exceptionally qualified," so much so that the executive vice-president saw his ascendency in jeopardy. With the chairman of the executive committee in Europe on an extended trip, the executive vice-president convinced the president to convene a board meeting, which resulted in the president's becoming chairman and the executive vice-president, president. The new president's first act was to fire Howell and cancel the search. Howell, of course, was well paid for his labors and since then the chemical company's new president has hired him for other searches.

Various reasons exist why a search might extend beyond average length. One obvious reason is that the recruiter may be incompetent. The recruiter, however, may be hindered by the reputation of the client company. The best-qualified executives may not wish for it or may want more money than the company wants to pay. Just as management consultants dislike ministering to sick businesses, executive recruiters dislike working for problem presidents. The ideal client is one with a rapidly expanding business, not only because of the ease with which candidates can be convinced to work for it, but also because an expanding company's need for additional executives will provide a constant source of assignments. Maichle & Wytmar once conducted thirty-three searches over a two-year period for an expanding $50 million electrical appliance company.

Occasionally an assignment will prove difficult for the recruiter because of a client's vacillation in deciding on the candidate. In one instance the president of a company in the heavy equipment field died without a successor. Five sons worked at the firm but not at a high enough level to step into the top job. The board chairman chose Maichle & Wytmar to locate a new president. The job offered a salary in excess of $100,000 and the recruiters eventually presented two candidates: one the vice-president of a division of a major automobile manufacturer and the other an executive vice-president at a competitor company.

However, at this point the president's widow, who still held considerable stock in the company, decided that one of her sons, who was thirty-five years old, should have the job. The board bowed to her will. It took three months for the son to prove himself incapable of holding the top job. By then the first candidate, the automotive vice-president, had lost interest in the job and the second had been promoted to the presidency of the competitor company. The recruiter had to begin his search anew.

Recruiting a president, however, can be a relatively easy task not only because the job is a desirable one, but the areas where a recruiter can find potential presidents are fairly clearly defined. "The hardest person to recruit," says R. J. Wytmar, "is the young tiger at $15,000 that everyone

The Business of Hiring the Boss

wants. There are no organization charts to define this fellow. He will have no track record of accomplishment to guide you." This is why, as executive recruiters establish their practice, they don't necessarily increase the size of their staff, but instead raise their goals and refuse to accept small recruiting assignments. As for fees,* it is better for a recruiter to be paid 25 per cent of $100,000, the salary of a president, than an equal percentage for a $15,000 junior executive. Also, if a recruiter helps to hire a president, that president presumably will have a predisposition to hire him to fill any future vacancies. Recruiters, like all other management consultants, thrive on repeat business.

Repeat business does not come automatically, however. Philip C. Martin, a recruiter who works from his home in suburban Chicago, discussed with me one job where a management consultant had been analyzing the problems of a small company in the equipment field. The consultant had recommended to the chairman of the board that a new president be hired; Martin got the assignment to find one, and did.

The new president took office and as one of his first acts fired his vice-president, his secretary, and the executive who had originally recommended the management consultant. The consultant himself was told not to return, as was Martin. "He decided I was too expensive," explained

---

* Although there are various means of determining fees, percentage of salary is the most popular one, used by more than 50 per cent of AERC members. Other types of billing include flat fees and straight time charges.

Martin. "Everyone else on the outside seems to think I picked the wrong man, but I can't criticize him. I admit I'm expensive."

"Our fees are realistic," adds E. B. Sollis. "Not all companies want us. If the client is too nervous about the compensation then we know we're better off, and they're better off, not working together. We think a company should hire us only if it gets outstanding value for its money. If a company pays us $60,000 and that's the best money they spent all year, then we'll do the eighty-seventh job with them."

Not all men recruited into new jobs succeed. Some recruiting firms guarantee to replace any man who either quits or is fired, while others will not. The manager of one employment agency told me of one company that spent $75,000 in six months with one recruiter and obtained only two engineers. The agency took the assignment and located a dozen engineers in a month. Obviously such cases don't happen very often, otherwise the recruiters would not stay long in business. Actually the reputation of executive recruiters has progressed so far beyond the "flesh-peddler" stage that many organizations in the personnel field now hide under the term "executive search firm" whether they do any actual recruiting or not.

Most reputable executive recruiters look down with distaste on those of lesser stature who would trade on their hard-won reputations. They wrinkle their noses at employment agencies as well as those among their own ranks who would accept contingency work, that is, getting paid only if you come up with a body. If a man can't possibly be found for a particular job, the recruiters want the freedom to say so, even to the point of maybe recommending somebody for promotion from within the company—while still getting paid. "With the security of payment, no matter what happens we can do a better and more honest job," says Edwin C. Johnson. "After all, if a lawyer loses your case he still gets paid. If a doctor operates on you and you die, he still deserves a fee."

Executive recruiting, despite all its connotations of piracy and raiding, seems to have established a very definite niche in the management consulting industry. The recruitment of executives, as well as job switching itself, has become at least semi-respectable in this age. Rudy Dallmeyer claims that there is no clear-cut ladder to success. "A man's business career," he says, "is more like floating on a raft down a wide river. The river twists and turns. You are assailed by currents from all sides. If your raft drifts out of the mainstream or is about to go under, you simply have to get off and find another raft."

In today's economy, the executive recruiter is the boat transferring men from raft to raft.

13

The Accountants Are Coming!
The Accountants Are Coming!

"We're specialists in change," the man wearing the vest and dark gray suit told me. "Probably only two or three times in a lifetime will the average business need to make major changes. It's difficult for executives to maintain technical competence in all areas of management so that they can make these changes smoothly. We find it difficult, and we're working in these areas all the time. So the average business-man faced with the necessity to make a change may un-cover problems he is unable to cope with. That's when he needs outside help. It's not that we're necessarily more competent than those who hire us; it's just that we're doing this kind of work all the time."

This was the kind of speech that might have been made by almost any management consultant—and the man mak-ing it *was* a consultant, but with a slightly different flavor. He worked for one of the certified public accounting firms. The mainstream management consulting firms face com-

The Accountants Are Coming!

petition from several areas. First, contract research firms such as Arthur D. Little, Stanford Research Institute, Battelle Memorial Institute, and IITRI (Illinois Institute of Technology Research Institute) have active management consulting divisions. Second, professors at many business schools consult to supplement their teaching salaries. Third, there are the accountants.

The Big Image management consulting firms don't greatly fear the contract research firms. Only Little and SRI rank high in total billings. Besides, since the largest ACME firm (Booz-Allen) has spread into the area of contract research, it is hardly in a position to complain. As for the professors, while perhaps many in number, they are essentially individual practitioners and thus don't compete head-on against ACME firms.

The certified public accounting firms present a different problem, and a growing threat. In the area of billings for management services, seven of the twenty-five top-earners are accounting firms, equal to the number of ACME firms so ranked. Moreover, the management services divisions of the larger CPA firms have been expanding so rapidly that, unless checked, they threaten to overwhelm the Big Image consulting firms. "We have approximately seven hundred professional people in our management services division," a partner in one of the Big Eight accounting firms informed me. "That's roughly 15 per cent of our professional staff— and we're growing."

Many members in ACME shudder convulsively when asked their opinion of the push by accountants into the area of management consulting. They consider it an invasion into an area where accountants, as auditors of industry's books, should not tread. On the other hand, the accountants insist that they *always* have been in consulting! One official of the American Institute of Certified Public Accountants told me that accountants were doing consulting work back in the 1500s. That may be stretching a point, but several of the Big Eight accounting firms actually began as "consultants" in the nineteenth century. Peat, Marwick, Mitchell & Co. dates their entry into management consulting as 1906.

But those consulting activities in which the accountants did engage were more or less incidental to their auditing functions. With the passing of the first Internal Revenue Act in 1913, the main thrust of CPA work, other than that related to the traditional auditing function, was directed toward taxes. After the Securities Act of 1933, CPA's began to concentrate even more on auditing corporate books for those "listed" companies for which outside audits became mandatory. It was only after World War II and particularly into the mid-fifties that the accounting firms began to expand into the previous dormant area of management services. Peat-Marwick's decision to increase the scope of its "other-than-accountant" services to industry came in 1952. Henry Gunders of Price Waterhouse & Company told me that if asked to supply a date for the transition within his firm, it would be 1946, when the function was established as a separate department; but he also indicated that their move into consulting areas was much more evolutionary than revolutionary.

The expansion by accountants into consulting areas coincided with the development of computer sciences. Certainly a great proportion of consulting by accounting firms involves the use of computers, but it would be wrong to cite electronic data processing as the reason for consulting by accountants. Business in general became much more complex following World War II, and the development of computer sciences became one way of solving complex business problems. For this same reason the management consulting firms *and* management services divisions of the accounting firms have grown and prospered during this era of business complexity. The decision by the accounting firm partners to enter consulting was motivated partly by a knowledge that firms such as McKinsey and Booz-Allen were providing certain services for their audit clients which they could provide very well themselves. As one accounting firm expanded its service to its clients, the other firms had to follow this lead for fear of losing their competitive edge. Estimates as to the volume of consulting work currently done by accountants range from 8 to 15 per cent of their business, and some sources anticipate that this may rise to 40 per cent by 1980.

Not only are accounting firms expanding, but they are expanding into the areas which the Big Image management consulting firms long had considered their private domain. "Ten years ago the scope of our work was in finance, accounting, data processing, and office operations," explains Peat-Marwick's James C. Cohrs. "Our work recently has led us into related areas: production control, inventory control, and marketing. We now work with our clients in the area of forecasting. They recognize the need to plan ahead and have some grasp of the future."

Many management consultants can cite various reasons why they feel the accountants should stick to their traditional roles as tax experts and auditors of the books. "I take a dim view of the entry of accountants into consulting," I was told by the president of one of the smaller ACME firms. "They're acting as both judge and jury. I don't think these activities go together. They say it's paperwork, that they're experts in paperwork. Bullshit! They do market studies and executive recruiting and get into a lot of other areas too. Any accountant can make final year-end adjustments to make the business look good or bad. If his management services division is taking a wad of dough out of the company, he will make it look good."

The accountants shrug off the charges that they can act as judge and jury by pointing to their code of ethics, which is so strict that an accounting firm will not even list itself in bold type in the phone book and its firm members, on their business cards, will have nothing more than the name of that firm to indicate what sort of work that individual does. "We don't consider ourselves management consultants," one accounting firm partner told me. "We never have and never will. We don't consider ourselves competitors of the ACME firms. Of course, there has to be some overlap."

The Accountants Are Coming!

"We don't intend to be a 'department store' where you can come in and get any sort of consulting service," adds Price Waterhouse's Henry Gunders. "In fact, some types of consulting engagements are, in our view, not even consistent with the postures of independent CPA's."

The various members of the Big Eight accounting firms vary in their approach toward consulting, some being quite conservative in the number of disciplines they cover, with others competing more directly with the ACME firms. Arthur Andersen and Haskins & Sells represent the conservative element among accountants. Peat-Marwick and Ernst & Ernst represent the forceful, broad-scope approach. The other four* among the Big Eight rank somewhere between. In recent years, however, Haskins & Sells has added executive recruiting to its list of disciplines, ostensibly to serve only its audit clients. The present trend among accounting firms is to embrace more rather than fewer disciplines.

Although all major accounting firms handle consulting assignments, and all agree that it is the coming thing, few seem to agree on what to call it. Peat-Marwick refers to their activities as "management consulting," but Ernst & Ernst calls the same animal "management services," and Arthur Andersen has an "administrative services department." Price Waterhouse calls it "management advisory services," reportedly to make clear that the function performed is one of advising rather than managing. Account-

* Lybrand, Ross Brothers & Montgomery; Price, Waterhouse & Company; Touche, Ross, Bailey & Smart; and Arthur Young & Co.

ants seemingly scorn the three-level hierarchy indigenous with many ACME firms and have their own four-level chain of command which, starting from the bottom, consists of: 1) junior and senior accountants (or consultants), 2) supervisors, 3) managers, and 4) partners and principals. The men in management services ordinarily fall into the three higher levels rather than the lowest one; their duties change less as they move upward in rank, as does their income.

A clear difference separates the "partner" from the "principal." To be a partner in an accounting firm, as a matter of policy, a person needs a CPA degree. If a non-CPA rises to the partner's level of authority and income, he receives the title of principal. Normally, policy also dictates that only a CPA will rise to the highest chair in each firm, which seemingly would put limits on the ambitions of those in the management services divisions. Spokesmen for the profession, however, indicate that should a consultant have designs on that top chair he probably will be ambitious enough to obtain a CPA degree sometime during his rise.

In recruiting members for their management services staff, the CPA firms stand at the doors of the business schools, just as do McKinsey and Booz-Allen, looking for men with master's degrees. They also hire men from the ranks of industry, and frequently men on their own staffs with accounting backgrounds may shift from the CPA area of the firm into the management services divisions. When the CPA firms first began to expand into consulting in the mid-fifties, there was a tendency at the upper levels to

The Accountants Are Coming!

recruit partners from ACME firms who weren't the top partners, and at the lower levels to hire as consultants men who for one reason or other couldn't get hired by McKinsey or Booz-Allen. The ACME firms frequently bad-mouthed the CPA firms, claiming that the accountants were obtaining lower-caliber men. With the management services divisions now firmly established within the accounting firms, this borrowing of ACME talent, if not having ceased entirely, has at least diminished so that accountants can be said to breed their own brand of consultant.

Whereas the average consulting firm hurls even its greenest recruit into the breech where he will be expected to sink or swim, the accounting firms more carefully preen him for his duties. At Arthur Andersen, a fresh recruit reportedly will be given a four-week course at firm headquarters before being introduced to client work. Then after six months of what Andersen refers to as on-the-job training, the novice returns to firm headquarters for another three to four months of formal classroom work. Andersen maintains a special staff with the prime responsibility of providing administrative services training with one partner in charge full time.

Unlike several management consulting firms, where the revolving door seems to be standard operating procedure, most accounting firms don't (or say they don't) consciously prune their staffs. Of course, as in any occupation a certain natural amount of pruning occurs. According to Peat-Marwick's James Cohrs: "A fellow with us five or six years who hasn't been promoted probably will decide at that time that the travel and other pressures are too much and he will do better in industry. We have no policy of forcing this. There's no timetable. It's strictly up to the individual. Actually, our practice is expanding so fast that there is a shortage of what I would call management talent throughout the firm."

If and when the accountant-consultant does decide to leave, he is not merely shown the door. Most ACME firms frown on their employees going to work for a client firm; the accountants not only do not frown on the practice, but even *encourage* their departing employees to settle with client firms. If they learn someone desires to return to industry, they will shop around and help to place him. While talking with the partner of one large accounting firm, I asked what if a company such as Lever Brothers were to recruit away one of his staffmen. The partner looked up with a broad grin. "I can't think of anything that would better cement our relationship with Lever Brothers than to have a comptroller come through here."*

One major difference between the management services divisions of many accounting firms and the ACME firms is that the accountants frequently handle more numbers-related assignments (particularly in the area of computer sciences); also, they often can do relatively minor assignments more conveniently. "The ACME firms are looking for the big ticket items," one accountant told me. "The tough jobs are the ones you have to get in, do the job, and

---

* Later, I learned that that particular accounting firm didn't have the Lever Brothers account. Perhaps he was trying to tell me something.

The Accountants Are Coming!

get out. The consulting firms would rather do the $30,000 and $40,000 jobs. It's easier than providing one- and two-day services for consulting clients."

Whereas the Big Image management consulting firms like to look toward the top 500 on *Fortune*'s list for their clients, the accounting firms anticipate particular success in accommodating companies who, if *Fortune* took notice of them, would rank anywhere from 1,000 to 5,000 in size. Although it is difficult to make sweeping generalizations, it frequently may be more practical for an accountant to accept assignments billable at less than $10,000, particularly when it involves an audit client. "The accounting firm has fewer start-up costs," says Henry Gunders. "We know a lot about our clients from the businessman's as well as from the auditor's point of view. Before starting an assignment with a company, consultants have to absorb a lot of information that, if the accountants working with that company are any good at all, they already know. Also, they know a lot of the problems."

"We don't have to locate the bathroom," is the way one accounting firm partner put it to me.

One other factor favoring the accounting firm in the rush to supply businessmen with consulting services is that most large accounting firms already have a built-up network of offices scattered throughout the world to serve their auditing clients. Given this network, they can add a one- or two-man office. Thus accountants can locate their consultants strategically closer to small companies, who will be increasingly in need of consulting services within the next two decades. This is less likely to have an impact on the business of the Big Image consulting firms than it may have on the smaller firms or individual practitioners in outlying cities.

Accountants have an edge over consulting firms in several other areas. Jim Cohrs of Peat-Marwick lists three reasons why a businessman should hire an accounting firm rather than a consulting firm: "First, there's the psychology of working with a firm you already know. You don't have strangers coming in in the night. Also, we're more familiar with the client's problems. We know the people and their personalities and can work with them effectively. In addition, we have a continuing thing riding. Year after year we do their audit work. We're not going to jeopardize this continuing relationship for a one-shot consulting assignment. We have a vested interest in seeing that we do a good job."

Perhaps one other related point that might appeal to some businessmen is that in the case of a badly handled assignment, he has little or no recourse with a consulting firm which has no connection with his business than that one assignment. If an ACME firm bungles a job, about all the businessman can do is pay the bill and complain to his friends at the club. If his accountant bungles a job he can have the satisfaction of firing that accountant from the profitable auditing work.

The management consultants counter, however, that it is exactly because the accountants have a vested interest in a continuing audit relationship that they are ineffective in dealing with certain assignments. One of the principal rea-

The Accountants Are Coming!

sons for hiring a management consultant is to obtain his objectivity, the opinions of an unbiased and impartial observer, the fresh point of view provided by the cold-eyed outsider who can appraise the inner workings of a company without fear of inner politics. An accounting firm that has been auditing a company's books for several decades may already have established itself as a member of the establishment. The accountant might not want to jeopardize that relationship by offering controversial advice, such as suggesting that the president be fired. An accountant who already knows where the bathroom is located may be unable to recognize that the bathroom should be located in another area of the plant.

The CPA firms have had to expand the scope of their business under the watchful eye of the Securities and Exchange Commission. The SEC in the past few years has been critical of the apparent inability of many accounting firms to detect fraud within companies and report it to the public. The SEC also has cast a questioning eye on the expanding management services practices of many CPA firms. At the annual meeting of the American Institute of Certified Public Accountants in Boston in 1966, Manuel F. Cohen, chairman of the SEC, commented: "A word of caution is in order with respect to what one of your prominent members describes as 'consulting services which cannot be related logically either to the financial process or to broadly defined information and control systems [such as] market surveys, factory layout, psychological testing, or public opinion polls.' And I am disposed to add, executive recruitment for a fee. An accountant who directs or assists in programs of this kind raises serious questions concerning his independence when it comes time to render to creditors, to investors, and to the public his opinion on the results of the programs."

The CPA firms naturally are concerned about charges that they are advising management what to do as well as reporting how well he does it. They believe that they still can retain their professional independence. "If I go to a doctor he may tell me on the one hand that I have an ulcer," says Henry De Vos of the AICPA. "With the next hand he opens it up. I don't know if I had an ulcer. I put my faith in him."

The accountants also insist that they do not serve as decision-makers, that they simply present the facts to management. According to Henry Gunders: "We don't want to drift gradually into the area where we actually make the decisions that management should make itself beyond developing the facts and analyzing their meaning. We don't think it is appropriate for us to participate in making the decisions by which managers set the major course of their companies." At the same time, one of the legitimate functions of the management consultant is to do just that: make decisions.

The accounting firms undoubtedly will continue to expand their business and bite off larger slices of the pie the consulting firms once had to themselves, but in the current expanding demand for consulting services there seems to be plenty of pie for all.

14

"You Have to Be Bullish About Consulting"

Without question the image most executives have of consulting firms is both projected and enhanced by the presence in the business world of ACME, the Association of Consulting Management Engineers. ACME considers itself a professional *association* rather than a professional *society*. Only firms belong, not individual members of those firms. McKinsey and Booz-Allen belong, as do Kearney and CMP. Proudfoot and May do not belong; but neither does Arthur D. Little, nor many smaller and less well known but reputable consulting firms such as The Boston Consulting Group, the Diebold Group, Planning Research Associates, or C. B. McLagan & Company, or individuals like Harvey Krentzman or Rufus Allen, whose work at least on certain levels of business and in certain areas matches and perhaps even betters the quality of work done by the blue-ribbon ACME firms. None of the accounting firms belong despite the fact that a majority of the ACME firms surprisingly do favor inclusion of management services divisions of CPA firms.

Many firms who possess ACME credentials might not be considered management consultants according to the present interpretation of that label, but could be more accurately classified as industrial engineers, specialists in the so-called dirty-fingernail work, which lies as far afield from the more cerebral practice of McKinsey & Company as the profession of medicine does from the profession of law. But then the "E" in ACME does stand for Engineers. The name "management engineers" actually became a part of the ACME name at the time of the Association's founding between 1929 and 1933, and this was done mainly to appease the predominantly engineering firms, especially Stevenson, Jordan & Harrison and Ford, Bacon & Davis. The name "consulting management engineers" thus persists in the Association's title, even though ACME now operates more as symbol and voice for what has become known today as the "management consulting profession."

The name ACME carries tremendous weight both in American and international business circles, but with only forty-five members it certainly can consider itself less representative of the entire consulting industry (which numbers 2,700 firms) than the American Medical Association is representative of the medical profession.

The functioning office for ACME is located on the twentieth floor of a trim but elderly building at 347 Madison Avenue within a few blocks of McKinsey and CMP headquarters and the New York offices of Kearney, Fry,

"You Have to Be Bullish About Consulting"

and Booz-Allen. There is nothing pretentious about ACME headquarters. It is a typical association office with four rooms occupied by two female employees and ACME executive director Philip W. Shay. One wall of Shay's office contains bookcases filled with volumes relating to business and the consulting profession. A Far Eastern atmosphere prevails. Japanese prints and wall scrolls add to this atmosphere, souvenirs from Shay's eighteen months in Japan, where he helped reorganize colleges and universities during the Army's occupation of that country following World War II. Shay's experience also includes college teaching, some industrial work, five years as a consultant with H. A. Hopf & Company, and four years as director of research and information services for the American Management Association. In 1954 he became executive director of ACME.

While researching this book I interviewed Shay several times. He is a quiet-talking, round little man and as I asked various questions he occasionally would rise and glide smoothly from room to room retrieving booklets and pamphlets containing information on the consulting profession. On one of my visits with Shay we discussed ACME, its membership requirements, and its size—or perhaps more aptly, its lack of size. "Our current membership is about forty-five firms," Shay had said. That was in 1966. "We're not looking for members. We don't solicit membership." He indicated that probably between fifty and sixty firms in North America, in addition to its present members, could meet the ACME standards. Every year ACME receives approximately two hundred inquiries about membership from consulting firms. At that time, ten to twelve applications were being studied by the ACME admissions committee.

Shay later expanded on his statements in a letter to me: "ACME is frequently accused of being a small group of elite firms with little or no sense of responsibility for the welfare of the total field of consulting in North America. Leadership in any field carries with it some responsibility for what is happening throughout the field. But this responsibility may be met in different ways. Instead of extending membership to a considerable number of consulting firms of questionable competence and integrity, ACME has chosen to exercise its leadership by the steady elevation of standards of professional conduct and performance. It has taken the lead in the development of ethics, professional practices, research, public relations, and publications. It provides aid to newly formed consulting firms, and it shares information on operating problems and practices with firms outside the membership. . . . While ACME does not actively solicit new members, any firm of management consultants in North America which meets the membership requirements is encouraged to apply. But it is essential that high standards for admission be maintained if the purposes of the Association and the welfare of clients are to be served."

Three years later, when I visited Shay in the spring of 1969, the ACME membership list actually had shrunk by one. Shay indicated that probably eight additional firms would be added within the year. "But we don't want to grow big," he added. He felt the maximum optimal size of ACME was around fifty-five firms.

The procedures for gaining admittance to the ACME inner sanctum are spelled out in a gray booklet that was among the documents retrieved for me by Shay during one of my visits. "If consultants are to be successful in their work with clients," says the booklet in the introduction to its Requirements for Membership, "their own competence and integrity must be beyond challenge. It was to insure this that ACME was incorporated in 1933, with high standards for membership and a strict code of professional ethics. Its purpose was twofold: first, to provide a professional association for consulting firms of demonstrated competence and reputation; and second, to provide prospective clients with standards by which they could differentiate well-qualified consultants from incompetent or unethical practitioners. The Association's present objectives still include the purposes envisioned by its founders."

ACME defines its membership requirements in broad terms which might be summarized to say that a candidate firm should work with management problems and have high principles. "A candidate firm must be serving clients in commerce, industry, government, or other institutions broadly on managerial and related operating and technical problems in one or more major areas of management," writes Shay. "In addition, it must meet specific require-

ments in terms of length of service, size of firm, competence of principals, financial stability, and professional-
type business offices."

Some of these specific requirements are spelled out in
the ACME booklets. But they are not defined too precisely.
The candidate "normally" should have been in business for
five years (or three years if its partners have had "substantial previous experience"). It must have at least three
full-time partners plus a supporting staff, and be financially
stable. It cannot engage men for specific assignments then
release them, or retain them on a reduced rate (or on fur-
lough basis), when an assignment is completed. "Finally,"
says the requirements booklet, "it must compensate its
professional men in a professional manner." What consti-
tutes a "professional manner" also does not get defined
precisely. The owner or owners must be active in the firm
and willing to follow ACME's Standards of Professional
Conduct and Practice. As one side point, "the candidate
firm must occupy business offices which are appropriate to
the practice of the profession of management consulting."

After approval of a preliminary application the firm sub-
mits a formal application and a complete list of clients
served during the previous three years. Executive director
Shay then checks these references and reports his recommendations to the admissions committee, which in turn
makes a recommendation to the nine-man ACME board of
directors. If more than one board member thumbs down
the candidate firm, its application fails. Thus it needs a
minimum of eight friendly votes out of nine.

"You Have to Be Bullish About Consulting"

Any ACME member who does not maintain "strict standards of professional conduct and practice" may be bounced from the club. Dismissal procedure is similar to admission procedure, at least in the number of votes required. Eight of the nine-member board must vote to dismiss. One ACME critic with whom I spoke insisted that you could count on one hand the number of firms kicked out of the Association. Whether or not he has more fingers than I, and whether or not they were expelled or left voluntarily, nine firms disappeared from the ACME ranks between 1960 and 1969. Fourteen firms have disappeared from membership since Shay first became executive director in 1954. Reportedly twenty-nine firms have disappeared from the ACME roster since its founding.

One firm was reportedly expelled from ACME for paying a percentage of gross billings on certain assignments to union officials who helped direct business to this firm. Bruce Payne & Associates, a New York firm with an international reputation, survived many years of criticism for promoting its services more actively than many ACME members considered professional. Some years ago, Bruce Payne was serving on the board of directors of Magnacord, Inc., a Chicago-based company that manufactured tape recorders. Magnecord was sold to a new group of investors, and the new owners received a bill for consulting services for approximately $130,000, which they considered exorbitant. When they did not pay the bill, the consulting firm sued for its fee, and the new owners countersued for $1.5 million. During the course of this law suit, Payne retained its membership in ACME because the Association's legal counsel advised the board of directors not to take any action against this firm until the court suit had been settled. Shortly after the suit was settled, this firm was dismissed from membership, the reason given being its repeated failure to pay its dues and assessments on time. Several firms have been asked to resign from ACME not for ethical reasons, but merely because ownership passed to other, outside hands. This happened to Barrington & Company and also to Wallace, Clark & Company. The most recent casualty to the bylaw stipulating that the owners must consult was Fry Consultants Incorporated. Fry became a wholly owned subsidiary of ARA Services Inc. and thus lost its ACME membership early in 1968. Many people within the consulting profession believe that public ownership of consulting firms may become common in the future. If so, ACME may have to reappraise its policies in this area.

As a result of the Association's Code of Professional Ethics and stiff admissions policy, the circular ACME emblem serves as a sort of *Good Housekeeping* seal of approval for businessmen in search of a consultant. It guarantees that the product bought—in this case, consulting services—will be of a certain level of competence. The ACME firms also list themselves together in the classified telephone directory of the major industrial cities in North America. A company president looking under the title "Management Consultants" in the yellow pages will discover the ACME emblem, a list of all ACME members (whether located in that city or not), their addresses and phone numbers, and the statement: "The following members are pledged to a strict code of professional conduct and practice. They serve clients in accordance with the highest standards of competence, objectivity, and integrity." Those desiring additional information are requested to call ACME headquarters in New York, where Phil Shay will listen to their problems, provide information and advice on hiring a consultant, and perhaps recommend several firms. (He also will mail them copies of the current "Directory of Membership and Services" and a basic brochure entitled "How to Get the Best Results from Consultants.")

On various visits to the ACME offices I overheard several telephone conversations that Shay had with businessmen seeking a consultant, and he seemed to speak impartially and favor no one firm. Several non-ACME consultants told me that on occasion they did work for clients who (at least indirectly) had been referred to them by Shay. More than likely, however, a businessman who seeks ACME advice will end up hiring an ACME firm.

Partly because of the possibility of obtaining business either through the Association or because of membership in it—but also because of a desire for status and acceptance as a professional—most non-member firms consider ACME as a pinnacle toward which to aspire. Not all of those on the outside admit this, but many do (at least off the record). While talking with several members of a growing non-ACME firm in Chicago, I raised the question of the Association. I learned that the firm had just made application for ACME membership. "There's no question in my mind that we'll be accepted," the number-two man in that firm informed me. He seemed to feel that their acceptance would occur in a matter of weeks. Two years later his firm was still waiting, although eventually it did join the club. For others, approval comes more rapidly. A consulting firm has to be in operation a minimum of three years before it can be considered. When I spoke with Don Booz he seemed visibly pleased that his firm had obtained ACME sanction after only four years.

The opinion of ACME held by the "outs," however, quite frequently differs from that of the "ins." According to one consultant with whom I spoke: "There's a tendency in ACME to self-serve, to protect the image. Once they take a guy into the club you automatically assume that all members are the same. Well, they aren't all the same."

The president of another consulting firm with about a dozen professional staff members called me while passing through the Midwest to arrange a later appointment for an interview. We briefly discussed the Association on the phone. "I don't care too much about ACME," he said. "It's such a hidebound, inflexible group. They're being out-flanked and if they continue to leave the smaller consulting firms on the outside it's going to hurt them. Actually, being a member of ACME doesn't help you much, except with a status-seeking company."

Later, while in the East, I spent most of a snowy Saturday morning with this same gentleman talking about the management consulting profession. During our discussion he sounded more mellow about ACME in person than he

"You Have to Be Bullish About Consulting"

had on the telephone: "About the worst thing that can be said about ACME is that they should be more actively enlisting into membership firms such as ourselves."

Individual practitioner Rufus Allen says: "I think the stated objectives of ACME are certainly worthy and that they have probably served a useful purpose in promoting high standards of conduct and competence. On the other hand, there was a time when the amount of political infighting among ACME's various members claimed more attention than did their main objectives. I think also that they are subject to some degree to the accusation that the membership requirements are written in such a way that only relatively large and prosperous firms can qualify. These, for the most part, are the firms who organized ACME to begin with, so it is easy to come to the conclusion that ACME was designed to perpetuate the success of its own members and to make it difficult for substantial competition to emerge. Whether this was a conscious input or an accidental by-product of the membership requirements, I don't know."

Surprisingly, not everyone within ACME would disagree with Allen's view. One member of the ACME board of directors told me: "If there are 2,700 consulting firms in this country and only forty-four of them belong to ACME, something's got to be wrong"

As befits a conservative association representing a conservative profession, ACME has moved slowly indeed in assimilating all competent and capable consultants. The Association listed thirty-nine members in 1960 and nearly ten years later, despite massive strides made within the profession, had increased in number only to forty-four. Since nine firms had relinquished membership, this meant fourteen new members, or an increase of less than two a year. Of the fifty-four firms engaged in management consulting that reportedly had grossed more than $1 million in 1968 (see Appendix B), only sixteen had ACME credentials. Perhaps more significant, ACME could claim only three of the top ten! By the end of the sixties it became increasingly evident that the Association could no longer continue to claim leadership with its head buried in the sand. ACME at last seemed ready to enact a program about which it had been talking since 1955: "The development of professional standards against which a consultant's performance can be measured." What this amounted to was the accreditation of individual consultants.

I had become aware of ACME's movements in this direction while writing a series of articles on the management consulting profession for United Features Syndicate in the summer of 1962. The following July an article in the New York *Herald Tribune* stated: "ACME . . . will announce this winter its long awaited program of minimum professional standards for individuals practicing in the management consulting field. 'It will enable the client to differentiate between the inexperienced, incompetent and improperly motivated firm from (*sic*) those fully qualified.' This program, which has been in the works for more than five years, will include a separate ACME unit which will test practitioners to qualify them."

"You Have to Be Bullish About Consulting"

But the winter of 1963 passed without the awaited announcement. The question of whether or not to form a separate ACME accrediting unit had split, at least temporarily, the ACME ranks. "We started to make the jump into accreditation and had to back off," the director of one of one of the older (and smaller) ACME firms explained to me. "The committees got ahead of the membership. ACME consists of forty-four diverse members. They're all experts. The more expert a person is, the harder it is to get him to agree. This had to be taken one step at a time. It didn't come to any final vote, because the program was not defined enough. It didn't get voted down; it simply was tabled."

When I pressed ACME's Shay for information on the controversy, he indicated that the movement had been slowed by "several of the medium- and large-sized consulting firms and engineering firms with management services departments." He also itemized the objections within the Association:

ᴧ-The success of management consultants depends on their judgment, and there is no way in which the judgment factor can be measured except by results attained. Certainly it can't be measured by written or oral examinations.

ᴧ-It is impossible or very difficult to establish professional standards for consultants because the common body of knowledge in this professional field is only beginning to be developed.

ʌ-Any program of professional standards for individual consultants would tend to de-emphasize the consulting firm in the light of its public because it would place primary emphasis on qualifications of individuals.

ʌ-Any program of professional standards would tend to accelerate action by state legislators to license or register management consultants.

ʌ-Managers show no signs of becoming a profession. Why then should consultants strive toward this end?

Why indeed? But the partners at the top of one or two of the Big Image firms sprinkle their talk with references to management consulting being just that: a profession. Neither McKinsey nor Booz-Allen (according to several insiders) showed much enthusiasm for the establishment of a standards program—and for understandable reasons. The Big Image firms in essence were delivering a branded product to their customers. They were selling a "McKinsey survey" or a "Booz-Allen survey," not a survey by consultants Jim, Ev, and Charlie, who just happened to work for McKinsey or Booz-Allen. Admitting that other consultants —whether within ACME firms or not—ranked equal to, or better than, their own personnel could only lessen their brand image. McKinsey and Booz-Allen could probably do without ACME, but ACME could not do without McKinsey and Booz-Allen—so the standards movement stalled.

Nevertheless, in its own publications ACME at least

"You Have to Be Bullish About Consulting"

indirectly admitted a need for the establishment of some form of professional standards. In the booklet "How to Get the Best Results from Management Consultants," Shay wrote: "There are as yet no professional standards of qualification which enable clients to differentiate well-qualified consultants from incompetent or unethical practitioners. Quacks and charlatans are less and less able to secure substantial blocks of business, but a number of unqualified consultants still offer other services. It is, therefore, wise to check carefully before you select a consultant. Furthermore, the dangers of mistakes in selection are often the result of too casual an assessment of a consultant in terms of the particular issue with which the company is faced."

Later in the booklet Shay suggests that the wary businessman should check standard investigating agencies such as the Better Business Bureau, Dun & Bradstreet, and credit associations as well as solicit recommendations from banks, law firms, public accountants, or advertising agencies. The advice seems sensible, but no easy means exists to differentiate *poor* from *good* from *excellent* consulting. I found that Better Business Bureau offices vary from city to city and may be either extremely vigilant or quite conservative, and even in the former case are geared toward detecting outright fraud rather than incompetence. Dun & Bradstreet deals even more superficially in the area of judging management consultants. It would do an inquiring businessman little good to learn (as I did from the report on one notorious firm) that the firm's operations were profitable and "a steady trend is indicated." As for banks, I once asked an officer at a large Chicago bank what he would do if someone asked him to recommend a consultant. "We operate on strict reciprocity," he said (meaning he would recommend only firms having accounts with his bank). As it turned out, that meant Booz-Allen.

Actually an astute businessman, through careful inquiry among other businessmen, often can determine the better consulting firms and the areas of operation in which they perform most ably. But even in the best consulting firms the quality of men may vary from excellent to merely mediocre. The quality of an assignment may depend, more than most large ACME firms would care to admit, on which principal or partner handles the assignment and how skillfully he selects his task force. Quality control becomes a vital factor, particularly the larger a firm gets. "It's more important to buy the man than the organization," I was told by one individual consultant. This isn't entirely true, of course, since some of the large firms manage to monitor the quality of their work quite effectively.

In talking with the members of dozens of management consulting firms, both inside and outside of ACME, I raised the subject of professional standards frequently. While I took no numerical poll, those consultants who might be classified as the "outs" (non-ACME members) seemed more eager to establish such a program than the "ins." This seemed only natural because it could only enhance their status. But many of the "ins" also felt standards to be necessary if management consulting were ever to obtain acceptance as a true profession.

"You Have to Be Bullish About Consulting"

ACME's Shay also seemed strongly to support such a program: "What the consultants in this country must do is establish some kind of program which serves the public interest by providing a recognized, acceptable means by which prospective clients and current clients can distinguish qualified practitioners from incompetent ones. It's one of the things that we're working on, and I think it will be a reality in about five years."

That discussion occurred in February 1966 and, considering what little I knew about the inner workings of ACME, I thought even a prediction of five years might prove optimistic. Approximately ten months later I lunched with the senior partner of a major consulting firm. He also was on the ACME board of directors. The subject of standards rose at about the time for the second cup of coffee. I expressed the opinion that standards were something ACME was always talking about without actually doing anything. "If you had said that a year ago I might have agreed with you," he acknowledged. "Since then there has been some action." He stated that the suggested time table was not unrealistic and that I return and talk to Shay once more.

When shortly afterward I did return to see Shay, I learned that progress indeed had been made and that an Institute of Management Consultants seemingly would become a reality as early as the spring of 1967. Part of the problem at that time still remained in defining the "common body of knowledge," possession of which would help qualify an individual to become a "certified public consultant." If four years in medical school qualified a person to become a doctor and three years in law school qualified a person to become a lawyer, then perhaps two years in business school might qualify a person to become a consultant. Unfortunately, the problem wasn't quite as simple as this. Other questions to be resolved were how many years of internship, whether in industry or with a consulting firm, would qualify an individual as a consultant and even what personal characteristics were involved? Also, at what point does a member of an established consulting firm become a member of the Institute? If he leaves the firm does he take his Institute membership with him?

Planning for the establishment of this professional group progressed under the leadership of ACME and with the cooperation of four other consulting associations: the Association of Management Consultants, Society of Professional Management Consultants, New England Society of Management Consultants, and Canadian Association of Management Consultants. A brief snag occurred when the New York state legislature refused to accept the name "Institute of Management Consultants" because of its being too general. For a while it was feared that the new group might have to incorporate itself under the title "National Academy of Management Consultants," which Shay and others felt sounded too scholarly. Fortunately for the profession's image, however, Governor Nelson Rockefeller intervened and the group was able to incorporate itself under the planned name, the Institute of Management Consultants.

"You Have to Be Bullish About Consulting"

Despite the progress now being made in this area, a certain number of grumblers within the ACME ranks do exist. One of these is James L. Allen of Booz, Allen & Hamilton. When I spoke with him in his office I raised the subject of professional standards. A frown crossed Mr. Allen's face.

"I've always had the feeling that it's stepping backward rather than forward," he said. "If you organized the practice of law or medicine today you wouldn't do it on the basis of individual specialties. You don't go to the Mayo Clinic and ask the qualifications of the individual doctors. You assume that the Mayo Clinic is going to have qualified men. So it is with us. None of our clients come in and worry about the qualifications of our people. They expect us to have qualified people, or we wouldn't be here."

Nevertheless, despite Mr. Allen's objections, ACME seems bound toward the establishment of professional standards for consultants. The Institute of Management Consultants, Inc., held its organizational meeting on Monday, January 6, 1969, at the Union League Club in New York. One hundred out of 142 founding members attended.* Marvin Bower was elected unanimously as the Institute's first president. A. M. Lederer and Harvey C. Krentzman (neither of them with ACME connections) became vice-president and secretary-treasurer, respectively. Of the twelve-member board of directors, only two have ACME connections. For the first year of its existence,

* One of those absent was planning committee chairman H. B. Maynard, whose airplane ironically suffered a mechanical failure.

the Institute intends to utilize the ACME offices and also use Phil Shay as its executive director, then presumably move forward on its own.

During its founding period the Institute of Management Consultants has been closely identified with ACME interests. "It's a defensive move on the part of ACME," one individual practitioner told me. "The organization had to start an accreditation program or lose its position as spokesman for the consulting industry." The question might be raised: can even the newly founded Institute establish itself as spokesman for the entire consulting industry? At the time of its establishment a significant percentage of that industry—members of contract research and CPA firms—had not been invited to join the club. When in the spring of 1969 I questioned Phil Shay as to whether or not consultants attached to accounting firms might become Institute members, he said that the subject was being discussed in committee. I received the impression that the subject might remain in committee for a considerable length of time.

After officers were elected at the Institute of Management Consultants' first organizational meeting, the members adjourned for cocktails and dinner. Afterward, president Marvin Bower gave a brief speech and there followed a short discussion on the Institute's first-year plans. The minutes of the meeting contain the notation: "It was also agreed that founding members refrain from using the initials 'PMC' (Professional Management Consultant)

"You Have to Be Bullish About Consulting"

after their name until the board suggests that this is in order."

Some years ago Justice Louis D. Brandeis defined a profession as follows: "An occupation requiring extensive preliminary intellectual training, pursued primarily for others and not merely oneself, and accepting as the measure of achievement one's contribution to society rather than individual financial reward." The management consulting industry currently is determining whether or not it can live up to Justice Brandeis's definition.

●

Without question, management consulting—whether it be considered an industry or a profession—has come a long way from the time following World War I when Edwin G. Booz established his practice in a small Chicago office. Perhaps the most concise description of the growth of management consulting was given to me by Bruce D. Henderson of The Boston Consulting Group. He described the twenties as being the decade of the efficiency experts, the thirties as the decade of the sick business doctors, the forties as the decade of production (particularly war production), the fifties as the decade of marketing, and the sixties as the decade of growth. Management consulting firms have grown tremendously since 1960, but it may take the hindsight of someone writing in the seventies to determine whether this decade should be labeled the decade of growth, the decade of computers, or maybe the decade of international expansion. Certainly the most striking aspect about consulting within the last few years has been the growth of consulting not just within the United States, but within Western Europe as well.

Originally, American consulting firms established offices abroad ostensibly to service their regular clients who had branches overseas, but they found European firms eager to hire the same brand of expertise that had helped make American business so successful. Presumably within the next decade or two, many of the European nationals who have joined the staffs of McKinsey and Booz-Allen will leave to open their own offices, and an entire new generation of consulting firms will emerge. "The ACME firms are indeed standard bearers," stated one recent article in *International Management Digest*. "But it is premature to say whether they bear the future international standards."

The prognosis for management consulting firms, however, is certainly up. "I see no end to the future of consulting if we can maintain professional standards and leadership," says Marvin Bower of McKinsey & Company. "Business is growing in size and complexity and the problems of business are multiplying." James L. Allen says: "From our standpoint I see nothing but continued opportunities for growth in the future if we can continue to organize and control the high standards we impose on our work." John Whitmore of Cresap, McCormick and Paget finally adds: "You have to be bullish about consulting. It thrives on change and this is an era where change is accelerating."

Despite certain flaws—some of them obvious, others not so obvious—management consulting firms undoubtedly have added stability to the managerial function. They give the top businessman a general staff corps from which he can seek advice. They have given the presidents of large companies a tool that they didn't have several decades ago. Formerly, if a president had a problem he had little time to do anything about it. Now he can call in an outside consultant and be able to know that within a certain period of time the problem will be solved. Because of the success of this process, the management consulting firms have carved themselves a very definite, and profitable, niche in today's business world.

APPENDIX A

What Management Consulting Is

Perhaps one of the most perplexing, though minor, problems faced by most management consulting firms is describing exactly what it is that they do. The Association of Consulting Management Engineers has made several attempts at defining "management consulting," the most recent being in its 1968–1969 Directory of Membership and Services.

> Management consulting is the professional service performed by specially trained and experienced persons in helping managers identify and solve managerial and operating problems of the various institutions of our society; in recommending practical solutions to these problems; and helping to implement them when necessary. This professional service focuses on improving the managerial, operating, and economic performance of these institutions.

Appendix A

The management consultant counsels the chief executive and other members of management on managerial and operating problems of the enterprise. His activity is not confined to solving these problems in a purely theoretical, abstract, or technical sense. He does these things, it is true; but the problems with which the consultant deals are action-oriented, and his thinking must be directed toward improved managerial and economic performance and results for the client. This must include the creation of understanding and commitment toward a particular change and methods whereby it can become integral to the client's organization. The consultant must urge and persuade the client and, when necessary, help him toward a sound course of action. The change program must include emotional and value as well as informational elements for successful implementation. Relying on rational persuasion is not sufficient. Most organizations possess the knowledge to cure many of their problems; the rub is utilization.

This is the art of management counsel, and it transcends the body of knowledge and skills the consultant possesses. This art includes at least four distinct aspects: *fidelity* and its concomitant responsibilities, *understanding, persuasion,* and *education.* The consultant is a fiduciary; that is, he stands at one end of a particular type of confidential relationship. He must think through what he owes his client in terms of responsibility, of candor, of ability and willingness to turn down an assignment which either exceeds his competence or, even more important, does not appear to him to be what the client really needs or should do. Fidelity to his client is his duty, including vigorous persuasion toward a sound course of action. In exercising this responsibility, the consultant must create a mutual understanding of the problem and persuade client executives to put his recommendations into effect so they will get lasting results. Finally, he has responsibility for the improvement and education of the client's employees.

These four aspects constitute the essence of the client-consultant relationship. In addition to these factors, three other ingredients play important parts in this relationship. They are proper communication, mutual cooperation, and confidence in each other. The professional practices employed by the consultant in the conduct of client engagements represent the technical part of this relationship.

APPENDIX B

Gross Billings
of Management Consulting Firms

Most firms engaged in management consulting dislike discussing either the size of their professional staffs or their annual gross billings. The following figures should be considered educated guesses at those figures for the year 1968. In cases where the firm also engages in non-consulting activities, the figure quoted represents only the consulting chunk of the pie.

FIRM	NUMBER OF PROFESSIONALS	GROSS BILLINGS IN MILLIONS OF DOLLARS
1. Stanford Research Institute	3,150	60
2. Planning Research Corporation	3,000	55
3. Booz, Allen & Hamilton Inc.	1,500	50

4. Peat, Marwick, Mitchell & Co.	700	30
5. McKinsey & Company, Inc.	462	22–25
6. WOFAC Company	550	16
7. Arthur D. Little, Inc.	230 (plus 150 part-time)	15
8. Alexander Proudfoot Company	300	15
9. URS Corporation	400	12.3
10. H. B. Maynard & Company	450	10
11. Ernst & Ernst	400	10
12. The Diebold Group	450	8
13. Lybrand, Ross Bros. & Montgomery	318	7.5
14. Management Science America, Inc.	300	7.5
15. A. T. Kearney & Company, Inc.	255	7
16. Kurt Salmon Associates, Inc.	200	6.5
17. Lester B. Knight & Associates, Inc.	225	6.5
18. Cresap, McCormick and Paget	160	6
19. Operations Research	240	5.27

20. Stone & Webster Management Consultants	275	**5**
21. Arthur Andersen & Company	150	**5**
22. Touche, Ross, Bailey & Smart	150	5
23. Auerbach Corporation	190	5
24. Price Waterhouse & Co.	125	5
25. Arthur Young & Company	150	5
26. Worden & Risberg	150	4
27. Haskins & Sells	180	3.8
28. EBS Management Consultants, Inc.	100	**3**
29. Harbridge House, Inc.	100	**3**
30. S. D. Leidesdorf & Company	60	3
31. Bonner & Moore Associates, Inc.	100	3
32. Glendinning Associates	100	3
33. The Fantus Company, Inc.	100	2.6
34. Case and Company, Inc.	100	2.5
35. Donahue, Groover and Associates	100	2.5

36. Woods, Gordon & Co.	125	2.5
37. George S. May International Company	400	2–10
38. Handley-Walker Company	60	2
39. S. J. Capelin Associates, Inc.	70	2
40. R. Dixon Speas Associates	63	2
41. Fry Consultants Incorporated	60	2
42. P. S. Ross & Partners	72	1.75
43. Checchi and Company	50	1.5
44. Albert Ramond and Associates, Inc.	80	1.4
45. Stevenson & Kellogg, Ltd.	70	1.4
46. Office of Graham Parker	60	1.25
47. Frank C. Brown & Company, Inc.	40	1.25
48. Edward N. Hay & Associates	40	1.2
49. William E. Hill & Company, Inc.	27	1.1
50. Commonwealth Services, Inc.	45	1
51. Corplan Associates	45	1

Appendix B

APPENDIX C

Fees Charged by Management Consulting Firms

Every three years ACME surveys both member and non-member firms to determine what they charge for their services. ACME published the most recent survey under the title "Professional Consulting Fee Arrangements" in 1966. A new study is under way as this book goes to press.

In addition to the billing rates given in the 1966 survey (reprinted below), ACME provided detailed information on how and why participants structured their fee arrangements. Because of the confidential nature of this survey, ACME identified none of the participating firms by name, but the survey provides good information on the value placed on consulting services by consultants and clients.

Some qualification probably is needed to compare the five-level division below with the more typical three-level hierarchy used by the firms to whom the majority of space in this book has been given. The term "Partner or Equivalent" speaks for itself. The "Principal Management Consultant" refers to a man with roughly eight years of consult-

Appendix C

ing experience. A "Senior Management Consultant" would be the equivalent of a consultant who has been with a firm about five years. A "Management Consultant" has three years' experience in consulting. The "Junior Management Consultant" is what's left.

The 1969 survey probably will indicate that per diem rates have increased in three years by an average of 12 per cent, except at the lowest level.

1. Per diem rates charged by twelve consulting firms, each with seventy or more professional staff men.

TITLE	MINIMUM per diem rate	MAXIMUM per diem rate	MEDIAN	AVERAGE
Partner or Equivalent	$200	$560	$338	$347
Principal Management Consultant	$225	$400	$250	$280
Senior Management Consultant	$175	$350	$213	$216
Management Consultant	$125	$350	$175	$184
Junior Management Consultant	$80	$160	$138	$132

2. Per diem rates charged by twenty consulting firms, each with from twenty to sixty-nine professional staff men.

Partner or Equivalent	$180	$400	$263	$271

Principal Management Consultant	$150	$350	$215	$226
Senior Management Consultant	$130	$280	$188	$195
Management Consultant	$90	$250	$190	$182
Junior Management Consultant	$60	$200	$125	$116

3. Per diem rates charged by twenty-three consulting firms, each with less than twenty professional staff men.

Partner or Equivalent	$150	$500	$250	$270
Principal Management Consultant	$175	$300	$225	$230
Senior Management Consultant	$94	$300	$225	$230
Management Consultant	$84	$225	$175	$160
Junior Management Consultant	$63	$175	$110	$118

4. Per diem rates charged in combined listing of fifty-five consulting firms in North America.

Partner or Equivalent	$150	$560	$275	$288
Principal Management Consultant	$150	$400	$225	$239

Appendix C

Senior Management Consultant	$94	$350	$200	$201
Management Consultant	$84	$350	$175	$175
Junior Management Consultant	$60	$200	$125	$122

5. Per diem rates reported by twenty-two consulting firms who participated in the 1963 study (for purposes of comparison).

Partner or Equivalent	$175	$500	$300	$290
Principal Management Consultant	$150	$350	$220	$225
Senior Management Consultant	$150	$350	$180	$185
Management Consultant	$100	$250	$150	$155
Junior Management Consultant	$80	$160	$119	$118

Several conclusions can be made from an examination of these figures. One is that, as with all other costs, the cost of management consulting services has risen. The actual percentage is not accurately reflected in comparing the final two charts, since the firms surveyed differ from 1963 to 1966. However, ACME also indicates that its forty-five member firms reported an average increase in rates of 15.2 per cent since January 1962. The median increase in rates was 15 per cent.

Also to be noted is that the larger the firm, generally the higher its billing rates. This reflects in part the higher overhead expenses of the bigger firms, but also relates to the fact that the larger the firm's size *and* reputation, the more it can charge.

crease in profits from our efforts, nor will we accept an engagement where the fee is related to any cost reduction that may result.

ARTICLE IV

We will accept only those engagements we are qualified to undertake and which are in the best interests of clients. We will assign personnel qualified by knowledge, experience, and character to give effective service in analyzing and solving the particular problem or problems involved. We will carry out each engagement under the direction of a principal of the firm.

ARTICLE V

We will charge reasonable fees which are commensurate with the nature of the service performed and the responsibility assumed, and which, whenever feasible, have been agreed upon in advance of the engagement. We will not allow any person to practice in our name who is not in our employ. We will neither accept nor pay fees to persons outside our firm for referral of clients. Nor will we accept fees, commissions, or other valuable consideration from individuals or organizations whose equipment, supplies, or services we may recommend in the course of our work with clients.

ARTICLE VI

We will guard as confidential all information concerning the business and affairs of clients coming to us in the course of professional engagements.

ARTICLE VII

We will not serve clients under terms or conditions which tend to interfere with or impair our objectivity, independence, or integrity.

ARTICLE VIII

We will negotiate for possible work with a client where another firm is currently engaged only when we are assured there is no reason for conflict between the two engagements.

ARTICLE IX

We will serve two or more competing clients at the same time on problems in a sensitive area only with their knowledge.

ARTICLE X

We will not make direct or indirect offers of employment to employees of clients. If we are approached by em-

Appendix D

ployees of clients regarding employment in our firm or in that of another client, we will make certain that we have our clients' consent before entering into any negotiations with such employees.

ARTICLE XI

We will make certain that the members of our professional staff, in order to insure their continuing objectivity, shall under no circumstances use a consulting engagement as a means of seeking new employment for themselves.

ARTICLE XII

We will not use data, technical material, procedures, or developments originated by other consulting firms but not released by them for public use, without their written permission.

ARTICLE XIII

We will review for a client the work of another consulting firm currently employed by him only with the other consultant's knowledge.

ARTICLE XIV

We will not make direct or indirect offers of employment

to consultants on the staffs of other consulting firms. If we are approached by consultants of other consulting firms regarding employment in our firm or in that of a client, we will handle each situation in a way that will be fair to the consultant and his firm.

ARTICLE XV

We will administer the internal and external affairs of our firm in the best interests of the profession at all times.

ARTICLE XVI

We will endeavor to safeguard clients, the public and ourselves against consultants deficient in moral character or professional competence. We will observe all laws, uphold the honor and dignity of the profession, and accept self-imposed disciplines. We will respect the professional reputation and practice of other consultants. But we will expose, without hesitation, illegal or unethical conduct of fellow members of the profession to the proper ACME authority.

ARTICLE XVII

We will strive continually to improve our knowledge, skills, and techniques, and will make available to our clients the benefits of our professional attainments.

Appendix D

Communications concerning any apparent departures from this Code of Professional Ethics may be addressed to the Chairman, Committee on Professional Ethics, ACME, 347 Madison Avenue, New York, New York 10017.

II: OBLIGATIONS OF GOOD PRACTICE

In order to promote highest quality of performance in the practice of management consulting, ACME has formulated the following standards of good practice for the guidance of the profession. The member firms subscribe to these practices because they make for equitable and satisfactory client relationships and contribute to success in management consulting.

1. We make it a practice to confer with an organization that is considering the use of a management consultant, to discuss the nature and scope of the assistance that may be required and to explore the benefits that may be attained. This preliminary discussion may be undertaken without obligation to the prospective client.

2. We recommend the engagement of our services only if we believe that real financial or other benefits will be realized by the client.

3. We make certain that the client receives a clear statement of the objectives and scope of the proposed engagement and when feasible its approximate cost, and cover this in writing by an initial proposal or a letter of confirmation when we accept the engagement.

4. We endeavor to accomplish our work expeditiously, consistent with professional thoroughness, and without disrupting the daily operations of the client organization.

5. We believe that the primary purpose of each engagement is to develop complete and practical solutions for the problems under study, including a realistic program for putting them into effect. Our professional staff is available to help implement them and to provide continuing counsel to management.

6. We discuss in detail with the client any important changes in the nature, scope, timing, or other aspects of an engagement, and obtain his understanding and agreement before we take any action on them.

7. We acquaint client personnel with the principles, methods, and techniques applied, so that the improvements suggested or installed may be properly managed and continued after completion of the engagement.

8. We maintain continuity of understanding and knowledge of clients' problems and the work that has been done to solve them by maintaining appropriate files of reports submitted to clients. These are protected against unauthorized access and supported by files of working papers, consultants' log-books, and similar recorded data.

9. We continually evaluate the quality of the work done by our staff to insure insofar as is possible that all of our engagements are conducted in a competent manner.

10. We endeavor to provide opportunity for the pro-

Appendix D

fessional development of those men who enter the profession, by assisting them to acquire a full understanding of the functions, duties, and responsibilities of management consultants, and to keep up with significant advances in their areas of practice.

11. We endeavor to practice justice, courtesy, and sincerity in our profession. In the conduct of our practice, we strive to maintain a wholly professional attitude toward those we serve, toward those who assist us in our practice, toward our fellow consultants, toward the members of other professions, and the practitioners of allied arts and sciences.

INDEX

Index

INDEX

Index

Index

About the Author

HAL HIGDON, a free-lance writer of many
interests, appears frequently in leading national
publications, such as the *New York Times Magazine,*
Good Housekeeping, Sports Illustrated, This Week,
the *Chicago Tribune Magazine,* and *Playboy.* This
is his fifth book. He lives in Michigan City, Indiana,
with his wife and three children.

DATE DUE